Table of Contents

Forms and Worksheets in this Book

Notes to Chapters 1–10

This new update of chapters 1–10 features a number of major additions, including notable additions to the sections discussing limited liability companies, estate tax planning, and emerging trends and issues. The list below identifies the most significant changes and additions to the text and gives you the chapter–section number where you will find the discussion.

What's New

- More studies confirm that failure rates among new businesses may be much lower than previously believed – 1.10

- More than 40 states have now enacted limited liability company (LLC) laws as this new type of business entity continues to catch on nationwide – 2.6

- Many states have recently repealed their bulk sales laws; yet another business trend that is rapidly spreading – 3.1, 9.14

- New 1994 OSHA regulations regarding reports of multiple injury accidents in the workplace now require employers to notify OSHA officials with 8 hours of such incidents, instead of the former 48 – 5.6

- There is a new notice, posting requirements under the Family and Medical Leave Act of 1993 – 5.8, 5.12

- The luxury tax on automobiles has been updated for indexed exemption – 7.2

- The IRS increased automobile standard mileage allowance to $0.29 (29 cents) a mile – 8.6

- There is an expanded discussion of estate tax planning and possible savings from use of bypass trusts – 8.10

- The U.S. Small Business Administration's (SBA) loan programs have expanded and updated coverage, including the SBA's new direct "microloan" program for very small businesses – 9.7

- The Federal Trade Commission's (FTC) mail order shipping rules have now expanded to also cover orders received by modem, fax, or telephone – 9.8

- Pending legislation may allow states to impose sales tax on some mail order sellers, if passed – 9.8

- Other pending legislation may increase medical insurance deduction for self-employed persons from 25% to 100%; however, income from S corporations may soon subject S corporation shareholders to self-employment tax on such income – 9.14

About the Author

The author of chapters 1–10 of the entire *Starting and Operating a Business* series, is Michael D. Jenkins. Mr. Jenkins, an attorney at law and a certified public accountant, is a graduate of Harvard Law School. He has worked in Los Angeles and San Francisco as an accountant and as an attorney with a prominent San Francisco firm well known in the venture capital arena. He is a member of the State Bar of California, the American Bar Association, the American Institute of Certified Public Accountants, and the California Society of Certified Public Accountants.

How to Use this Book

0.1 Getting the Most Out of this Book

To most effectively use this book, become acquainted with the many helpful features it provides. Remember that each edition is updated annually to provide you with the most current information available. To find the most recent changes made to federal laws, refer to the Notes to Chapters 1–10: What's New page. For similar state information, refer to the Notes to State Chapter: What's New page, which immediately precedes Chapter 11.

0.2 Numbered Section Heads Correspond to Table of Contents and Index

Text

Discussions range from explaining how to start and operate your business to examining such practical issues as insurance, marketing, cash-flow management, internal financial controls, and much more. This book also explains federal and state government requirements and tax laws, as well as a number of emerging trends and issues your business may face.

Topics Noted in Margins

To make the information in this workbook easily accessible to busy people, the primary topics discussed within each numbered section are identified by "sideheads" in the margin beside the text.

Smaller Heads for Subtopics

When subsections of primary topics are discussed, the sideheads are slightly smaller.

Lists

- This small bullet helps you easily locate lists of requirements, things to do, and aspects of a particular subject or law.

Checklists

☐ Small boxes encourage you to enter a check, so that you can clearly see those items you've considered and dealt with — and those left to do.

Worksheets

Where the Action Begins

A number of worksheets are provided for you to answer questions and fill in numbers that form the basis for action plans, self-evaluation, budgeting, personnel policies, marketing feasibility studies, and the like.

The worksheets are set apart by boxes to clearly show where your interaction is required, to focus your thoughts, to record information, and to create the plans and reports that will help you establish and guide your business.

Resources

Sources and Data   Resources are set in tabular form to highlight the many agencies and companies listed to assist you.

Contacts
Addresses
Phone numbers
(listed in directory style)

Table of Contents

The detailed Table of Contents will help you quickly find any specific section of the book you wish to refer to. The first digit of the chapter–section number indicates the chapter, followed by a period and the section number.

Endnotes

The endnotes follow each chapter and are provided to assist you in accessing specific statutes, cases, regulations, and publications and to use this book as a starting place for legal research.

Index

The subject-matter index, organized alphabetically with cross-referenced entries, provides an exhaustive list of the topics, indexed not only by the terms actually used in the entries but also by various other terms you might think of instead. The Index is referenced by the chapter–section number, not by page number, to help you find the corresponding discussion in the text.

Related Resources

At the back of this book, you will find a compendium of additional resources that will save you valuable research time and money.

Appendix

The Appendix features a checklist of tax and various other major requirements for most businesses and a checklist of official government posters and notices required to be displayed by a business.

Forms

Since many business requirements depend on submitting specific forms to various government agencies, some samples of these forms are included for your reference and listed in the Table of Contents.

Post Cards

At the back of this book, you will also find post cards preaddressed to government agencies and other sources so you can request additional information, posters, and forms.

Preface

Anyone who runs a small business today, or who is thinking about starting one, knows that he or she faces serious and growing challenges. The hurdles one must get over to start or continue to operate a business seem to have grown a little higher each year since this series of books was first introduced in 1981. In particular, the government has shifted more and more responsibilities onto the shoulders of employers in recent years, a trend that seems likely to continue. As a result, many large and small firms are currently putting off expansion and hiring plans until the new Clinton universal health care proposals are finalized, since mandated health care benefits could well become the biggest financial responsibility ever thrust upon the nation's businesses — especially upon smaller businesses.

Despite the growing complexities of running a business, the slow-growth economy, and the fact that according to Dun & Bradstreet, more than 420,000 businesses failed in the last decade, small businesspeople have not been deterred. Quite to the contrary — business start ups are flourishing in this tough environment. According to an August 1993 article in *Investor's Business Daily*, for every business that failed in the "wave of creative destruction" in the 1980s, at least 15 new businesses sprang up to take its place. While many in the mass media have bemoaned the rash of takeovers, leveraged buyouts, mass layoffs, downsizing, corporate restructuring, and other wrenching changes in the 1980s and early 1990s, all this ferment seems to have provided fertile ground for new, small, and nimble businesses.

In fact, according to Dun & Bradstreet, the number of "total concerns in business" almost tripled in the 1980s to more than eight million by 1990. That compares very favorably to the 1970s, when the total number of businesses increased by just 13.8%, to 2.8 million by the end of that decade. The desire of Americans, especially many recent immigrants from all corners of the world, to start and run their own businesses seems indomitable, obstacles or no.

The publisher and I would like to think this 51-book *Starting and Operating a Business* series — which features a book for each state and the District of Columbia — might have played a significant part in empowering many of the millions of people who have started their own businesses since our first edition in 1981. A more modest view would suggest that we were merely on the leading edge of change, part of a huge expansion in the resources that have arisen in recent years to provide help to new and small firms.

We must confess, however, to being very pleased when, in April 1994, *Inc.* magazine chose *Starting and Operating a Business* as one of the best small business books available. After an exhaustive survey of hundreds of small business self-help books, as described in the cover article entitled, "In Search of the Small Business Bible," *Inc.* chose our book (series) as one of the six overall winners. We are also pleased with the award we received from the Small Business Administration "in recognition of significant contributions to the nation's small business." In fact, *Starting and Operating a Business* is featured in each of the eleven SBA Business Information Centers (BICs) in the U.S. and will also be featured in the 20 new BICs projected for the next year.

At the time we introduced this series, there were only a few useful small business self-help books available, and relatively few government resources devoted to helping new enterprises get off the ground.

Today, however, there are books and software programs offering assistance on almost every aspect of running a large, small or medium-sized business. In fact, this book series is now only part of a much larger series of business self-help books on a wide array of subjects offered by the publisher, The Oasis Press. In addition, there are now Small Business Development Centers (SBDCs) and "one-stop" business permit offices in almost every state, and while state governments are cutting services left and right, most are expected to maintain or even increase their business services and economic development and other assistance to small businesses.

Why the turnaround? State governments recognize that new and existing small businesses are the backbone of their economies and the only sector of the economy that is currently providing growth in jobs for their residents. Thus, it should not be surprising that the states are doing as much as possible to encourage business growth, expansion, and relocation.

I became involved in this trend after advising small and large businesses over the years — first as an economic and management consultant; then later, as a tax attorney; and more recently, as a certified public accountant. After years of helping many small businesses and venture capital start ups get off the ground, I had become increasingly aware of the need for a single, authoritative, and practical guide that would serve people starting and operating a business in a particular state — and acutely aware that no such guides existed, except in a few states.

Thus, in 1980, I was particularly receptive when my neighbor and publisher, Emmett Ramey, approached me with the idea of writing a nuts-and-bolts guidebook for the state of California that would guide a small business person or entrepreneur through the maze of red tape at both the federal and state levels of government, as well as provide the basic steps and advice needed to get a new business off the ground.

We decided to create an operating manual that would draw together — in a readable, usable, and nontechnical format — the practical facts of life a person needed to know when establishing a business in California. Since first publishing that California edition, we have enlisted local experts in each of the other states to work with us and coauthor the books for those states.

By and large, tax, legal, and business information is useless when it is out of date. As a result, we update each state chapter (Chapter 11) and the federal section (chapters 1–10) in this series approximately every twelve months.

So, if you want an up-to-date guide to the basic financial, legal, and tax ground rules that apply to most businesses operating in your state, the *Starting and Operating a Business* series has been designed with you in mind as a self-help tool. It is also intended to be a useful (and footnoted) reference source to the attorney who has only a limited knowledge of business taxation and the basic regulatory requirements of a large number of federal, state, and local government agencies. Accountants will also find this series a useful resource for understanding the broad scope of government regulations that affect their small business clients.

While the *Starting and Operating a Business* books provide an authoritative discussion of many legal and tax matters regarding small business, they are not intended to be a substitute for professional legal or tax advice. On the contrary, they are designed to help you focus on key points to explore in greater depth with your attorney, accountant, benefits consultant, or other adviser. By being better informed, you can use your professional advisers' time more efficiently.

Many of the items covered in this book have been added at the request of readers who have written to us with their suggestions. This series is not a "finished" project, but is under constant revision. Accordingly, as the principal author, I invite and welcome your feedback or suggestions as to improvements we might make. Your letters should be addressed either to me or my coauthor for the state chapter of this edition, in care of the publisher.

Michael D. Jenkins
July 1994

Dedication

To America's entrepreneurs — tenacious, courageous men and women — whose contribution to the variety, richness, and quality of our lives is immeasurable.

Preliminary Considerations

Part I

Chapter 1

Making the Decision to Go into Business

Entrepreneurship is the last refuge of the troublemaking individual.

— James K. Glassman

1.1 Introduction

Neither this book nor any other book can tell you whether or not you should take the plunge and go into business for yourself. You alone must make that difficult decision. Before you make the decision, carefully consider some of the key points discussed in this chapter. Some of the points discussed you may not have considered yet, while others may assist you in dealing successfully with some initial problems you may face.

One of the first points to consider when starting your business is the major financial risk you will be taking. Once you have committed yourself financially, it will not be a simple or easy thing to change your mind and back out.

In addition, be aware there is a high failure rate among new businesses. Don't assume just because you are an expert in your field, you will be an automatic success. You will need to have strengths in other areas as well. In fact, statistics show that a very high percentage of those business failures result from poor management. Poor or ineffective management is usually a lack of balanced experience and competence in three areas:

- Marketing strategies — Know what kind of product or service to sell, how to target and reach your customers, and how to sell your product or service at a price that maximizes your profits.
- Technical ability — Be able to get the work done and do it right, so you will have satisfied customers. If you are going into the auto repair

business, for example, you better know a lot about how to keep autos running right, or you will not be in business very long.

- Financial knowledge — While you do not necessarily have to be a financial wizard, you do need to know how to plan and control your business' cash flow, raise or borrow the money you will need to start your business, and get through tight periods without being caught short of cash. A certain amount of financial sophistication is becoming more and more important in today's increasingly complex financial world, even for the small business owner.

If you are lacking experience or knowledge in one or more of these three critical areas, the odds of your business succeeding are greatly reduced.

This chapter engages you in the process of realistically evaluating your entrepreneurial strengths and weaknesses. It is also intended to cause you to focus on some of the typical start-up problems and choices you are likely to face, as well as assist you in dealing effectively and rationally with those issues.

Worksheets are provided at the end of the chapter. While reading the text, pick up a pencil and write in your responses when appropriate. Often, the simple process of writing down your thoughts on specific problem areas may provide significant new insights.

1.2 Advantages and Disadvantages of Owning Your Own Business

Have you realistically considered both the advantages and the disadvantages of owning and operating your own business? If not, the time to do so is before, not after, you have committed yourself.

Advantages

If you are actively considering going into business for yourself, you most likely have already thought about the potential advantages, such as:

- Being your own boss and not having to report to a superior;
- Having the independence and authority to make your own business decisions;
- Direct contact with customers, employees, suppliers, and others;
- The personal satisfaction and sense of achievement that comes with being a success, plus the recognition that goes with it;
- The opportunity to create substantial wealth and job security for yourself;
- The opportunity to be creative and to develop your own idea, product, or service;
- The chance to make a living doing something you truly enjoy; and

- Doing something that contributes to others, whether it be providing an excellent product or service, providing employment, paying dividends to stockholders, or doing something else that is useful or that creates value.

Disadvantages

If you are like most people, you may not have thought much about the downside of going into business; however, awareness of the potential disadvantages should not discourage you from your goal of going into business for yourself, if you have a strong commitment to that goal.

Seriously consider whether you and your family are prepared to handle the disadvantages that often come with being an entrepreneur.

- In many ways, you are still not your own boss. Instead of having one boss, you will have many — your customers, the government agencies to whom you must report, and in some cases, your key suppliers.

- There is a large financial risk. The failure rate is high in new businesses, and you may lose not only your own money but also that of your friends and relatives who may have bankrolled you.

- The hours are long and hard. When you start your business, you will no longer be working 9 to 5. Count on working 10- to 12- or even 15-hour days, often six or seven days a week.

- You will not have much spare time for family or social life. And you can forget about taking any long vacations for the first few years since the business is unlikely to run itself without your presence for any long length of time.

- Your income may not be steady like a salary. You may make more or less than you could working for someone else, but in either case, your income may fluctuate up and down from month to month.

- The buck stops with you. If a problem arises, there is no boss you can take it to and say: "What do we do about this?" You are the boss and all the responsibility is yours. If anything goes wrong, the cost comes out of your pocket.

- You may be stuck for years doing work you do not like. Unlike an employee, you cannot simply quit and look for a better job. It may take you years to sell the business or find some other way to get out of it without a major financial loss.

- As a business grows, the amount of activity not associated with the primary business objective will increase. You will spend more time on personnel, administrative, and legal matters and less doing what you may have wanted most to do in your business.

- Increasing legislation and litigation make owning a business very risky. You can work a lifetime to build a business only to have it lost because of a lawsuit or a new law or regulation.

1.3 Typical Characteristics of the Successful Entrepreneur

A good deal is known about what it takes to be a successful entrepreneur. For the most part, it seems the one overriding factor is a tremendous need to achieve. In short, attitude seems to have almost everything to do with success in business, while factors, such as intelligence, education, physical appearance, and a pleasing personality, are much less important. Characteristics of typical successful entrepreneurs include:

- An overpowering need to achieve, as opposed to a need to be liked or to exercise power; the form in which different individuals measure their achievement varies widely, ranging from amassing wealth to building a larger organization to creating a better mousetrap than anyone else;

- The trait of following through on a commitment, not quitting halfway through when the going gets tough: in short, perseverance;

- A positive mental attitude or the ability to remain optimistic in new and unfamiliar situations, which essentially grows out of being self-confident about one's abilities;

- Objectivity — the ability to accurately weigh and assess risks associated with a particular course of action, as well as being realistic about one's own abilities and limitations;

- A respectful attitude toward money, but a tendency to look upon money as a means for accomplishing things, or a way of keeping score in the game of business, rather than as a thing to be sought as an end in itself;

- The tendency to anticipate developments and to make things happen rather than constantly reacting to problems as they arise;

- Resourcefulness — the ability to solve unique problems in unique ways and to be able to handle things that come up for which the entrepreneur has no previous experience to rely on as a guide;

- Strong personal relations skills — the characteristics of being cheerful and cooperative, and usually getting along well with, without necessarily being close to, employees and associates;

- Well-developed communication skills, both in oral and written presentations; and

- Well-rounded technical knowledge with emphasis on the knowledge about the physical process of producing goods and services.

How do your personal characteristics stack up against the foregoing profile of the typical successful entrepreneur? If that profile doesn't sound very much like you, maybe you had better give some long, hard thought as to whether you are cut out for making it as a business owner.

Running a business is not like working for someone else. No one is there to tell you what to do when something goes wrong. You are responsible for everything.

Are you capable of handling that kind of total responsibility? Are you a self-starter, capable of planning, organizing, and carrying out projects on your own? If not, you may find that starting and running a successful business is not for you.

Running a business demands a great deal in the way of initiative, hard work, self-discipline, and resourcefulness. On the other hand, solving the problems that arise from day to day and making it all work out can be a source of immense satisfaction, as well as be financially rewarding.

Before reading further, complete Worksheet 1, which is a useful questionnaire that may help you to get a better idea of your suitability for playing the role of entrepreneur in the real world. Worksheet 1 is located at the end of this chapter.

1.4 Knowing Your Market

One of the most important questions you should ask yourself is whether you feel that you know and understand the market for the particular kind of products or services you intend to sell. Do you know who your competition is and whether the particular market you intend to appeal to is large enough for both you and the existing competition? Also, how will your products or services measure up against those of your competitors in terms of quality and price?

If your product or service is something new or unusual, you need to have a sense of whether you will be selling an item that is wanted and needed in the marketplace. Or, even if you intend to sell a product or service that you know there is a need for, you should be satisfied in your own mind that you are going to be making it available at the right place at the right time.

Few sights are sadder than the boarded-up mom-and-pop store or restaurant — in which the owners have sunk their life savings — that never got off the ground for some obvious reason, such as lack of visibility from the street, lack of substantial foot traffic by its doors, or some other fatal flaw the inexperienced owners overlooked.

To succeed, you must find the right business opportunity. If you do not have a clear idea of what business you want to go into and where you want to operate it, you will need to do some intelligent investigation of all possible opportunities that might be suitable for you.

If you already have a concept of what you want to do, you will still need to do a great deal of investigating to make sure it is as good an opportunity as it appears to be. In either case, a lot of initial research and footwork is advisable, unless you want to close your eyes and indulge in wishful thinking.

Determining Market Feasibility

In other words, to quote a well-known brokerage firm: "Investigate before you invest." This often entails doing your own marketing feasibility study before committing yourself to opening a new business.

A marketing feasibility study is simply a systematic analysis of any information you can obtain about the potential market for your product or service. This information can include the competition you face, the amount of sales you can reasonably expect to obtain in that particular market, and whether that level of sales will be adequate for your business to operate at a reasonable profit. For example, if you are planning to build homes in a small community where there is only a demand for five homes a year, and you need to build and sell ten homes a year to survive, doing a marketing feasibility study might help you realize your proposed business venture is not feasible, even if you were to capture 100% of the local housing market. Investigate first, then invest.

Alternatively, if you have several thousand dollars to spend and a well-defined idea of what it is you want to do, you can hire a professional economist or marketing consultant to do a feasibility study. In every major city, there are several firms that can do a thorough marketing and demographic study for you. Such a feasibility study can be quite valuable, but it will also be fairly expensive. Most people starting a new business tend to do their own marketing feasibility study, which is usually done very informally, if at all. The exception would be for people who create a formal, written business plan. A thorough analysis of the market for a new business' product or service is always a key portion of any such business plan. The Oasis Press publishes books and software that can assist you in creating a written business plan. See the list of publications in the back of this book for ordering information.

Before doing a marketing feasibility study, you obviously need to know what business you want to go into. When choosing your type of business, keep these thoughts in mind:

- If you see that a particular business is doing quite well and you want to go in and compete head-to-head with it, don't make the mistake of adopting a me-too approach and going in with the assumption that you can take away a lot of their business by competing on a price basis. Other than price, you better have a lot of good reasons why you think another business' customers will switch over to you. Other good reasons could include a distinctly better product, service, or location.

- Keep your eyes open for developing social, economic, and technological trends that will create new markets that you can move into at an early stage. It will help if you are a voracious reader of magazines such as *Time*, *Newsweek* (social trends); *Forbes*, *Business Week* (economic trends); or *Omni* or *Discover* (technological innovations).

An example of how observing social trends can translate into profits — in this instance stock market profits — is the case of an investment analyst in the 60s who noticed the trend toward mini-skirts and correctly anticipated that the spread of mini-skirts among women would create a boom market for panty hose. The analyst made a killing by buying shares of panty hose stock.

So how do you go about analyzing the market for your product or service once you have focused on a particular business you might want to start? Worksheet 2 will help you pinpoint the kind of information you need to develop to satisfy yourself that a good market exists for whatever it is you are planning to sell. Before you read any further, spend some time writing down your responses to each of the items on Worksheet 2.

Market Data Resources

Once you have identified your most likely potential customers, find out how to locate your business or structure and to direct your advertising and promotional efforts to most efficiently reach them. Fortunately, there is a great deal of published data you can use if you need to do this type of research. One of the best sources is *Sales and Marketing Management Magazine*, which publishes *Survey of Buying Power* each year. This survey provides breakdowns in population, households, retail sales by type of business, and total purchasing dollars for each county in the United States and for cities with a population of more than 10,000. To request information on *Survey of Buying Power*, see Statistical Information in Section 10.4.

Some of the printed sources of market information you can use in your research are:

- A.C. Nielsen market studies
- McGraw-Hill research studies from McGraw-Hill Publishing
- *National Trade and Professional Association (NTPA) Directory*
- Newspapers
- Statistical abstracts
- Trade magazines

Many of these items can be found in your local business or university library. The *NTPA Directory* can be ordered from:

National Trade and Professional Association Directory
Columbia Books
Washington, DC
(202) 898-0662

Various industry and government sources of information to consider are:

- Trade associations
- U.S. Chamber of Commerce
- U.S. Department of Commerce
- U.S. Small Business Administration

Another excellent source is the 1990 U.S. census data, which gives vast amounts of detailed information on the U.S. population and its buying habits by individual census tract. You may want to obtain a couple of useful pamphlets from your nearest U.S. Small Business Administration field office. Ask for the pamphlet entitled, *Researching Your Market*, for guidance on how to do your own market research.

Finding the Optimum Site

Even more important in your local community may be studies and future projections as to population and income trends that have been done by local groups, such as your local chamber of commerce or, in some areas, the local planning commission. If finding the optimum site to locate is important to your marketing effort, do the following:

- Talk to a knowledgeable person at your local chamber of commerce about business and other trends in the area where you intend to locate.
- Talk to a staff person at your local planning commission about census tract projections of future population growth, income trends, and economic development in the area you are considering. Also, they — or some other local agency, such as a traffic or streets department — will usually have done traffic counts showing how many cars pass certain points every day. This information can be very useful if you are opening a retail business. Also, consult any trade association, which serves your business and may have available information tailored exactly to your needs.
- Obtain a copy of the Small Business Administration's publication, *Choosing a Retail Location*.

For a complete guide to specifying, ranking, and evaluating the factors you must consider when choosing an optimum site for your new or relocating business, obtain a copy of *Company Relocation Handbook*. This handbook features a list of related reference publications and economic development organizations. Get your copy through your local book source or:

The Oasis Press
(800) 228-2275

1.5 Knowing the Business

Do you have any experience in the area of business in which you will be engaged? Of course, it is possible to learn while doing, but it helps a great deal to know a business before you start. Often, the most successful businesses are started by people who have worked in a particular line of business for years and who finally decide that they know the ropes well enough to leave their employer and start their own similar operation.

It helps to have experience in the particular business you propose to enter, but in most cases, your experience working in some other line of business will also have considerable carryover value. If you have neither type of experience, you may find you have a lot to learn once you begin the business.

A major management weakness that causes businesses to fail is the inability to get the job done and to do it right, on time, and efficiently enough to charge a competitive price for your product or service and still make a profit. For example, with the tremendous proliferation of personal computers, you may have decided to go into business repairing small computers. You may be absolutely right, but unless you have the technical capability to do such repairs, or the ability to properly select and hire employees who can do the job, you had better look for some other kind of business.

In many cases, if you know you lack the technical experience you need to open a particular kind of business, your best approach will be to get a job in that industry and work for someone else for a few years until you learn what you need to know. This may require a lot of patience, but it is definitely preferable than getting into a business you do not know well and losing your shirt in the process.

1.6 Knowing How Much Money It Will Take to Succeed

Can you afford to start a full-time business, if it will mean giving up your current employment and income? Many small businesses never really have a chance to succeed because the owners run out of money before the business becomes a viable operation. As a result, the owners often wind up having to go back to work for someone else again, disappointed and broke.

Carefully calculating and scheduling out, in as much detail as possible, the income and expenses you can reasonably expect for at least the first year of operation, as well as your living expenses and a reserve for emergencies, is a helpful step when determining how much money it will take to start and maintain your business.

You want to have enough money to last until the business reaches the point where you expect to make enough profit to live on. Remember a lot of expenses are involved in starting up almost any kind of business, and most businesses start out operating in the red for a time.

Completing worksheets 3 through 5 will help you plan your cash flow for the crucial first year of business. Worksheet 3 will help you to project your monthly sales revenue in terms of actual cash to be received. Worksheet 4 projects your monthly operating expenses for the first year of business, plus one-time, start-up expenses. Worksheet 5 is a schedule of your estimated personal living expenses during the first year.

Once you have completed worksheets 3 through 5, enter the monthly totals from the bottom line of each onto Worksheet 6, which is a summary of your cash needs. This will show you how much cash you will have to put into the business each month — and on a cumulative basis — during the first year of business. Once you have completed Worksheet 6, you will have a pretty good handle on how much money it is going to take to get your business started and approximately when you will need it.

If, under your most realistic projections, you are still running a deficit in cash flow each month at the end of the first year, you may want to do a similar projection out into the second year of operation.

If it appears you will need to borrow or raise money to keep the business operating until it gets into the black, find out well in advance how much you will be able to raise and whether or not you will be able to get that amount. If you plan to borrow, do you know how to put together a strong presentation to demonstrate to the prospective lender how you will be able to repay the loan? If not, see Section 9.7 and Chapter 10 for sources of information and help in obtaining financing for a small business.

Several books are available to help you along this process. One book, *The Loan Package*, can help you put together a loan application package for a small collateralized business loan. *Raising Capital: How to Write a Financing Proposal* can help you raise larger amounts of money for both equity and debt financing. Another book, *The Money Connection: Where and How to Apply for Business Loans and Venture Capital* provides an up-to-date list of federal, state, county, and community loan programs.

Affordable and easy-to-use software programs are also available to help your small business. Two noteworthy titles are *Small Business Expert* and *Start A Business*. Both of these programs complement this *Starting and Operating a Business* book. For more information on the software or the books above, call:

The Oasis Press
(800) 228-2275

1.7 Signing a Lease

If you will need to lease space for your business location, have you located a suitable place that is available? If so, there are a number of critical points you need to consider before you sign a lease with a landlord.

Remember that a lease is a binding legal contract, and if you agree to pay rent of $1,000 a month for two years, you are on the hook for $24,000, unless you can sublease or assign the lease to someone else, which could be difficult or impossible to do, depending on the terms of the lease. Key points to consider when signing a lease agreement include:

- What are the terms of the lease? Most businesses tend to start off by either growing rapidly or folding quickly. Thus, except in a retail or service business, you will probably be better off initially leasing on a month-to-month basis or for as short a lease term as you can get, such as three or six months, even if the monthly rent is higher than for a longer lease. You will already have enough financial problems if your business fails, without being saddled with a long-term lease obligation.

- Can you put up the kind of sign you must have on the building? A business like a restaurant can be devastated if the landlord doesn't permit a sign that is sufficiently visible to passersby.

- Will the landlord permit you to make necessary improvements and alterations to the leased premises?

- Will the local health department, fire and police departments, air pollution control authorities, and zoning rules permit operation of your particular type of business at the location you have chosen?

- Is your location in a high-crime area that will require expensive burglary insurance and security precautions?

- Is there enough parking nearby or good public transit access for customers?

- Is the location appropriate to the kind of business you will conduct? There is usually no need to locate a manufacturing operation in a busy, high-traffic area. On the other hand, retail businesses are usually heavily dependent on the number of people passing nearby on foot or by car. For example, the Pillsbury Company reportedly selects its sites for Burger King fast food restaurants by looking for locations that have at least 16,000 cars passing by each day at an average speed of about 30 miles per hour.[1]

- Does the lease provide you with an option to renew — and at what rental price — after the initial term expires?

- If the lease is for more than just a few months, do you have the right to sublease or assign the lease? If so, under what conditions or restrictions?

1.8 Will You Hire Employees?

In certain kinds of businesses, during the initial start-up phases — and perhaps even afterwards — you may be able to operate without employees by either doing all your work yourself, with the help of family members, or by contracting out certain functions to independent, outside contractors. To the extent you can do so, you may find your life is much simpler by doing it yourself or with independent contractors.

Once you hire even one employee, you take on a great many responsibilities as an employer, over and above meeting a payroll every week or two. These responsibilities include paying and filing tax returns for federal and state unemployment taxes, Social Security taxes, and income tax withholding from wages. In addition, you will need to comply with workers' compensation laws, employee health and safety laws, anti-discrimination laws, U.S. immigration law restrictions on hiring, and a variety of other federal and state labor laws and regulations that may apply once you hire employees. These and other employer requirements are discussed in Chapter 5.

This section reviews some of the legal restrictions on your hiring practices and provides you with a working outline of what you will need to consider in the way of personnel policies once your business reaches the point where you will have to hire employees.

Hiring Practices

Hiring personnel can be complicated because of the broad array of state and federal laws designed to prevent an employer from hiring on the basis of discriminatory factors, such as age, sex, race, or religion. Most of these laws affect all but the smallest employers, so you will have to be alert to most of these rules to avoid even the appearance of discrimination in your hiring practices.

While anti-discrimination rules apply to promotions, job assignments, firing, and other aspects of the employment relationship as well as to hiring, the focus here is mainly on hiring practices. This is the area where most small business owners are likely to stumble into trouble, even when they have no intention to discriminate.

Things Not to Do

All questions or information you express should relate to job qualifications only and not to extraneous factors, such as age, race, sex, or physical size or condition.

If there are special occupational requirements — for example, hard physical labor that might preclude hiring certain handicapped individuals — be sure to carefully document such unusual situations or requirements.

Help Wanted Ads

Use the list below to guide you when writing a help wanted advertisement.

- Do not mention race or national origin or any attribute of national origin, such as native language.
- Do not refer to sex classifications, such as "girl wanted."
- Avoid any type of reference to age, such as "young boy" or "recent high school graduate."

Job Application Forms

Your employment application forms should avoid any questions or information on these topics:

- Arrest record;
- Whether the applicant has ever filed for unemployment benefits;
- Place of birth or where parents were born;
- Physical characteristics, such as height or weight;

- Social Security number;
- Marital status;
- Labor union affiliation;
- Request for photograph;
- Religious affiliation;
- Mode of transportation to work;
- Sex;
- Race or national origin;
- Clubs or organizations, unless you instruct the applicant not to list organizations that indicate race or national origin; and
- Native language or how the applicant learned a foreign language.

A sample employment application form is provided for your review on page 30. If you wish to add additional questions to it, be careful not to indirectly request anything that would reflect on the applicant's race, religion, sex, age, marital status, national origin, or physical condition. Because state laws differ, check with your legal adviser or state employment department before preparing your employment application.

Employment Interviews

During interviews with potential employees, refrain from asking questions, such as:

- Are you a U.S. citizen?
- When did you attend grade school, high school, or college?
- Do you have children, and who will care for them while you are working?
- Do you have any physical or mental handicap?
- What does your spouse do for a living, and are you likely to move elsewhere?
- Would your religion prevent you from working on holidays or certain days of the week?

Federal law generally bans the use of any kind of lie detector tests in most private employment situations, except for drug manufacturers and distributors and certain security firms.[2] Many state laws are even more stringent.

In addition, questions on possible felony convictions, previous military service, and drug or alcohol addiction are not necessarily illegal in all cases, but they may entail difficulties and probably should be avoided.

Checking References

As a general rule, former employers have no legal obligation to give you any information about a former employee. As a practical matter, however, most former employers will at least verify the former employee's employment and the date of employment. Since a former employer can get into trouble for giving you negative information that they cannot substantiate, don't expect them to volunteer much information or to put anything negative in writing. For that reason, you should generally do reference checks by phone. Acceptable questions would include:

- Verifying information given by the applicant;
- Asking about the applicant's principal strong points, weak points, and degree of supervision needed;
- Asking about the applicant's attitude;
- Asking how the applicant's performance compared with others; and
- Asking if the applicant would be rehired.

Personnel Policies

Even before you hire your first employee, you will need to outline some basic personnel policies. Better yet, if you write down your policies on matters such as hours, vacation time, and sick leave and can give such a written summary to new employees, it will greatly help to clarify the employment relationship. Perhaps it will even prevent a misunderstanding that could lead to legal action against you by an employee.

Worksheet 7 provides a series of questions that will help you focus on different personnel policies that are typical in a small to medium-sized business. For a more thorough treatment of this area, and if you wish to develop a personnel policy manual for your business, you may want to obtain a copy of *A Company Policy and Personnel Workbook* from The Oasis Press.

Related Information

To supplement the information you have just read in this chapter, you may want to read the following sections which discuss more related information:

- Employee or Independent Contractor? — Section 9.11
- Fair Employment Practices — Section 5.8
- Sexual Harassment — Section 5.8
- Immigration Law Restrictions on Hiring — Section 5.9
- Hiring a Spouse as an Employee — Section 8.12
- Employee Wage-Hour and Child Labor Laws — Section 5.7
- The Americans with Disabilities Act — Section 5.11
- Mandatory Family and Medical Leave Requirements — Section 5.12

In addition, to get an overview of other legal obligations that come with the territory when you have employees, scan through Chapter 5.

1.9 Other Questions You Need to Ask

- Will or should you advertise? If you do, you need to decide what kind of advertising will be the most cost-effective for your business, whether it be newspaper ads, direct mail, radio, posters, handbills, or other forms of advertising and promotion.
- Do you understand what will be involved in purchasing, managing, and restocking your inventory of goods?
- How will you go about selling? Will you hire sales clerks or outside salespeople, or will you do most of the selling yourself?
- Will you sell to customers on credit? If so, how will you protect yourself from bad credit risks and outright deadbeats?
- How much of your personal savings are you putting at risk by going into business? Are you willing to risk losing all of it if the business is a failure?
- Can you run the business alone — or with help from family members — or would you do better with one or more partners or business associates to provide additional capital and skills and to divide up some of the responsibilities of running the business?

Again, the questions posed in this chapter are not intended to discourage you from going ahead with starting your business. Chances are you have already considered most of the points raised in this chapter and are reasonably confident that you will be able to do what is necessary to make your business work. If so, many of the questions raised above probably seem rather elementary and obvious to you, as they will to most individuals seriously considering going into business, and you will now want to proceed to the discussions in the remainder of this book.

If you have not previously given serious thought to most of the above points that are relevant to the type of business you are planning to start, now is the time to take a long, hard look at whether you are adequately prepared to embark upon such a venture.

1.10 How Likely Are You to Succeed?

One of the chief deterrents to starting your own business is the fear of failure. This fear has long been enforced by scary statistics that state approximately four out of five new businesses fail after only a short period of time. Given those kinds of frightening odds, it is surprising that anyone is brave enough to start a business.

However, a recent in-depth study of business failure rates done at the New Jersey Institute of Technology (NJIT) suggests the grim statistics on new firm failures may be little more than myth. According to the study, no more than 18% of new firms fail during the first eight years of being in business. Over half (54%) of all start ups survive over eight years with either their original owners (28%) or with a change in ownership (26%). The other 28% of new firms voluntarily terminate operations without losses to creditors.

The author of the study, Bruce A. Kirchoff, professor of entrepreneurship at NJIT and former chief economist for the U.S. Small Business Administration, states, "I suspect entrepreneurs have known the truth about survival and success for some time. While economists argue that entrepreneurs are foolish to start new businesses because the risk of failure is so high, 400,000 or more new firms are formed every year in the U.S. All these entrepreneurs cannot be stupid; they look around and talk to others and realize that their chances of survival and success are far better than academic economists have estimated. It's the economists that look foolish."[3]

According to Kirchoff, the greater survival rate is consistent with the evidence that small firms are the primary job creators in the U.S. economy. While other, even more recent, studies have suggested that most *net* new jobs are created by mid-sized businesses, rather than by either small or large businesses, a 1994 Dun & Bradstreet (D&B) study strongly backs Kirchoff's conclusion that the failure rate for new businesses is much lower than previously believed. The D&B study of 249,768 businesses that started up in 1985 showed that 177,133 (about 71%) were still going strong in early 1994.[4] The Kirchoff and D&B studies are not reasons to become foolhardy or overconfident about your prospects for success. On the other hand, they do indicate that starting your own business may not be the five-to-one long shot gamble you may have been told it was.

Endnotes

1. San Francisco *Chronicle*, Aug. 3, 1980.

2. The Employee Polygraph Protection Act, 29 U.S.C. 2001, *et seq.*

3. Kirchoff, Bruce A., Ph.D. *Assessing Firm Failure Fictions*. New Jersey Institute of Technology, 1993.

4. *Forbes,* June 6, 1994.

Worksheet 1 – Self-Evaluation Checklist for Going into Business

Under each question, check the answer that says what you feel or comes closest to it. Be honest with yourself.

Are you a self-starter?

☐   I do things on my own. Nobody has to tell me to get going.

☐   If someone gets me started, I keep going all right.

☐   Easy does it. I don't put myself out until I have to.

How do you feel about other people?

☐   I like people. I can get along with just about anybody.

☐   I have plenty of friends; I don't need anyone else.

☐   Most people irritate me.

Can you lead others?

☐   I can get most people to go along when I start something.

☐   I can give the orders if someone tells me what we should do.

☐   I let someone else get things moving; then I go along if I feel like it.

Can you take responsibility?

☐   I like to take charge of things and see them through.

☐   I'll take over if I have to, but I'd rather let someone else be responsible.

☐   There's always some eager beavers around wanting to show how smart they are. I say let them take the responsibility.

How good of an organizer are you?

☐   I like to have a plan before I start. I'm usually the one to get things lined up when the group wants to do something.

☐   I do all right unless things get too confusing; then I quit.

☐   Just when I'm all set, something comes along and presents too many problems, so I just take things as they come.

How good of a worker are you?

☐   I can keep going as long as I need to. I don't mind working hard for something I want.

☐   I'll work hard for a while, but when I've had enough, that's it.

☐   I can't see that hard work gets me anywhere.

☐   If I make up my mind to do something, I don't let anything stop me.

☐   I usually finish what I start if it goes well.

☐   If it doesn't go right away, I quit. Why beat my brains out?

Worksheet 1 – Self-Evaluation Checklist for Going into Business (continued)

How good is your health?

☐   I never get run down.

☐   I have enough energy for most things I want to do.

☐   I run out of energy sooner than most of my friends seem to.

Count the checks you made.

How many checks are there beside the first answer to each question? _____

How many checks are there beside the second answer to each question? _____

How many checks are there beside the third answer to each question? _____

If most of your checks are beside the first answers, you probably have what it takes to run a business. If not, you are likely to have more trouble than you can handle by yourself. You may want to find a partner who is strong on the points you are weak on. If many checks are beside the third answer, not even a good partner will be able to shore you up.

Source: U.S. Small Business Administration.

Worksheet 2 – Marketing Feasibility Study Checklist for Your Product or Service

Your Product

Briefly describe the nature of the product or service you will offer:

_____

_____

_____

Most products or services have a life cycle, beginning with very rapid growth in the introductory stage, which slows down in the maturity stage, flattens out in the saturation stage, and finally begins shrinking in the declining stage. Which stage of its market cycle do you believe your product or service is in?

☐ introductory (high growth)   ☐ saturation (little or no growth)

☐ maturity (slower growth)   ☐ declining (negative growth in demand)

If you believe your product is in one of the earlier, faster growing stages of its life cycle, what edge do you believe your product will have over similar products that may be introduced by new competitors who may come into the field?

_____

_____

_____

If you are entering at a fairly late stage of the product marketing cycle, why is it you believe that you can succeed in taking away others' market share with your product or service?

_____

_____

_____

How is your product or service different in terms of quality and price from what is already on the market?

_____

_____

_____

Is there good reason to believe that your customers will recognize the difference? _____ If so, why?

_____

_____

_____

What is different about your marketing strategy or distribution strategy that will enable your product or service to succeed in a market where there is little, if any, growth?

_____

_____

_____

Worksheet 2 – Marketing Feasibility Study Checklist for Your Product or Service (continued)

Your Potential Customers

Not everyone is a potential customer. Certain age groups, income levels, geographic areas, ethnic groups, and educational levels will be more likely than others to be your customers. You need to focus on who will need your product and be most likely to buy it and then where to locate your business or how to structure your marketing approach to reach those segments of the market that you are most interested in reaching. Spell out below, as clearly as you can, who your customers are most likely to be.

The particular area from which I will be able to draw most of my customers is:

_____

_____

_____

_____

In addition, I should draw a significant number of customers from the following area or areas:

_____

_____

_____

My plan or strategy for reaching potential customers in the above areas can be summarized as follows:

_____

_____

_____

_____

The target market for my product or service, in terms of demographics, should be among the following persons (Describe your ideal customer's age, gender, educational level, and geographical location.):

_____

_____

_____

_____

In terms of income groups, my particular product or service should appeal primarily to people in the following income levels:

- ☐ Under $25,000 a year household income
- ☐ $25,000 – $35,000 a year
- ☐ $35,000 – $50,000 a year
- ☐ $50,000 – $75,000 a year
- ☐ $75,000 – $100,000 a year
- ☐ More than $100,000 a year

My product or service is likely to be more in demand by certain social, cultural, and ethnic groups than others. The groups that are most likely to be customers, if any, are:

_____

_____

_____

_____

_____

_____

_____

The groups that are least likely to be customers are:

_____

_____

_____

_____

_____

Your Competition

Even though you may have done a great job in pinpointing and studying your market segment, the job isn't done until you have considered your competition.

Main competitors in my market area are (list firms by name):

1. _____

_____

2. _____

_____

3. _____

_____

4. _____

_____

5. _____

_____

6. _____

_____

Worksheet 2 – Marketing Feasibility Study Checklist for Your Product or Service (continued)

Based on my market research of statistical data, such as *Sales Marketing and Management Magazine*, the amount of buying power per business represented in my area is $ _____.

If I can generate that amount of sales, it: will ☐, will not ☐ be sufficient for me to operate successfully.

Five reasons why customers would buy from me rather than my competitors are:

1. _____
2. _____
3. _____
4. _____
5. _____

Five weaknesses my business will have when compared to my competitors are:

1. _____
2. _____
3. _____
4. _____
5. _____

To overcome these weaknesses, I will:

_____
_____
_____
_____
_____
_____
_____
_____
_____
_____
_____
_____
_____
_____
_____

Worksheet 3 – Estimated Cash Inflow from Sales for Year _____

	Jan.	Feb.	Mar.	Apr.	4-month Total
Gross Sales for Month					
Less: Credit Sales Made					
Subtotal: Cash Sales					
Plus: Collections on Prior Credit Sales					
Less: Bad Debts*					
Total: Net Cash Flow from Monthly Sales					

	May	June	July	Aug.	4-month Total
Gross Sales for Month					
Less: Credit Sales Made					
Subtotal: Cash Sales					
Plus: Collections on Prior Credit Sales					
Less: Bad Debts*					
Total: Net Cash Flow from Monthly Sales					

	Sept.	Oct.	Nov.	Dec.	4-month Total
Gross Sales for Month					
Less: Credit Sales Made					
Subtotal: Cash Sales					
Plus: Collections on Prior Credit Sales					
Less: Bad Debts*					
Total: Net Cash Flow from Monthly Sales					

Total Net Cash Flow from Monthly Sales for Year $ _____

* Consider using some percentage, say 1 or 2% of credit sale collections, to estimate your uncollectible debts.

Worksheet 4 – Estimated Business Cash Outlays for Year _____

	Jan.	Feb.	Mar.	Apr.	May
Monthly Expenses					
Rent					
Salaries and wages (except owner)					
Payroll taxes					
Advertising and promotion					
Insurance					
Federal estimated income tax					
State estimated income tax					
Owner's FICA or SE tax					
Telephone and utilities					
Inventory replacement purchase					
Interest on loans					
Maintenance					
Legal and accounting fees					
Office supplies					
Delivery expense					
Miscellaneous					
One-time Expenses					
Fixtures and equipment					
Decorating and remodeling					
Initial stock of inventory					
Utility and lease deposits					
Licenses and permits					
Other					
Total Expenses for Month					
Plus: Loan principal payment					
Less: Purchases on credit					
Plus: Payment on prior credit					
Net Monthly Cash Outlay					

June	July	Aug.	Sept.	Oct.	Nov.	Dec.	Annual Totals

Worksheet 5 – Estimated Personal and Living Expenses for Year _____

	Jan.	Feb.	Mar.	Apr.	May
Regular Payments					
Rent or house payment					
Property taxes					
Condo owner's dues					
Car payments					
Furniture and appliance payments					
Loan payments					
Health insurance					
Other insurance					
Household Expenses					
Food – restaurants					
Food – at home					
Telephone and utilities					
Water					
Personal Expenses					
Clothing and laundry					
Medical, dental, and drugs					
Education					
Dues and subscriptions					
Gifts and charity					
Gasoline and auto					
Entertainment and travel					
Miscellaneous spending					
Total Personal Expenses (Draw Required)					

June	July	Aug.	Sept.	Oct.	Nov.	Dec.	Annual Totals

Worksheet 6 – Summary of Estimated Cash Requirements for Year _____

	Jan.	Feb.	Mar.	Apr.	4-month Total
Net cash for month from sales – Worksheet 3					
Less: Net monthly cash outlay – Worksheet 4					
Subtotal: Net operating cash flow (or deficit)					
Less: Owner's draw for living & personal expenses – Worksheet 5					
Add: Money borrowed					
Add (or subtract): Equity capital paid in (or withdrawn) from the business					
Total: Net cash flow (or deficit) for month					
Cumulative* cash flow (or deficit)					

	May	June	July	Aug.	4-month Total
Net cash for month from sales – Worksheet 3					
Less: Net monthly cash outlay – Worksheet 4					
Subtotal: Net operating cash flow (or deficit)					
Less: Owner's draw for living & personal expenses – Worksheet 5					
Add: Money borrowed					
Add (or subtract): Equity capital paid in (or withdrawn) from the business					
Total: Net cash flow (or deficit) for month					
Cumulative* cash flow (or deficit)					

	Sept.	Oct.	Nov.	Dec.	4-month Total
Net cash for month from sales – Worksheet 3					
Less: Net monthly cash outlay – Worksheet 4					
Subtotal: Net operating cash flow (or deficit)					
Less: Owner's draw for living & personal expenses – Worksheet 5					
Add: Money borrowed					
Add (or subtract): Equity capital paid in (or withdrawn) from the business					
Total: Net cash flow (or deficit) for month					
Cumulative* cash flow (or deficit)					

* Add each month's net cash flow to the previous month's cumulative total.

Annual Totals: To get your total figures for the list below, add the three, four-month totals together for each item.

Net cash for month from sales – Worksheet 3   _____

Less: Net monthly cash outlay – Worksheet 4   _____

Subtotal: Net operating cash flow (or deficit)   _____

Less: Owner's draw for living & personal
expenses – Worksheet 5   _____

Add: Money borrowed   _____

Add (or subtract): Equity capital paid in (or
withdrawn) from the business   _____

Annual cumulative cash flow (or deficit)   _____

Sample Employment Application Form

Employment Application

Personal Data

Name: _____
　　　　　　(last)　　　　　　　　　　　　　　　　(first)　　　　　　　　　　　　　(middle)

Present address: _____
　　　　　　　　(street address)　　　　　　　　　　　(city)　　　　　(state)　　(zip)

Telephone numbers: _____　　_____
　　　　　　　　　　　(home)　　　　　　　　(work)

Education

High school: _____　Graduated? Yes ☐ No ☐　Location: _____

College or University: _____　Graduated? Yes ☐ No ☐　Degree(s): _____

Other (specify type): _____　Graduated? Yes ☐ No ☐　Certificate(s): _____

_____　Graduated? Yes ☐ No ☐　Certificate(s): _____

Work Experience

List below all present and previous employment, starting with the most recent.

Company name: _____　From (mo/yr): _____　Type of work: _____

Address: _____　To (mo/yr): _____　Name of supervisor: _____

_____　Reason you left: _____

Company name: _____　From (mo/yr): _____　Type of work: _____

Address: _____　To (mo/yr): _____　Name of supervisor: _____

_____　Reason you left: _____

Company name: _____　From (mo/yr): _____　Type of work: _____

Address: _____　To (mo/yr): _____　Name of supervisor: _____

_____　Reason you left: _____

Company name: _____　From (mo/yr): _____　Type of work: _____

Address: _____　To (mo/yr): _____　Name of supervisor: _____

_____　Reason you left: _____

May we contact the employers above?　Yes ☐　No ☐　If yes, list any employers you do not wish us to contact:

_____

_____

Remarks: _____

_____

_____

Worksheet 7 – Defining Your Company's Personnel Policies

Working Hours

Describe briefly the policy you will set for working hours, including:

Starting time? _____

_____

How much time will be allowed for lunch? _____

_____

Quitting time? _____

_____

Which days of the week employees will be expected to work? _____

_____

If, like many companies these days, you will adopt some kind of "flex-time" system, spell out how it will work.

_____

_____

_____

_____

Overtime

Outline your policy on overtime work. Refer to Section 5.7 of this book for legal requirements for paying overtime premiums. See also Section 11.5 regarding state wage laws. Points to consider here include:

Will you pay exempt employees (administrative or professional) overtime if they work extra hours? _____

_____

Will you require employees to obtain permission to work overtime? _____

_____

Compensation

Make a list of the job positions in the company other than your own and the compensation level for each. On a separate piece of paper, write out a specific job description for each position, outlining duties and responsibilities. Refer to sections 5.7 and 11.5 of this book for a description of hourly minimum wage requirements.

Position	Hourly Wage	Salary	Total Monthly Pay
_____	_____	_____	_____
_____	_____	_____	_____
_____	_____	_____	_____
_____	_____	_____	_____
_____	_____	_____	_____

Worksheet 7 – Defining Your Company's Personnel Policies (continued)

Vacation Policy

Describe how much paid vacation employees will have and how this may increase after a certain number of years of service. _____

_____

Will vacation time and sick leave time off be combined into a single category for employees (as some companies now do to reward employees who do not abuse sick leave and to discourage others from using sick leave as additional vacation by playing hooky)? _____

_____

Will you pay employees, who terminate, for unused vacation? (The laws of many states require you to do so.)

_____

_____

Family and Medical Leave Policy

Outline your policy for both paid and unpaid sick leave and family and medical leave. (If you have more than 50 employees, the federal Family and Medical Leave Act may apply to you. See Section 5.12.)

Sick leave: _____

_____

Family/medical leave: _____

_____

Birth or adoption of a child? _____

_____

Leaves of Absence

What will your policy be towards employees who request unpaid leaves of absence? _____

_____

_____

Time Off with Pay

Will you provide other time off with pay for such eventualities as funerals, jury duty, and training?

Funerals or family emergencies? _____

_____

Jury duty? _____

_____

Attend work-related seminars and training sessions? _____

_____

Promotions and Evaluations

Outline your policy for evaluating employees' performance and determining when promotions will be made.

_____

_____

_____

_____

_____

Fringe Benefits

Consider which employee fringe benefits you will provide and specify your policy for each.

Medical insurance: _____

_____

Long-term disability insurance: _____

_____

Life insurance: _____

_____

Dental insurance: _____

_____

Medical expense reimbursement: _____

_____

Child care benefits: _____

_____

Maternity benefits: _____

_____

Pension or profit-sharing plans: _____

_____

Paid holidays: _____

_____

Automobiles or allowances: _____

_____

Expense accounts: _____

_____

Worksheet 7 – Defining Your Company's Personnel Policies (continued)

Fringe Benefits (continued)

Education assistance programs: _____

_____

_____

_____

Employee discounts on purchases: _____

_____

Stock options (if incorporated): _____

_____

Incentive bonus plan: _____

_____

Other: _____

_____

_____

_____

Placement Fees

If you hire employees through a personnel agency or "headhunting" firm, will you pay the placement fee?

_____

_____

Other Company Policies

_____

_____

_____

_____

_____

_____

_____

_____

_____

_____

_____

_____

Chapter 2

Choosing the Legal Form of the Business

The hardest thing in the world to understand is Income Tax.

— Albert Einstein

2.1 General Considerations

A business venture can be structured in several ways; however, the law classifies businesses so that most fall into one of three legal forms — the sole proprietorship, the partnership, or the corporation. There are also certain variations on some of these basic legal forms, such as the S corporation and the limited partnership. In addition, the limited liability company (LLC), a relatively new form of business organization, has gained legal status in more than 40 states. See Section 2.6 for more on LLCs.

If you are planning to start a business, consider the following questions when deciding your business' legal form:

- Will someone else share in ownership of the business? If so, it will not be a sole proprietorship. The choice will be between a partnership arrangement and a corporation, or possibly a limited liability company.

- How important is it to limit personal liability for debts or claims against the business? If this is a major consideration, incorporating the business would generally be the best means of limiting your liability.

- Which form of business organization will result in the least taxes? While there is no universal answer to this question, the rest of this chapter explains when it is and isn't beneficial to incorporate for tax reasons.

Before choosing the legal form of your business, it is important to realize that you may need to change to a different form at some time in the

Changing Legal Forms

future. Changing legal forms is easier to do with some forms of business than with others. As a broad generalization, it is usually a simpler matter to change from a sole proprietorship to a partnership, or to change from a sole proprietorship or partnership to a corporation, than it is to move in the opposite direction. (An LLC is usually treated like a partnership.)

For example, converting a corporation into a sole proprietorship or partnership may result in substantial individual and corporate-level taxes when the corporation is liquidated. This would occur if the value of the business, when transferred to the stockholders of the corporation, was greater than the cost or tax basis for their stock, resulting in taxable gains to the stockholders. If some of the corporate assets have value in excess of their tax basis, the corporation will also have taxable gains and will pay a corporate tax on such gains when it transfers the assets to its stockholders.

While there are almost always some expenses and complications in changing the legal form of a business, such changes are quite routine transactions. Many businesses start off as sole proprietorships, develop into partnerships, and later incorporate, if tax and other considerations indicate that it no longer makes good business sense not to be incorporated. Thus, the choice of one legal form when starting a business should not be considered a final choice.

2.2 Advantages and Disadvantages of Sole Proprietorships

The great advantage of operating a new business as a sole proprietorship is that it is simple and does not require any formal action to set it up. You can start your business today as a sole proprietorship — there is no need to wait for an attorney to draft and file documents or for the government to approve them.

Of course, you will need a business license, and a few states require you to register to do business. As a sole proprietor, you are the sole owner of your business. If married, however, your spouse will usually have a one-half interest in the business in a state which has community property laws.

Personal Liability

As the owner of the sole proprietorship, you will be personally liable for any debts or taxes of the business or other claims, such as legal damages resulting from a lawsuit. This is one reason why many entrepreneurs prefer to use a corporation rather than a sole proprietorship. Unlimited personal liability is perhaps the major disadvantage of operating a business in the form of a sole proprietorship.

Profit (or Loss) Is Yours

All of the profit or loss from your business belongs to you and must be reported on your federal income tax return, *Schedule C, Income (or Loss) from a Business or Profession*, on *Form 1040*. This can either be an advantage or a disadvantage for income tax purposes, depending on the circumstances.

If operating the business results in losses or significant tax credits, you may be able to use the tax losses or tax credits to reduce taxes on income from other sources. Or, if your sole proprietorship generates modest profits — but not more than about $60,000 to $75,000 a year — overall taxes may be less than if incorporated, assuming you need most of the income to live on.

Unemployment Tax Savings

As a sole proprietor, you are not considered an employee of your business. As a result, you will avoid having to pay unemployment taxes on your earnings from the business. Both the state and federal governments impose unemployment taxes on wages or salaries, but not on self-employment income. Note that a corporation would normally get an income tax deduction for the unemployment tax it paid on your salary, so that the actual after-tax savings from operating as a sole proprietorship would be somewhat less than the unemployment taxes you would avoid paying. Refer to sections 5.3 and 11.5 regarding the unemployment taxes you must pay for each employee.

Withdraw Assets Tax-Free

Another advantage of a sole proprietorship is that you can shift funds in and out of your business account or withdraw assets from the business with few tax, legal, or other limitations. In a partnership or a limited liability company, you can generally withdraw funds only by agreement and, in the case of a corporation, a withdrawal of funds or property will usually be taxable as a dividend or capital gain and may violate some states' corporation laws.

Limited Tax Savings for Fringe Benefits

A major disadvantage of sole proprietorships and partnerships is they cannot obtain a number of significant tax benefits regarding group-term life insurance benefits, long-term disability insurance coverage, and medical insurance or medical expense reimbursements. To qualify for favorable tax treatment regarding such fringe benefit plans, it is necessary to incorporate. A self-employed individual is allowed to deduct 25% of his or her health insurance in computing adjusted gross income.[1] This deduction expired on December 31, 1993, but Congress will very likely extend it again.

The special advantages of corporate pension and profit-sharing plans have largely been eliminated. There are now virtually no differences in the tax treatment of self-employed (Keogh) plans of sole proprietorships and partnerships, as compared with corporate retirement plans. See Section 8.3.

See the table at the end of this chapter which summarizes the key characteristics of sole proprietorships, partnerships, corporations, and limited liability companies.

2.3 Advantages and Disadvantages of Partnerships

General Partnerships

In general, any two or more individuals or entities who agree to contribute money, labor, property, or skill to a business and who agree to share in its profits, losses, and management are considered to have a partnership. You can choose to have a general partnership or a limited partnership.

Creating a partnership can be a very simple matter since the law does not require any formal written documents or other formalities for most partnerships. As a practical matter, however, it is much sounder business practice for partners in a business to have a written partnership agreement that, at a minimum, spells out their agreement on such basic issues as:

- How much and what kind of property each partner will contribute to the venture;
- What value will be placed on the contributed property;
- How profits and losses will be divided among the partners;
- When and how profits will be withdrawn;
- Whether or how certain partners will be compensated for their services to the partnership or for making capital available to the partnership; and
- How changes in ownership of interests in the partnership will be handled.

A written partnership agreement should be prepared by an attorney and, if possible, should be reviewed by a tax accountant before it is put into effect. Partnerships are a bit like marriages; they usually start out with a great deal of trust but have a high break-up rate. Be advised that partnerships are easy to get into, require a lot of patience and understanding to live with, and are often costly and painful to get out of.

Liability of Partners

As a partner, you are an agent for the partnership and can do anything necessary to operate the business, such as hire employees, borrow money, or enter into contracts on behalf of the partnership. You and each of your partners — except for a limited partner in a limited partnership — have personal liability for the debts, taxes, and other claims against the partnership.

If the partnership's assets are not sufficient to pay creditors, the creditors can satisfy their claims out of your personal assets. In addition, when any partner fails to pay personal debts, the partnership's business may be disrupted if his or her creditors proceed to satisfy their claims out of his or her interest in the partnership by seeking what is called a charging order against partnership assets.

State and Federal Tax Requirements

While a partnership must file federal and usually state information returns — *Form 1065* is the federal form — it generally pays no income tax. Instead, the partnership reports each partner's share of income or loss on the information return, and each partner reports the income or loss on *Schedule E* of his or her individual income tax return, *Form 1040*.

Certain partnerships are allowed to use a fiscal year, rather than the calendar year, for tax filing purposes; however, these partnerships may have to report and pay income taxes directly if the use of a fiscal year results in a tax-deferral benefit to their partners.[2] The exceptionally complex accounting required to determine this tax is part of the price a partnership must pay if it elects to have a fiscal tax year.

In addition, partnerships are required to file a special report, *Form 8308*, with the IRS each time a sale or exchange of an interest in the partnership occurs.[3]

Like a sole proprietor, a partner is not generally considered an employee of the partnership for income tax and payroll tax purposes. The income tax advantages and disadvantages of a sole proprietorship are equally applicable to a partnership since a partner's share of income from a partnership is treated essentially the same as income from a sole proprietorship. For example, your income from a partnership may be subject to federal self-employment tax but not to federal and state unemployment taxes as discussed in Section 2.2.

Dissolution

Unless a partnership agreement provides otherwise, a partnership usually terminates when any partner dies or withdraws from the partnership. This is in contrast to a corporation which, theoretically, has perpetual existence. Under the laws of most states, bankruptcy of a partner or the partnership itself will cause the dissolution of the partnership, regardless of any agreement.

Limited Partnerships

The law provides for a special kind of partnership in which partners have limited personal liability: the limited partnership. The limited partnership is more regulated than the more common general partnership, but it allows investors who will not be actively involved in the partnership's operations to become partners without being exposed to unlimited liability of the business' debts, if it should go out of business.

A limited partner risks only his or her investment but must allow one or more general partners to exercise control over the business. In fact, if the limited partner becomes involved in the partnership's operations, he or she may lose his or her protected status as a limited partner. The general partners in a limited partnership are fully liable for the partnership's debts. Every limited partnership must have one or more general partners as well as one or more limited partners.

State law requires certain formalities in the case of a limited partnership that are not required for other partnerships. To qualify for their special status, limited partnerships must usually file a *Certificate of Limited Partnership* with the secretary of state or other state and county offices. Establishing a limited partnership also requires a written partnership agreement. See Section 11.2 regarding special filing requirements for partnerships under state law.

2.4 Advantages and Disadvantages of Corporations

A corporation is an artificial legal entity that exists separately from the people who own, manage, control, and operate it. It can make contracts, pay taxes, and is liable for debts. Corporations exist only because state statutory laws allow them to be created.

A business corporation issues shares of its stock, as evidence of ownership, to the person or persons who contribute the money or business assets which the corporation will use to conduct its business. Thus, the stockholders or shareholders are the owners of the corporation, and they are entitled to any dividends the corporation pays and to all corporation assets — after all creditors have been paid — if the corporation is liquidated.

Limited Personal Liability

The main reason most businesses incorporate is to limit owner liability to the amount invested in the business. Generally, stockholders in a corporation are not personally liable for claims against the corporation and are, therefore, at risk only to the extent of their investment in the corporation. Likewise, the officers and directors of a corporation are not normally liable for the corporation's debts, although in some cases, an officer whose duty it is to withhold federal income tax from employees' wages may be liable to the IRS if the taxes are not withheld and paid over to the IRS as required.

Potential Loss of Limited Personal Liability

The advantage of limited liability is not always completely available through incorporation. For example, don't start a corporation on a shoestring. If your corporation is capitalized too thinly with equity capital (your money) as compared to debt capital (borrowed money), the courts may determine that your corporation is a thin corporation and hold you and your stockholders directly liable to creditors.

Failure to observe corporate formalities and the separate legal existence of the corporation can have a similar result. This is called "piercing the corporate veil" by the courts, and means if a corporation is not adequately capitalized and properly operated to protect the interests of creditors, the courts can take away the veil of limited liability that normally protects the stockholders.

Piercing the corporate veil is relatively uncommon. A much more frequent problem is that many banks and other lenders will not loan money to a small incorporated business unless someone, usually the stockholders of the corporation, personally guarantees repayment of the loan.

Despite this common business practice, the limited liability feature can still be an important protection from personal liability for other debts, such as accounts payable to suppliers and others who sell goods or services to the corporation on credit, typically without requiring any personal guarantee of payment by the owners.

Even this partial protection is a significant advantage of incorporating for most small business owners. Being incorporated can also protect you from personal liability regarding lawsuit damages not covered by your corporation's liability insurance policies; for example, someone slips on a banana peel in your store and sues the corporation for ten million dollars. To help you avoid personal liability for corporate acts, consult your attorney and keep thorough and specific records of your corporation's operations, policies, and meetings.

Continuous Existence

Unlike a sole proprietorship or partnership, a corporation has continuous existence and does not terminate upon the death of a stockholder or a change of ownership of some or all of its stock. Creditors, suppliers, and customers, therefore, often prefer to deal with an incorporated business because of this greater continuity.

Naturally, a corporation can be terminated by mutual consent of the owners or even by one stockholder in some instances.

Cost of Incorporating

To set up a corporation, you must file articles of incorporation with the state office that grants and approves corporate charters. See Section 11.2 for more information on state incorporating requirements.

Legal fees usually run between $500 and $1,000, even for a simple incorporation, and if it is necessary to obtain a permit from the state to issue stock or securities, legal fees can be much more.

Thus, it should be apparent that one of the disadvantages of incorporating is the cost involved, which will be substantial even for the simplest incorporation. In addition to the costs of establishing a corporation, there will be recurring costs, often including annual franchise or corporate income taxes.

Federal Corporate Income Taxes

Corporations filing their income tax returns on *Form 1120-A* or *Form 1120* will be taxed at different rates depending on the amount of their taxable income. The following table lists the current federal corporate income tax rates, which are 39% in the highest bracket.

Corporate Tax Rate Table

Taxable Income	Tax Rate
Not more than $50,000	15%
$50,000 to $75,000	25%
$75,000 to $100,000	34%
$100,000 to $335,000	39%
$335,000 to $10 million	34%
$10 million to $15 million	35%
$15 million to $18,333,333	38%
More than $18,333,333	35%

As an owner, you will most likely draw a salary from your corporation. This salary will be subject to FICA (Social Security) taxes and state and federal unemployment taxes. These unemployment taxes, however, are not imposed on your income when you own a sole proprietorship or partnership. FICA taxes are generally the same (in total) on the wages of a corporate employee/owner as would be the self-employment tax on the same amount of business income if you were a sole proprietor or a partner.

For certain types of unincorporated businesses, however, such as a firm whose income is from interest or real estate rentals, or both, there is no self-employment tax on the income. By incorporating such a firm, you would unnecessarily incur FICA (Social Security) taxes of 15.3% on your earnings from the business.

Personal Service Corporations

Certain kinds of corporations called qualified personal service corporations (QPSCs) are taxed at a flat rate of 35%, instead of the graduated tax rates listed above.[4] While it may not always be clear whether an incorporated service business is a QPSC, the IRS defines a QPSC by these characteristics:

- At least 95% of the value of its stock is held by employees or their estates or beneficiaries; and
- The employees perform services at least 95% of the time in the following fields: health, law, engineering, architecture, accounting, actuarial science, performing arts, or consulting.

Double Taxation of Corporate Earnings

Regular corporations, which are also called C corporations, have one major potential disadvantage that usually does not exist for other legal forms of doing business — the problem of potential double taxation of the earnings of the corporation. This problem arises because a C corporation must pay corporate income taxes on its taxable income. Then, the after-tax earnings may be subject to a second tax on either the individual stockholders, if the earnings are distributed as dividends, or as a corporate penalty tax, if the earnings are not distributed as dividends.

The main ways in which a corporation's earnings can be subject to double taxation are:

- Payment of taxable dividends — Shareholders will be taxed when the corporation pays dividends to them out of earnings that have already been taxed once at the corporate level. In this case, the shareholders would pay individual federal income taxes (plus state tax, in most states) on the dividends they receive. If, for example, the corporation has already paid tax at a marginal rate of 34% on its income, and individual federal income tax of roughly 40% is paid by the stockholders on the remaining 66% of corporate income that is distributed to them as dividends, then less than 40% of the profit earned by the corporation will end up in the owners' bank accounts after taxes. Even less would remain after taxes in a state that has corporate or individual income taxes, or both.

- Corporate accumulated earnings tax — Corporations that retain too much of their after-tax earnings, instead of paying out the earnings as dividends, risk being hit by the accumulated earnings tax. This tax rate can be up to 39.6% of the accumulated income.

- Certain other C corporations that are considered to be "personal holding companies" under the federal tax law are exempt from the accumulated earnings tax; however, they may instead be subject to a 39.6% personal holding company tax on their undistributed income that is derived from certain sources, such as rents, royalties, and interest or dividends received from stock investments.

- Even if a corporation avoids all of the above double taxation problems during its existence, double taxation may yet arise if the corporation is liquidated and either the value of the corporate assets or the stock is greater than the tax basis. In that case, the stockholders will usually have to pay capital gains taxes if the amount they receive in liquidation exceeds the tax basis of their shares of stock.

As a practical matter, few small incorporated businesses ever encounter actual double taxation, except when the corporation is liquidated. Most small corporations do not pay dividends, and there are many tax-planning approaches that will enable a company and its shareholders to avoid the accumulated earnings tax or personal holding company tax on their undistributed earnings.

See Section 8.9 for a discussion of various tax-planning techniques that will permit you to avoid the problems of potential double taxation listed above.

Income Splitting

By using a corporation, it may be possible to split your overall profit between two or more taxpayers so that none of the income gets taxed in the highest tax brackets. Thus, the total tax paid by the two taxpayers — you and your corporation — may be less than if all of the income were taxed to you, as in a sole proprietorship.

See Section 8.2 for a more detailed discussion of how income splitting can help reduce your income and estate taxes.

Fringe Benefit Plans

Federal and state tax laws permit you, as a corporate employer, to provide a number of different fringe benefits to employees on a tax-favored basis. These tax-favored fringe benefits include medical insurance plans, self-insured medical reimbursement plans, disability insurance, and group-term life insurance. An unincorporated business receives the same tax treatment for its employees, but not for its owners. In an unincorporated business, the payments made on behalf of the sole proprietor or partners for these fringe benefits are generally not deductible as expenses of the business, in contrast to fringe benefits paid for by a corporation for its shareholders/employees. So the tax benefits of employee fringe benefits, such as those listed above, are another reason for incorporating your business and becoming an employee of the corporation.

Note, however, that if your corporation is an S corporation, it will be treated much like a partnership for fringe benefit purposes, with regard to its shareholders who own 2% or more of its stock.[5] An exception to this partnership treatment of S corporation shareholders is for medical insurance premiums paid on their behalf, which can be deducted by the S corporation. However, the amount deducted by the corporation for medical insurance must be reported as taxable compensation income on the shareholder/employee's *Form W-2*, for income tax purposes,[6] but not for FICA (Social Security) tax purposes if the insurance plan covers employees generally.[7]

Unlike an unincorporated business, a corporation — other than an S corporation — can generally deduct the insurance premiums or other fringe benefit payments it makes on behalf of an employee who is an owner of the business, while the employee is not taxed on the value of the benefit provided. This is far more favorable than payments of salary to an employee, which are fully taxable.

The major types of fringe benefit plans, other than retirement plans, that allow for tax deductions to the corporation and no taxable income to the employee are discussed in more detail in Section 8.3.

Tax Break for Dividends Received by a Corporation

Another important tax advantage of a C corporation is that, in general, it can deduct 70% of the dividends it receives from stock investments from its federal taxable income.[8] This tax benefit, called the dividends received deduction, is discussed in more detail in Section 8.2.

Tax Break for Investing in Small Business Stock

The Clinton tax package that was enacted in August 1993 provides a major tax incentive for investing in the stock of certain small corporations. This incentive is not available for investments in unincorporated businesses or in stock of S corporations.

A noncorporate investor who purchases "qualified small business stock" after August 10, 1993 and holds it for five years or more will be allowed to exclude from his or her taxable income up to 50% of any capital gain reported on the sale of stock.[9] If the current maximum tax rate on capital gains remains at 28%, this would translate into a very low effective tax rate of only 14% on gains from qualified small business stock.

Qualified small business stock is stock of a C corporation that meets an active business test during the period the stock is held. Stock in a special entity, such as a Domestic International Sales Corporation (DISC), regulated investment company, or a real estate investment trust, is ineligible. In addition, the corporation must not have more than $50 million in gross assets before or immediately after the stock is issued to the investor.

To meet the active business test, a corporation must use at least 80% of its assets in the conduct of one or more qualified trades or businesses. Personal service firms, banks, finance or investment businesses, insurance companies, and farming businesses are not considered qualified trades or businesses; neither are companies in certain extractive industries, or in the hotel, motel, or restaurant businesses.

While this section has outlined a number of important tax advantages of incorporating a business, the picture is not all that one-sided. Some of the potential tax disadvantages of corporations are discussed in more detail in Section 8.9. Most of those disadvantages are not applicable if you elect S corporation status. Deciding whether to incorporate in this state or elsewhere is discussed in Section 9.12.

Corporate Income Tax Disadvantages

2.5 Advantages and Disadvantages of S Corporations

The first thing to understand about S corporations — formerly referred to as Subchapter S corporations — is they are just like any other corporation in terms of corporate law requirements, limited liability of shareholders, and all other corporate aspects, except regarding tax treatment. An S corporation is simply a regular corporation that meets certain requirements and which has elected to be treated somewhat like a partnership for federal income tax purposes. Most, but not all, states also allow this special tax treatment for S corporations. See Section 11.2 for a discussion of how S corporations are treated for tax purposes in this state.

Once a corporation has made an election with the IRS to be treated as an S corporation, its shareholders will generally report their share of the corporation's taxable income or loss on their individual tax returns. That is, the corporation "passes through" its income or loss and tax credits to the shareholders in proportion to their stock holdings in the corporation, much like a partnership.

The S corporation does not usually pay tax on any of its income.[10] Any domestic S corporation, however, must file *Form 1120S, U.S. Income Tax Return for an S Corporation*, regardless of any tax due. *Form 1120S* must be filed by March 15, if filing under a calendar-year basis, or the 15th day of the third month following the close of a fiscal year.

An S corporation must furnish a copy of *Schedule K-1, Shareholder's Share of Income, Credits, Deductions* to each shareholder. By not providing *Schedule K-1* before filing *Form 1120S*, the S corporation could incur penalties.

In certain instances, an S corporation may be subject to tax on "built-in gains." Built-in gains are untaxed gains on the assets of a corporation that would have been recognized as taxable if the assets had been sold at fair market value on the day a corporation became an S corporation.

Profits are deemed to be distributed to the shareholders on the last day of the corporation's tax year, whether or not the profits are actually distributed.[11] Thus, if profits of an S corporation are distributed as dividends, the distribution itself is ordinarily not taxable, so there is no double taxation of distributed profits.

The Clinton Deficit Reduction tax package enacted in August 1993 has made S corporations somewhat less attractive because it raised individual tax rates to a new maximum rate of 39.6%, up from 31%. In addition, the top corporate rate remains at 34%, except for corporations with more than ten million dollars of taxable income. These corporations now pay 35%. Shareholders of an S corporation may now pay individual income tax at a higher rate than would a C corporation in some income brackets and at a lower rate in other brackets. Thus, from a tax-rate standpoint, S corporations no longer enjoy a clear advantage over C corporations.

In addition, capital gains on sale of the stock of an S corporation will not qualify for the new 50% capital gain exclusion that is discussed in Section 2.4.

S Corporation Requirements

To qualify for S corporation treatment, your corporation must meet the following requirements:

- It must be a domestic corporation — that is, incorporated in the United States.[12]
- No shareholder can be a nonresident alien individual.[13]
- All of its shareholders must generally be individuals, although certain trusts, called Qualified Subchapter S Trusts and Grantor Trusts, may hold stock under certain circumstances. No shareholder can be a corporation or a partnership.[14]
- The corporation can have only one class of common stock and no preferred stock.[15]
- There cannot be more than 35 shareholders.[16] For this purpose, a husband and wife who are both stockholders will be counted as only one stockholder, whether or not they hold the stock in joint ownership.[17]
- The corporation cannot be a member of an affiliated group of corporations.[18] If it owns stock in a subsidiary that is considered an affiliate, it may not be able to qualify under the S corporation provisions.
- Less than 25% of the corporation's gross receipts during three successive tax years must be from passive sources, such as interest income, dividends, rent, royalties, or proceeds from the sale of securities.[19] The passive income limit does not apply at all for a brand new corporation or an existing corporation that has no accumulated earnings and profits when it elects S corporation status.[20]

Electing S Corporation Status

To become an S corporation, your company must meet the above requirements and file an election on *Form 2553* with the IRS. The election must be signed by all of the corporation's shareholders,[21] including your spouse, who may have a community property interest in stock that is in your name. The S corporation election must be filed during the first two months and 15 days of the corporation's tax year for which the election is to go into effect or at any time during the preceding tax year.[22]

Since a newly formed corporation that wants to start out as an S corporation does not have a preceding tax year, it has to file an election in the two-month and 15-day period after it is considered to have begun its first tax year. Its first tax year is considered to start when it issues stock to shareholders, acquires assets, or begins to do business, whichever occurs first. Filing of articles of incorporation with the secretary of state usually does not begin the first taxable year.

Care must be taken to file the election at the right time, which can be tricky, since it is sometimes difficult to determine when a corporation first begins to do business. There can be some horrendous tax consequences if you operate the corporation as though it were an S corporation, and the election is later determined to have been filed too early or too late.

Extreme care must also be taken if a regular C corporation elects to change over to S corporation status; this should not be done without consulting a competent tax adviser. A regular corporation that elects to become an S corporation will generally be subject to an eventual corporate-level tax on any built-in gains on its assets — assets with a value greater than their tax basis — if assets are sold for a gain within ten years.

Terminating an S Corporation Election

If it becomes desirable to revoke or terminate S corporation status after a few years, as is often the case, this can be done if shareholders owning more than half the stock sign and file a revocation form.[23] A revocation is effective for the tax year it is filed, if it is filed during the first two months and 15 days of that tax year.[24] If it is filed later in the year, it does not become effective until the next tax year.[25]

Doing anything, however, that causes the corporation to cease to qualify as an S corporation — such as selling stock to a corporate shareholder — will also terminate the election, effective on the first day after the corporation ceases to qualify as an S corporation. In that case, the company must file two short-period tax returns for the year, the first — up to the date it ceased to qualify — as an S corporation, the second as a regular taxable corporation.

Once a corporation terminates an S corporation election, it cannot re-elect S corporation status for five years, unless it obtains the consent of the IRS.[26]

Reasons for Electing S Corporation Status

For a corporation, electing S corporation status can be very advantageous in some instances, and less so, or even disadvantageous in other situations. An S corporation election should not be made without the advice and assistance of a tax professional, since it is a very complex and technical area of the tax law.

Electing S corporation treatment for a corporation is usually most favorable in these types of situations:

- Where it is expected that the corporation will experience losses for the initial year or years of doing business and where the shareholders will have income from other sources that the "passed through" losses can shelter from tax. If S corporation losses are passive losses — such as losses from real estate investments — they can only be used to offset other passive activity income, except for certain shareholders who are real estate professionals.

- Where, because of the low tax brackets the shareholders are in, there will be tax savings if the anticipated profits of the corporation are passed through to them rather than being taxed at corporate tax rates.

- Where the nature of the corporation's business is such that the corporation does not need to retain a major portion of profits in the business. In this case, all or most of the profits can be distributed as dividends without the double taxation that would occur if no S corporation election were in effect.

- Where a corporation is in danger of incurring an accumulated earnings penalty tax for failure to pay out its profits as dividends.

It will often be advantageous for your corporation to operate as an S corporation in its early years, when losses can be passed through to shareholders, or when income is not so great as to push the shareholders into higher tax brackets. Also, the nontax advantage of being incorporated and protected from personal liability if the business fails is generally most important during the early years of operation, when the risk of failure is highest.

Many businesses initially start off as S corporations, obtaining the advantage of limited liability while being taxed much like an unincorporated business. Later, when or if the profit from the business becomes very substantial, the S corporation election can be terminated, and the C corporation can be used to split income between the corporation and its stockholder/employees.

Disadvantages of S Corporation Election

While there are some significant advantages to operating as an S corporation, the S corporation election is frequently not advisable under some circumstances. Some of the possible disadvantages of operating your business in the form of an S corporation are:

- The change to S corporation status may eventually result in a large corporate-level tax on built-in gains or an immediate last in, first out (LIFO) recapture tax.

- The tax law regarding S corporations is very complex and you should expect to pay fairly substantial additional legal or accounting fees to your tax adviser, compared to what would be necessary with a regular corporation.

- S corporations are now treated almost exactly like regular corporations with respect to pension and profit-sharing plans. One important difference remains; any employee who owns 5% or more of the stock and participates in the S corporation's pension or profit-sharing plan is prohibited from borrowing from the plan, unlike a participant in a regular corporation's retirement plan.[27]

- Certain built-in gains of an S corporation may be taxed to the corporation and the shareholder for federal tax purposes.[28]

- Fringe benefit payments for medical, disability, and group-term life insurance for 2% shareholders are deductible, to the corporation, but are taxable to the shareholder/employee.[29]

- Unlike many regular corporations, very few newly electing S corporations may now have a fiscal tax year that ends earlier than September.[30]

For your convenience, a sample of *Form 2553, Election by a Small Business Corporation*, and a summary of key characteristics regarding business organization forms are provided at the end of this chapter.

2.6 Advantages and Disadvantages of Limited Liability Companies

The S corporation and the limited partnership may soon become endangered species due to the appearance of a new form of legal entity that has a number of advantages over both and that is proliferating across the country. This new type of entity is called a limited liability company (LLC). An LLC closely resembles and is taxed as a partnership, but it offers the benefit of limited liability like corporations. It is also similar to a limited partnership, except that in an LLC, all partners have the benefit of limited liability.

In 1988, the IRS concluded in Revenue Ruling 88-76 that a Wyoming limited liability company could be classified as a partnership for federal income tax purposes, despite its limited liability, because it lacked continuity of life. Under Wyoming law, LLCs have to terminate in a specified period of years, usually 30 years or less.

Another reason for this classification is because interests in the LLC were not freely transferable. This ruling was highly favorable, from a taxpayer's standpoint, because LLCs offer the corporate benefits of limited liability, while retaining the flexible flow-through tax treatment of a partnership. This is generally preferable even to an S corporation for income tax purposes.

Because this favorable IRS ruling opened the floodgates, more than four-fifths of the states have followed Wyoming's lead in adopting similar LLC laws, and approximately 45 states will probably have adopted LLC laws by early 1995.

Despite the obvious advantages of LLCs, do not be in a rush to set one up, even if you are located in one of the states that has adopted a limited liability company law. At present, if you set up an LLC in State X that allows LLCs and you do business in State Y, which does not, your LLC may not provide any limited liability protection from creditors in State Y. This is a severe risk, and one you won't face if your business is incorporated.

Under the LLC laws in almost every state, an LLC must have at least two owners, and thus is not a viable choice for a sole proprietor who wishes to change to a business entity that offers limited liability. Even if you were to create a single-owner LLC under the laws of a state that permits one-person LLCs — Arkansas, for example, permits such LLCs — the tax treatment is unclear at present. Every favorable IRS tax ruling to date on LLCs has involved a multi-owner LLC that the IRS "blessed" as being the tax equivalent of a partnership. A one-person LLC is clearly not like a partnership, so unless or until the IRS says such, an LLC is taxable as a sole proprietorship, and setting one up will have very uncertain tax consequences. Unless you want to become a pioneer, it may be prudent to shy away from creating a one-person LLC until the IRS rules on this issue. This brings to mind the old saying about how to spot a pioneer in a crowd — the pioneers are always the ones with the arrows in their backs.

In most states, LLCs can engage in any business that is permissible for a corporation to engage in, with certain limited exceptions, including professions. However, a number of states that recognize LLCs do not yet allow professional LLCs for physicians, attorneys, or other such professionals.

Another potential drawback is that a subcommittee of the U.S. House Ways and Means Committee is already looking into the possibility of enacting federal legislation that would cause LLCs to be taxed as corporations in order to prevent the loss of significant federal tax revenues. Such legislation, if enacted, would defeat the whole purpose of setting up an LLC and could even leave you in a considerable tax predicament if you put your business into an LLC and the law changed subsequently. You might even have to pay a large capital gains tax if you then decided to liquidate the LLC. Extreme caution is advised before adopting LLC status. Consult a good tax adviser before you even consider setting up an LLC, despite their obvious attractions. See Chapter 11 for more specific information on LLCs in this state.

Endnotes

1. I.R.C. § 162(l).
2. I.R.C. §§ 444 and 7519.
3. I.R.C. § 6050K.
4. I.R.C. § 11(b)(2).
5. I.R.C. § 1372(a).
6. Rev. Rul. 91-26, 1991-1 C.B. 184.
7. I.R.S. Ann. 92-16, 1992-5 I.R.B. 53.
8. I.R.C. § 243(a).
9. I.R.C. § 1202.
10. I.R.C. § 1374.
11. I.R.C. § 1366.
12. I.R.C. § 1361(b).
13. I.R.C. § 1361(b)(1)(C).
14. I.R.C. § 1361(b)(1)(B).
15. I.R.C. § 1361(b)(1)(D).
16. I.R.C. § 1361(b)(1)(A).
17. I.R.C. § 1361(c).
18. I.R.C. § 1361(b)(2)(A).
19. I.R.C. § 1362(d)(3).
20. I.R.C. § 1362(d)(3)(B).
21. I.R.C. § 1362(a)(2).
22. I.R.C. § 1362(b).
23. I.R.C. § 1362(d)(1)(B).
24. I.R.C. § 1362(d)(1)(C)(i).
25. I.R.C. § 1362(d)(i)(C)(ii).
26. I.R.C. § 1362(g).
27. I.R.C. § 4975(d).
28. I.R.C. § 1374(a).
29. Rev. Rul. 91-26, 1991-1 C.B. 184.
30. I.R.C. § 1378(a).
31. I.R.C. § 162(1).

Key Characteristics of the Various Legal Forms of Business Organization – Summary

	Proprietorship	General or Limited Partnership
Simplicity in Operation and Formation	Simplest to establish and operate.	Relatively simple and informal, except that a limited partnership must have a written agreement.
Liability for Debts, Taxes, and Other Claims	Owner has unlimited personal liability.	General partners have unlimited personal liability; limited partners are only at risk to the extent of their investment.
Federal Income Taxation of Business Profits	Taxed to the owner at individual tax rates of up to 39.6% or more, depending on exemptions and deductions which may phase out.	Taxed to partners at their individual tax rates.
Double Taxation if Profits Withdrawn from Business	No.	No.
Deduction of Losses by Owners	Yes. May be subject to "passive loss" restrictions.	Yes. But limited partner's deductions cannot exceed amount invested as a limited partner — except for real estate, in some instances. Losses are generally restricted by the "passive loss" rules.
Social Security Tax on Earnings of Owner from Business	15.3% of owner's self-employment earnings in 1994 on first $60,600 of income, plus 2.9% on earnings of more than $60,600, half of which is now deductible for income tax purposes.	15.3% of each partner's share of self-employment earnings from the business in 1994 on up to $60,600 in earnings are taxed, plus 2.9% tax on earnings over $60,600. Half of tax is deductible for income tax.
Unemployment Taxes on Earnings of Owner from Business	None.	None.
Retirement Plans	Keogh plan. Deductions, other features now generally the same as for corporate pension and profit-sharing plans. But proprietor cannot borrow from Keogh Plan.	Keogh plan. Same as for proprietorships. A 10% partner cannot borrow from Keogh Plan.
Tax Treatment of Medical, Disability, and Group-Term Life Insurance on Owners	Not deductible, except part of medical expenses may be an itemized deduction on owner's tax return, including medical insurance premiums. However, 25% of medical insurance on an owner is allowed as a deduction from adjusted gross income — at least until December 31, 1993.[31]	Not deductible, except part of medical expenses may be an itemized deduction on owner's tax return, including medical insurance premiums. However, 25% of medical insurance on an owner is allowed as a deduction from adjusted gross income — at least until December 31, 1993.
Taxation of Dividends Received on Investments	Dividends received on stock investments are fully taxable to owner.	Dividends taxable to individual partners. See proprietorship.

Limited Liability Company	Regular Corporation	S Corporation
Generally similar to a partnership, but required to file articles of organization.	Requires most formality in establishment and operation.	Same as a regular corporation but requires close oversight by a tax adviser (an additional cost).
Members are generally not liable for an LLC's debts, but they often have to guarantee loans, as a practical matter, which is similar to a corporation.	Stockholders are not generally liable for corporate debts, but often have to guarantee loans, as a practical matter, if the corporation borrows money. Also, corporate officers may be liable to the IRS for failure to withhold and pay withholding taxes on employees' wages.	Stockholders are not generally liable for corporate debts, but often have to guarantee loans, as a practical matter, if the corporation borrows money. Also, corporate officers may be liable to the IRS for failure to withhold and pay withholding taxes on employees' wages.
Taxed to owners at their individual tax rates, unless the IRS treats the LLC as a corporation.	Taxed to the corporation, at rates higher than those of individuals — maximum of 34% or 39% in 1993, except for very large corporations.	Taxed to individual owners at their individual rates — certain gains are taxable to the corporation as well.
No, unless the LLC is treated as a corporation.	Yes, but not on reasonable compensation paid to owners who are employees of the corporation.	No, in general.
Yes, generally, if treated as a partnership by IRS. No, if treated as a corporation by IRS.	No. Corporation must carry over initial losses to offset future profits, if any.	Yes, in general, for federal tax purposes. But not for state tax purposes in all states. Loss for a shareholder limited to investment in stock plus amount loaned to the corporation. Losses may be subject to "passive loss" restrictions.
Not clear yet. Probably same as for a partnership, if treated as partnership by IRS. Same as a corporation, if the LLC is treated as a corporation.	Owner/employee of corporation pays 7.65% on his or her salary and corporation pays 7.65%. Total Social Security (FICA) tax on employer and employee is 15.3% of employee's first $60,600 of wages (in 1994). Employee and corporation each pay 1.45% on wages above $60,600.	Owner/employee of corporation pays 7.65% on his or her salary and corporation pays 7.65%. Total Social Security (FICA) tax on employer and employee is 15.3% of employee's first $60,600 of wages (in 1994). Employee and corporation each pay 1.45% on wages above $60,600.
Not clear yet, but probably none, if treated as a partnership for income tax purposes by IRS.	Yes. State and federal unemployment taxes apply to salaries paid to owners.	Yes. State and federal unemployment taxes apply to salaries paid to owners.
Not clear yet, but probably same as a partnership, if treated as a partnership by IRS.	Corporate retirement plans are no longer significantly better than Keogh plans. Deduction limits are same now as for Keogh, but participants can borrow from plan.	Plans now essentially identical to regular corporate retirement plans, except that shareholder/employee (5% shareholder) of S corporation cannot borrow from plan.
Not clear yet, but probably same as a partnership, if treated as a partnership by IRS.	Corporations may be allowed to deduct corporation medical insurance premium or reimbursements paid under medical reimbursement plan. Generally not taxable to the employee, even if employee is an owner. Similar treatment for disability and group-term life insurance plans.	Fringe benefits for 2% shareholders are deductible by corporation, but must be included in income of the shareholder who may be allowed to deduct 25% of medical insurance from adjusted gross income.
Dividends taxable to individual members, if the LLC is treated as a partnership.	Dividends are taxable to the corporation. However, 70% of the dividends received are generally free of federal income tax (unless stock is purchased with borrowed money), an important tax advantage.	Dividends taxable to individual shareholders of the S corporation, as in the case of a partnership.

Instructions for Form 2553: Sample

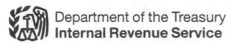 **Department of the Treasury**
Internal Revenue Service

Instructions for Form 2553
(Revised September 1993)
Election by a Small Business Corporation
Section references are to the Internal Revenue Code unless otherwise noted.

Paperwork Reduction Act Notice.—We ask for the information on this form to carry out the Internal Revenue laws of the United States. You are required to give us the information. We need it to ensure that you are complying with these laws and to allow us to figure and collect the right amount of tax.

The time needed to complete and file this form will vary depending on individual circumstances. The estimated average time is:

Recordkeeping	6 hr., 13 min.
Learning about the law or the form	2 hr., 59 min.
Preparing, copying, assembling, and sending the form to the IRS	3 hr., 13 min.

If you have comments concerning the accuracy of these time estimates or suggestions for making this form more simple, we would be happy to hear from you. You can write to both the **Internal Revenue Service,** Attention: Reports Clearance Officer, T:FP, Washington, DC 20224; and the **Office of Management and Budget,** Paperwork Reduction Project (1545-0146), Washington, DC 20503. **DO NOT** send the tax form to either of these offices. Instead, see **Where To File** below.

General Instructions

Purpose.—To elect to be an "S corporation," a corporation must file Form 2553. The election permits the income of the S corporation to be taxed to the shareholders of the corporation rather than to the corporation itself, except as provided in Subchapter S of the Code. For more information, get **Pub. 589,** Tax Information on S Corporations.

Who May Elect.—A corporation may elect to be an S corporation only if it meets **all** of the following tests:

1. It is a domestic corporation.

2. It has no more than 35 shareholders. A husband and wife (and their estates) are treated as one shareholder for this requirement. All other persons are treated as separate shareholders.

3. It has only individuals, estates, or certain trusts as shareholders. See the instructions for Part III regarding qualified subchapter S trusts.

4. It has no nonresident alien shareholders.

5. It has only one class of stock (disregarding differences in voting rights). Generally, a corporation is treated as having only one class of stock if all outstanding shares of the corporation's stock confer identical rights to distribution and liquidation

proceeds. See Regulations section 1.1361-1(l) for more details.

6. It is not one of the following ineligible corporations:

a. A corporation that owns 80% or more of the stock of another corporation, unless the other corporation has not begun business and has no gross income;

b. A bank or thrift institution;

c. An insurance company subject to tax under the special rules of Subchapter L of the Code;

d. A corporation that has elected to be treated as a possessions corporation under section 936; or

e. A domestic international sales corporation (DISC) or former DISC.

7. It has a permitted tax year as required by section 1378 or makes a section 444 election to have a tax year other than a permitted tax year. Section 1378 defines a permitted tax year as a tax year ending December 31, or any other tax year for which the corporation establishes a business purpose to the satisfaction of the IRS. See Part II for details on requesting a fiscal tax year based on a business purpose or on making a section 444 election.

8. Each shareholder consents as explained in the instructions for Column K.

See sections 1361, 1362, and 1378 for additional information on the above tests.

Where To File.—File this election with the Internal Revenue Service Center listed below.

If the corporation's principal business, office, or agency is located in ▼	Use the following Internal Revenue Service Center address ▼
New Jersey, New York (New York City and counties of Nassau, Rockland, Suffolk, and Westchester)	Holtsville, NY 00501
New York (all other counties), Connecticut, Maine, Massachusetts, New Hampshire, Rhode Island, Vermont	Andover, MA 05501
Illinois, Iowa, Minnesota, Missouri, Wisconsin	Kansas City, MO 64999
Delaware, District of Columbia, Maryland, Pennsylvania, Virginia	Philadelphia, PA 19255
Florida, Georgia, South Carolina	Atlanta, GA 39901
Indiana, Kentucky, Michigan, Ohio, West Virginia	Cincinnati, OH 45999
Kansas, New Mexico, Oklahoma, Texas	Austin, TX 73301
Alaska, Arizona, California (counties of Alpine, Amador, Butte, Calaveras, Colusa, Contra Costa, Del Norte, El Dorado, Glenn, Humboldt, Lake, Lassen, Marin, Mendocino, Modoc, Napa, Nevada, Placer, Plumas, Sacramento, San Joaquin, Shasta, Sierra, Siskiyou, Solano, Sonoma, Sutter, Tehama, Trinity, Yolo, and Yuba), Colorado, Idaho, Montana, Nebraska, Nevada, North Dakota, Oregon, South Dakota, Utah, Washington, Wyoming	Ogden, UT 84201
California (all other counties), Hawaii	Fresno, CA 93888
Alabama, Arkansas, Louisiana, Mississippi, North Carolina, Tennessee	Memphis, TN 37501

When To Make the Election.—Complete and file Form 2553 **(a)** at any time before the 16th day of the third month of the tax year, if filed during the tax year the election is to take effect, or **(b)** at any time during the preceding tax year. An election made no later than 2 months and 15 days after the beginning of a tax year that is less than 2½ months long is treated as timely made for that tax year. An election made after the 15th day of the third month but before the end of the tax year is effective for the next year. For example, if a calendar tax year corporation makes the election in April 1994, it is effective for the corporation's 1995 calendar tax year. See section 1362(b) for more information.

Acceptance or Nonacceptance of Election.—The Service Center will notify the corporation if its election is accepted and when it will take effect. The corporation will also be notified if its election is not accepted. The corporation should generally receive a determination on its election within 60 days after it has filed Form 2553. If box Q1 in Part II is checked on page 2, the corporation will receive a ruling letter from the IRS in Washington, DC, that either approves or denies the selected tax year. When box Q1 is checked, it will generally take an additional 90 days for the Form 2553 to be accepted.

Do not file Form 1120S until the corporation is notified that its election has been accepted. If the corporation is now required to file **Form 1120,** U.S. Corporation Income Tax Return, or any other applicable tax return, continue filing it until the election takes effect.

Care should be exercised to ensure that the IRS receives the election. If the corporation is not notified of acceptance or nonacceptance of its election within 3 months

Cat. No. 49978N

Instructions for Form 2553: Sample (continued)

of date of filing (date mailed), or within 6 months if box Q1 is checked, please take follow-up action by corresponding with the Service Center where the corporation filed the election. If the IRS questions whether Form 2553 was filed, an acceptable proof of filing is: **(a)** certified or registered mail receipt (timely filed); **(b)** Form 2553 with accepted stamp; **(c)** Form 2553 with stamped IRS received date; or **(d)** IRS letter stating that Form 2553 has been accepted.

End of Election.— Once the election is made, it stays in effect for all years until it is terminated. During the 5 years after the election is terminated under section 1362(d), the corporation (or a successor corporation) can make another election on Form 2553 only with IRS consent. See Regulations section 1.1362-5 for more details.

Specific Instructions

Part I

Part I must be completed by all corporations.

Name and Address of Corporation.—Enter the true corporate name as set forth in the corporate charter or other legal document creating it. If the corporation's mailing address is the same as someone else's, such as a shareholder's, please enter "c/o" and this person's name following the name of the corporation. Include the suite, room, or other unit number after the street address. If the Post Office does not deliver to the street address and the corporation has a P.O. box, show the box number instead of the street address. If the corporation changed its name or address after applying for its EIN, be sure to check the box in item G of Part I.

Item A. Employer Identification Number.—If the corporation has applied for an employer identification number (EIN) but has not received it, enter "applied for." If the corporation does not have an EIN, it should apply for one on **Form SS-4,** Application for Employer Identification Number, available from most IRS and Social Security Administration offices.

Item D. Effective Date of Election.—Enter the beginning effective date (month, day, year) of the tax year requested for the S corporation. Generally, this will be the beginning date of the tax year for which the ending effective date is required to be shown in item I, Part I. For a new corporation (first year the corporation exists) it will generally be the date required to be shown in item H, Part I. The tax year of a new corporation starts on the date that it has shareholders, acquires assets, or begins doing business, whichever happens first. If the effective date for item D for a newly formed corporation is later than the date in item H, the corporation should file Form 1120 or Form 1120-A, for the tax period between these dates.

Column K. Shareholders' Consent Statement.—Each shareholder who owns (or is deemed to own) stock at the time the election is made must consent to the election. If the election is made during the corporation's tax year for which it first takes effect, any person who held stock at any time during the part of that year that occurs before the election is made, must consent to the election, even though the person may have sold or transferred his or her stock before the

election is made. Each shareholder consents by signing and dating in column K or signing and dating a separate consent statement described below.

An election made during the first 2½ months of the tax year is effective for the following tax year if any person who held stock in the corporation during the part of the tax year before the election was made, and who did not hold stock at the time the election was made, did not consent to the election.

If a husband and wife have a community interest in the stock or in the income from it, both must consent. Each tenant in common, joint tenant, and tenant by the entirety also must consent.

A minor's consent is made by the minor or the legal representative of the minor, or by a natural or adoptive parent of the minor if no legal representative has been appointed.

The consent of an estate is made by an executor or administrator.

If stock is owned by a trust that is a qualified shareholder, the deemed owner of the trust must consent. See section 1361(c)(2) for details regarding qualified trusts that may be shareholders and rules on determining who is the deemed owner of the trust.

Continuation sheet or separate consent statement.—If you need a continuation sheet or use a separate consent statement, attach it to Form 2553. The separate consent statement must contain the name, address, and employer identification number of the corporation and the shareholder information requested in columns J through N of Part I.

If you want, you may combine all the shareholders' consents in one statement.

Column L.—Enter the number of shares of stock each shareholder owns and the dates the stock was acquired. If the election is made during the corporation's tax year for which it first takes effect, do not list the shares of stock for those shareholders who sold or transferred all of their stock before the election was made. However, these shareholders must still consent to the election for it to be effective for the tax year.

Column M.—Enter the social security number of each shareholder who is an individual. Enter the employer identification number of each shareholder that is an estate or a qualified trust.

Column N.—Enter the month and day that each shareholder's tax year ends. If a shareholder is changing his or her tax year, enter the tax year the shareholder is changing to, and attach an explanation indicating the present tax year and the basis for the change (e.g., automatic revenue procedure or letter ruling request).

If the election is made during the corporation's tax year for which it first takes effect, you do not have to enter the tax year of any shareholder who sold or transferred all of his or her stock before the election was made.

Signature.—Form 2553 must be signed by the president, treasurer, assistant treasurer, chief accounting officer, or other corporate officer (such as tax officer) authorized to sign.

Part II

Complete Part II if you selected a tax year ending on any date other than December 31

(other than a 52-53-week tax year ending with reference to the month of December).

Box P1.—Attach a statement showing separately for each month the amount of gross receipts for the most recent 47 months as required by section 4.03(3) of Revenue Procedure 87-32, 1987-2 C.B. 396. A corporation that does not have a 47-month period of gross receipts cannot establish a natural business year under section 4.01(1).

Box Q1.—For examples of an acceptable business purpose for requesting a fiscal tax year, see Revenue Ruling 87-57, 1987-2 C.B. 117.

In addition to a statement showing the business purpose for the requested fiscal year, you must attach the other information necessary to meet the ruling request requirements of Revenue Procedure 93-1, 1993-1 I.R.B. 10 (updated annually). Also attach a statement that shows separately the amount of gross receipts from sales or services (and inventory costs, if applicable) for each of the 36 months preceding the effective date of the election to be an S corporation. If the corporation has been in existence for fewer than 36 months, submit figures for the period of existence.

If you check box Q1, you must also pay a user fee of $200 (subject to change). Do not pay the fee when filing Form 2553. The Service Center will send Form 2553 to the IRS in Washington, DC, who, in turn, will notify the corporation that the fee is due. See Revenue Procedure 93-23, 1993-19 I.R.B. 6.

Box Q2.—If the corporation makes a back-up section 444 election for which it is qualified, then the election must be exercised in the event the business purpose request is not approved. Under certain circumstances, the tax year requested under the back-up section 444 election may be different than the tax year requested under business purpose. See **Form 8716,** Election To Have a Tax Year Other Than a Required Tax Year, for details on making a back-up section 444 election.

Boxes Q2 and R2.—If the corporation is not qualified to make the section 444 election after making the item Q2 back-up section 444 election or indicating its intention to make the election in item R1, and therefore it later files a calendar year return, it should write "Section 444 Election Not Made" in the top left corner of the 1st calendar year Form 1120S it files.

Part III

Certain Qualified Subchapter S Trusts (QSSTs) may make the QSST election required by section 1361(d)(2) in Part III. Part III may be used to make the QSST election only if corporate stock has been transferred to the trust on or before the date on which the corporation makes its election to be an S corporation. However, a statement can be used in lieu of Part III to make the election.

Note: *Part III may be used only in conjunction with making the Part I election (i.e., Form 2553 cannot be filed with only Part III completed).*

The deemed owner of the QSST must also consent to the S corporation election in column K, page 1, of Form 2553. See section 1361(c)(2).

Ⓢ *Printed on recycled paper*

*U.S. Government Printing Office: 1993 — 301-628/80221

Form 2553 – Election by a Small Business Corporation: Sample

Form **2553** (Rev. September 1993) Department of the Treasury Internal Revenue Service	**Election by a Small Business Corporation** (Under section 1362 of the Internal Revenue Code) ▶ For Paperwork Reduction Act Notice, see page 1 of instructions. ▶ **See separate instructions.**	OMB No. 1545-0146 Expires 8-31-96

Notes: 1. *This election, to be an "S corporation," can be accepted only if all the tests are met under **Who May Elect** on page 1 of the instructions; all signatures in Parts I and III are originals (no photocopies); and the exact name and address of the corporation and other required form information are provided.*

   2. *Do not file **Form 1120S**, U.S. Income Tax Return for an S Corporation, until you are notified that your election is accepted.*

Part I   Election Information

Please Type or Print	Name of corporation (see instructions)	**A** Employer identification number (EIN)
	Number, street, and room or suite no. (If a P.O. box, see instructions.)	**B** Date incorporated
	City or town, state, and ZIP code	**C** State of incorporation

D Election is to be effective for tax year beginning (month, day, year) . . . . ▶ ___/___/___

E Name and title of officer or legal representative who the IRS may call for more information | **F** Telephone number of officer or legal representative ( )

G If the corporation changed its name or address after applying for the EIN shown in **A**, check this box . . . . ▶ ☐

H If this election takes effect for the first tax year the corporation exists, enter month, day, and year of the **earliest** of the following: (1) date the corporation first had shareholders, (2) date the corporation first had assets, or (3) date the corporation began doing business . . . . ▶ ___/___/___

I Selected tax year: Annual return will be filed for tax year ending (month and day) ▶ . . . .

If the tax year ends on any date other than December 31, except for an automatic 52-53-week tax year ending with reference to the month of December, you **must** complete Part II on the back. If the date you enter is the ending date of an automatic 52-53-week tax year, write "52-53-week year" to the right of the date. See Temporary Regulations section 1.441-2T(e)(3).

J Name and address of each shareholder, shareholder's spouse having a community property interest in the corporation's stock, and each tenant in common, joint tenant, and tenant by the entirety. (A husband and wife (and their estates) are counted as one shareholder in determining the number of shareholders without regard to the manner in which the stock is owned.)	K Shareholders' Consent Statement. Under penalties of perjury, we declare that we consent to the election of the above-named corporation to be an "S corporation" under section 1362(a) and that we have examined this consent statement, including accompanying schedules and statements, and to the best of our knowledge and belief, it is true, correct, and complete. (Shareholders sign and date below.)*		L Stock owned		M Social security number or employer identification number (see instructions)	N Share-holder's tax year ends (month and day)
	Signature	Date	Number of shares	Dates acquired		

*For this election to be valid, the consent of each shareholder, shareholder's spouse having a community property interest in the corporation's stock, and each tenant in common, joint tenant, and tenant by the entirety must either appear above or be attached to this form. (See instructions for Column K if a continuation sheet or a separate consent statement is needed.)

Under penalties of perjury, I declare that I have examined this election, including accompanying schedules and statements, and to the best of my knowledge and belief, it is true, correct, and complete.

Signature of officer ▶ | Title ▶ | Date ▶

See Parts II and III on back. | Cat. No. 18629R | Form **2553** (Rev. 9-93)

Form 2553 – Election by a Small Business Corporation: Sample (continued)

Form 2553 (Rev. 9-93)   Page **2**

Part II   **Selection of Fiscal Tax Year (All corporations using this part must complete item O and one of items P, Q, or R.)**

O   Check the applicable box below to indicate whether the corporation is:

   1. ☐ A new corporation adopting the tax year entered in item I, Part I.

   2. ☐ An existing corporation retaining the tax year entered in item I, Part I.

   3. ☐ An existing corporation changing to the tax year entered in item I, Part I.

P   Complete item P if the corporation is using the expeditious approval provisions of Revenue Procedure 87-32, 1987-2 C.B. 396, to request: **(1)** a natural business year (as defined in section 4.01(1) of Rev. Proc. 87-32), or **(2)** a year that satisfies the ownership tax year test in section 4.01(2) of Rev. Proc. 87-32. Check the applicable box below to indicate the representation statement the corporation is making as required under section 4 of Rev. Proc. 87-32.

   1. Natural Business Year ► ☐ I represent that the corporation is retaining or changing to a tax year that coincides with its natural business year as defined in section 4.01(1) of Rev. Proc. 87-32 and as verified by its satisfaction of the requirements of section 4.02(1) of Rev. Proc. 87-32. In addition, if the corporation is changing to a natural business year as defined in section 4.01(1), I further represent that such tax year results in less deferral of income to the owners than the corporation's present tax year. I also represent that the corporation is not described in section 3.01(2) of Rev. Proc. 87-32. (See instructions for additional information that must be attached.)

   2. Ownership Tax Year ► ☐ I represent that shareholders holding more than half of the shares of the stock (as of the first day of the tax year to which the request relates) of the corporation have the same tax year or are concurrently changing to the tax year that the corporation adopts, retains, or changes to per item I, Part I. I also represent that the corporation is not described in section 3.01(2) of Rev. Proc. 87-32.

Note: *If you do not use item P and the corporation wants a fiscal tax year, complete either item Q cr R below. Item Q is used to request a fiscal tax year based on a business purpose and to make a back-up section 444 election. Item R is used to make a regular section 444 election.*

Q   Business Purpose—To request a fiscal tax year based on a business purpose, you must check box Q1 and pay a user fee. See instructions for details. You may also check box Q2 and/or box Q3.

   1. Check here ► ☐ if the fiscal year entered in item I, Part I, is requested under the provisions of section 6.03 of Rev. Proc. 87-32. Attach to Form 2553 a statement showing the business purpose for the requested fiscal year. See instructions for additional information that must be attached.

   2. Check here ► ☐ to show that the corporation intends to make a back-up section 444 election in the event the corporation's business purpose request is not approved by the IRS. (See instructions for more information.)

   3. Check here ► ☐ to show that the corporation agrees to adopt or change to a tax year ending December 31 if necessary for the IRS to accept this election for S corporation status in the event: (1) the corporation's business purpose request is not approved and the corporation makes a back-up section 444 election, but is ultimately not qualified to make a section 444 election, or (2) the corporation's business purpose request is not approved and the corporation did not make a back-up section 444 election.

R   Section 444 Election—To make a section 444 election, you must check box R1 and you may also check box R2.

   1. Check here ► ☐ to show the corporation will make, if qualified, a section 444 election to have the fiscal tax year shown in item I, Part I. To make the election, you must complete **Form 8716**, Election To Have a Tax Year Other Than a Required Tax Year, and either attach it to Form 2553 or file it separately.

   2. Check here ► ☐ to show that the corporation agrees to adopt or change to a tax year ending December 31 if necessary for the IRS to accept this election for S corporation status in the event the corporation is ultimately not qualified to make a section 444 election.

Part III   **Qualified Subchapter S Trust (QSST) Election Under Section 1361(d)(2)****

Income beneficiary's name and address	Social security number
Trust's name and address	**Employer identification number**

Date on which stock of the corporation was transferred to the trust (month, day, year) . . . . ►   /   /

In order for the trust named above to be a QSST and thus a qualifying shareholder of the S corporation for which this Form 2553 is filed, I hereby make the election under section 1361(d)(2). Under penalties of perjury, I certify that the trust meets the definitional requirements of section 1361(d)(3) and that all other information provided in Part III is true, correct, and complete.

_____   _____

Signature of income beneficiary or signature and title of legal representative or other qualified person making the election   Date

****Use of Part III to make the QSST election may be made only if stock of the corporation has been transferred to the trust on or before the date on which the corporation makes its election to be an S corporation. The QSST election must be made and filed separately if stock of the corporation is transferred to the trust after the date on which the corporation makes the S election.

   Printed on recycled paper   *U.S. Government Printing Office: 1993 — 301-628/80216

Notes

Chapter 3

Buying an Existing Business

Trust in Allah. But always tie your camel.

— Arab proverb

3.1 General Considerations

Obviously, it may not be necessary for you to build your business from the ground up. If you wish to go into a particular type of business, you may find an appropriate existing business that is for sale. Buying an existing business can have considerable advantages over starting one from scratch, and one of the most important of these is the chance to start out with an established customer base. It is also sometimes possible to have the seller stay on as an employee or consultant for a transitional period to help you become familiar with the operation of the business.

Other advantages of purchasing a going business include:

- You may be able to take a regular draw or salary right from the start, if it is a profitable operation. This is usually not the case in a start-up operation, which typically starts off losing money.

- Your risk is frequently less when you buy an established, profitable business. You know that it has a viable market if it is already profitable. Your main risk would be that something would change after you acquire the business, such as new competition or product obsolescence, and this would adversely affect your business. Another risk is that you will mismanage the business.

- Getting started is simpler. By buying an established business, you can focus your attention on giving good service and operating profitably. Since most facilities, operating systems, and employees will already be in place, your efforts will not be diluted by remodeling the premises, trying to hire employees, setting up accounting systems, acquiring initial inventory, and the like. With an existing business, in most cases, you should be able to step right into an operation that has already been established by someone else.

While there are some definite advantages to buying an established business, as compared to starting a new business, it can also be a lot more complicated and involves many potential pitfalls that you must avoid. The watchword in buying any kind of business should be *caveat emptor* — let the buyer beware.

Because the process of buying and selling businesses is very complicated even for experts, do not attempt it without retaining the services of a reliable attorney and, usually, a good accountant. Even skilled professionals, however, can generally only protect you from certain legal, financial, or tax pitfalls that arise in connection with the purchase of a business. Many of the potential problems that would not become obvious until it is too late can only be spotted in advance, if at all, by the exercise of your good judgment and as a result of your doing the necessary homework. Important pitfalls you should look out for in connection with buying an existing business are discussed in Section 3.3.

3.2 Finding a Business for Sale

How do you go about finding a business that is for sale? You have a number of ways to approach the problem, none of which are ideal, so you will probably want to use two or more of the approaches discussed below to find and buy an existing business.

Advertisements

The business opportunities section of your local newspaper, regional magazine, or trade association journal can be a major source of leads to businesses that are for sale. Such ads often do not tell you very much about the nature of the business, but at least they can be a starting point in your search. In many cases, the ads will have been placed by a business broker rather than the owner. The business broker will often be representing people who are seeking to sell their businesses.

Business Brokers and Realtors

Business brokers and realtors can be excellent sources in your search for a business that is for sale. The main drawback of going through a business broker or realtor is that his or her fee (paid by the seller) is usually a percentage, often 10%, of the sales price of the business; so the broker or realtor, like the seller, is trying to get the highest possible price for the business. At the same time, the seller will usually want more than he or she would if the sale were made without a broker, since he or she knows that the broker will take a healthy commission out of the negotiated sales price.

Your local chamber of commerce can usually tell you a great deal about the local business community and also provide you with leads to firms that are for sale.

Local Chambers of Commerce

Professionals, such as accountants, attorneys, and bankers, can often provide leads regarding good businesses even before they are on the market. Frequently, a business client will tell his or her accountant, attorney, or banker that he or she is planning to sell out or retire, long before making any formal attempt to put the business up for sale. So, if you have friends who are accountants, attorneys, or bankers, take them to lunch and tell them what you have in mind. Typically, they will have a vested interest in finding a friendly buyer for a retiring client's business, since they may loose that account if the firm is sold to buyers who have their own professional advisers.

Accountants, Attorneys, and Bankers

Certified public accountants (CPAs) can be excellent sources of leads. Not only will they usually not charge you any kind of finder's fee, but they usually know which of their clients' businesses are little gold mines. In some cases, a CPA who has a very profitable client who wishes to sell out may even want to go into the business with you as a financial partner, leaving the day-to-day operations to you. In these cases, you can generally be sure that if the CPA is putting up his or her money, he or she has studied the client's business carefully and feels that it is a real money-maker. In short, the CPA will have already done much of the prescreening for you.

Often, if you see a small business you think you might like to buy, the simplest approach will be to talk to the owner and see if he or she is interested in selling. While an owner may have had no serious thoughts about selling the business before, the appearance of an interested potential buyer is not only somewhat flattering, but it may even cause him or her to decide to sell out to you. Many businesses are bought and sold this way.

The Direct Approach

3.3 What to Look for Before You Leap

One of the first questions you may want to ask is: "Why are you selling your business?" Often, the response will be the owner wants to retire or is in poor health. While such an explanation may be true in many cases, it is also quite likely to be a well-rehearsed cover story. The real reason may be the business is in a declining neighborhood and the owner has been robbed several times recently and wants out. Or, the owners of a profitable little corner grocery store may be anxious to sell out while they can because they have learned that a major chain-store supermarket will

Why Is the Business for Sale?

be opening in the neighborhood in a few months. Another common reason behind a planned sale is that the business is either losing money or is not sufficiently profitable to make continuing worthwhile.

Whatever the real reason behind the owner's attempt to sell the business, you are unlikely to discover it without rolling up your sleeves and doing some independent and in-depth investigation. Perhaps the best way to find that needle in the haystack is to talk to a number of other businesspeople in the vicinity of the business you are investigating, particularly competitors in the same business. The business' suppliers can also be a source of important information.

Even if you are very diligent and thorough, you may not be able to discover the hidden reason — if there is one — underlying an owner's desire to sell out. You may simply have to rely on your intuition in deciding whether the seller's reason for getting out of the business is the real reason. Just remember that in most cases a good and profitable small business is not something that most people walk away from, unless there is a very good reason to do so or the price offered is too good to turn down.

What Kind of Reputation Does the Business Have?

One of the great advantages of taking over an existing business can be the opportunity to enjoy the reputation and goodwill that the existing owner has built up with customers and suppliers over the years. On the other hand, you may be much better off starting your own business from scratch than acquiring a business that has a poor reputation because of inferior work or merchandise or inferior service. It could take you years of hard work and reduced profits to overcome a former owner's poor reputation.

Even if the present owner has an excellent business reputation, you will want to know whether or not that goodwill is based on personal relationships built up between the owner and customers. These types of relationships aren't easily transferable. If the business relies heavily on a few key customers with whom the owner has very favorable business arrangements based on personal relationships, you may find those business arrangements could be lost when you attempt to take the owner's place. In short, satisfy yourself the goodwill you are buying is not based solely on personal relationships.

How Profitable Is the Business Now?

Unless you have some very good reasons to believe that you can operate the business more profitably than the current owner, you should not purchase a going business that does not produce a satisfactory profit under its current ownership. Thus, it is extremely important to find out how the business has fared financially for the last few years. This is where the services of a good accountant, who has knowledge of the particular type of business, will be invaluable.

Insist on having the seller make available the business' financial and business records to your accountant. Be particularly wary of a business that keeps poor records. Often, the most reliable sources of financial information can be the owner's income tax and sales tax returns, since it is not very likely that a business owner will report more income than was actually earned for tax purposes.

If the owner is not willing to make financial records available, make it clear that you are not willing to negotiate any further. Buying a business is a lot like buying a used car; you want to make sure it runs before you pay for it.

Assets and Liabilities

You will need to review both the tangible and intangible assets of the business to see if they are worth the price you will be paying and also to determine just what assets you will be acquiring under the sales agreement.

Personally inspect the business premises, and look for things like obsolete or unsalable inventory, out-of-date or rundown equipment, or furniture or fixtures that you may have to repair or replace. Also, determine whether the business is able to expand at its present location or if it is already too cramped. What you determine might require you to buy or lease additional facilities, if you wish to expand.

Review the terms of any leases. Some businesses close because of the imminent expiration of a favorable long-term lease or because the landlord plans to either raise the rent drastically or not renew the lease at all when the current lease expires.

If you will be acquiring the accounts receivable of the business, review them in detail. An aging of the accounts should be performed to determine how long various receivables have been outstanding. As a general rule, the longer a given receivable has been outstanding, the more likely it will prove to be uncollectible.

If a few large accounts of credit customers make up a significant portion of the receivables, you will want to particularly focus on those accounts and perhaps even have credit checks run on those customers. The bankruptcy of a major credit customer can ruin an otherwise successful business.

Part of your job in investigating a business that you want to buy is to find out what makes it tick — and make sure you will be getting whatever it is. For example, a business that has well-developed customer or mailing lists should ordinarily include those lists in the sales agreement. If there is a favorable lease, make sure it can and will be assigned to you. If patents, trademarks, trade names, or certain skilled employees are vital to the business, be sure that you will get them as part of the package.

You also need to be aware of potential problems with the government that the seller is experiencing or expects to experience in the near future, such as zoning problems or new environmental restrictions that may hamper the business' profitability.

Hidden Liabilities

Liabilities of the business may not always show up on its accounting records. There may be any number of hidden claims against the business, such as security agreements encumbering the accounts receivable, inventory, or equipment; unpaid back taxes of various kinds; undisclosed lawsuits or potential lawsuits; or simply unpaid bills.

If you are going to assume the liabilities of the business, the written agreement of sale should specify exactly which liabilities are being assumed and the dollar amount of each.

Other examples of hidden liabilities to look out for are:

- Pension liabilities — You may be taking on significant termination liability as a successor employer if the seller maintains or contributes to a pension fund and has unfunded pension fund liabilities.
- Vacation liabilities — If you are a successor employer, you may be liable for accrued but unpaid vacation leave of employees, which can be a significant hidden liability in some cases.
- Environmental liabilities — In many instances, environmental law imposes liability for past environmental abuses on current land owners or lessors. Many banks and savings and loans have recently learned about this the hard way, after foreclosing on land which had been contaminated over the years by toxic substances, and being held liable for clean-up costs as the contamination problems came to light.

  Many companies, when buying land or other companies that own land, now require the sellers to make detailed representations and warranties concerning environmental matters and to undertake extensive and costly environmental audits as a condition to buying a business. See Section 9.9 for a more detailed discussion of these issues.

If you intend to buy a corporation, you will be well advised to buy the business assets from the corporation rather than purchase its stock. The latter approach will subject the business to all hidden or contingent liabilities of the old corporation, whether or not you have agreed to pay for any liabilities of the corporation that predated the sale.

One exception to this general rule would be for a corporation that had substantial tax loss or tax credit carryovers that you might be able to utilize if you bought the stock of the corporation rather than the assets. Be aware, however, the tax law is a minefield when it comes to taking over someone else's tax loss or credit carryovers.

So before you do so, seek good advice from a tax attorney or tax accountant. If you don't, you may find that the carryovers you thought you were acquiring have evaporated like a mirage.

A change in ownership of more than 50% of the stock of a corporation in a three-year period will generally result in a severe restriction on the amount of its prior net operating losses that can be deducted in any subsequent taxable year.

3.4 Should You Consider a Franchise Operation?

Many small businesses, particularly fast food restaurants and print shops, are operated under franchises from a large national company (a franchisor). There can be substantial advantages to operating a franchised business, such as the benefits of national advertising, training programs, and assistance in setting up and running the business. If you are investigating a franchise, determine whether the franchise can be transferred to you, and if so, provide for the transfer as part of the sale in the sales agreement.

Carefully review the franchise agreement with the help of your attorney to determine whether the franchisor must approve the transfer, what the costs of operating are under the franchise, and the other terms of the agreement.

If the franchisor is not a well-known and respected company, contact your local Better Business Bureau or an appropriate state agency to see if they have any information regarding the history, ethics, and reputation of the franchisor. You do not want to sign on with one of the less-than-reputable franchising operations that charge substantial franchising fees for very little in the way of useful services.

The Federal Trade Commission (FTC) and a number of states provide franchising laws and regulations that offer you protection. These laws and regulations mandate the timing and content of the various disclosures which the franchisor must make to you, as the potential franchisee. You or your attorney should make sure that you ask for all of these disclosures on a timely basis, and be wary of any franchisor who does not provide these disclosures to you unless you ask for them.

A number of excellent publications, including *Franchise Bible* by Erwin J. Keup, can be obtained to help you evaluate various franchise opportunities. *Franchise Bible* explains what the franchise system entails and presents how both the franchisor and the franchisee should approach a franchising venture or opportunity.

For more information on *Franchise Bible* and additional franchise publications, refer to Section 10.9.

If you acquire a franchise, either from the franchisor or as a transfer from another franchisee, you may be able to amortize (write off) the cost of acquiring the franchise, under certain circumstances, for federal income tax purposes. Consult your tax adviser as to whether or not this will be possible in your case. If it is amortizable, you may want to allocate a significant part of the purchase price for the business to the cost of the franchise, which could save you major tax dollars in the long run.

Once you have focused on a particular franchise opportunity, you will find the checklist located at the end of this chapter very useful for evaluating the franchise operation.

3.5 Negotiating the Purchase

The Purchase Price

No book can tell you how much you should pay for the business you are planning to buy. You are on your own on that one. If, however, you have done your homework thoroughly in investigating the business in question and have talked to bankers and other businesspeople about what the normal purchase price for a business of that type and size should be, you should have a fairly good basis for determining whether the purchase price is a reasonable one.

For example, you may find that small businesses of the type you are considering generally sell for about one and one-half times their annual gross sales. That could be very important to know if the seller is asking three times last year's gross sales.

Even if you conclude the purchase price is a fair one, or even a bargain, you still must decide whether the price is one you can afford. Assuming that you can get the purchase price together, will it so deplete your liquid resources that you will not have enough working capital to make the business go or put you in a bind if income from the business drops off while you are at the learning stage? Or, if you are financing a substantial part of the purchase price, will your operating budget be able to stand the cost of making the payments on the debt and still leave enough for you to live on?

Remember, just because you can get the purchase price or down payment together does not necessarily mean that you can afford to buy a particular business even when the price is right.

Disclosure of Financial Information

At an early stage in the negotiations, specify that you want access to tax returns, books of account, and other financial records of the business, and make it clear that you have no interest in continuing the negotiations unless the seller cooperates fully in this respect.

Additionally, be sure this condition is expressed in any informal "memorandum of understanding" or letter of agreement between you and the seller that is written up before the final contract of sale.

Allocation of Purchase Price

One very important item that is often omitted in business sales agreements, perhaps because it is not absolutely necessary, is a provision in the agreement that shows how the parties agree to allocate the purchase price between the various assets that are being acquired.

For tax purposes, however, it is often very important to both you, as the purchaser, and the seller to have a written allocation agreement.

Since you and the seller usually have opposing interests in making an agreed allocation, the courts and IRS have generally been willing to abide by any allocation agreement between the parties.

The passage of the Clinton Deficit Reduction tax legislation on August 10, 1993 has greatly simplified the allocation process and made it easier, on an after-tax basis, to acquire a business when a significant portion of its assets are intangibles.[1]

Under the 1993 tax law, a broad new category of amortizable assets, called "Section 197 Intangibles," has been created. Section 197 Intangibles may be amortized over a 15-year period for assets purchased after August 10, 1993. Taxpayers may elect to have the new law apply retroactively to acquisitions of intangible assets that occurred after July 25, 1991. Consider amending your tax returns if you have recently purchased a business, after the latter date, and acquired any intangible assets that were not amortizable under prior law.

Before passage of this new law, a business buyer would seek to allocate as much of the purchase price as possible to depreciable tangible assets and amortizable intangible assets, such as technical know-how, customer lists, or covenants not to compete. In addition, buyers usually sought to minimize the portion of the purchase price allocated to other intangible items, such as goodwill or going concern value, which could never be amortized.

However, there was often little choice but to allocate most of the purchase price to intangibles because the value of tangible assets, such as office equipment and furniture and a few supplies, made up only a small portion of the purchase price. Since the IRS clearly would not accept a purchase price allocation that put a $50,000 value on $5 worth of paper clips, buyers were forced to become creative and try to define some asset, such as a customer base or insurance renewals list, and allocate some part of the purchase price to that asset.

In the past, when a buyer attempted to write off the cost of such intangible assets, the IRS often disallowed the amortization deduction. To sustain the deduction, the buyer often had to litigate the issue with the IRS and prove to a court that the intangible assets had a short, reasonably ascertainable economic life, and could thus be amortized for tax purposes. The courts frequently allowed taxpayers to write off various types of intangible assets over various periods of time, but only when the taxpayers convincingly demonstrated that such assets lost their economic value over a given period. The costs of such litigation, however, are usually prohibitive for small businesses.

Thankfully, the new law should put an end to most such disputes with the IRS over intangible assets. For the first time ever, the tax law allows goodwill and going concern value to be amortized as Section 197 Intangibles over 15 years. Also included in the definition of Section 197 Intangibles are:

- Workforce in place;
- Information base;
- Any license, permit, or other right granted by a governmental unit or agency;

1993 Tax Law Simplifies Allocations

- Know-how, such as patents, copyrights, formulas, designs, patterns, or similar items (special rules apply to computer software and interests in films, tapes, books, and videos);
- Any customer-based intangible, such as customer lists, depositor lists, subscribers, and insurance expirations;
- Any supplier-based intangible, such as favorable supplier contracts;
- Covenants not to compete; and
- Any franchise, trademark, or trade name.

Computer software is considered an intangible asset, but it is generally not subject to the 15-year amortization requirement of Section 197. Software that is readily available for purchase by the general public is not considered a Section 197 Intangible asset and can now be amortized over three years rather than the five-year period that previously applied.[2] Other computer software is a Section 197 Intangible asset only if acquired in a transaction that involves the purchase of a whole business or a substantial portion of a business.

Section 197 will benefit most business buyers by preventing many disputes with the IRS regarding the purchase price of a business and by allowing amortization of the cost of intangible assets that were not deductible in the past. The new law, however, is not entirely favorable. Previously, business buyers who were allowed to amortize certain intangibles were often able to do so over a period of only a few years, which was far better than the new 15-year amortization requirement.

Allocation Agreements Are Still Important

Do not assume that the new law makes a purchase price allocation agreement unnecessary or unimportant. Certain assets that might be acquired in a business purchase, such as land, are still not depreciable or amortizable, so it will be advisable to try to allocate as little as possible to the cost of land in a purchase price allocation agreement. Also, it will still be advantageous to allocate as much as possible of the purchase price to inventories or depreciable assets whose costs can be written off in a time frame shorter than the 15-year amortization period for Section 197 Intangibles.

A tax deduction you can take today or in the near future is almost always worth a great deal more than a tax deduction 15 years from now.

Required Filing

Tax regulations require both you and the seller to file *Form 8594* with the IRS any time a business is bought or sold.[3] *Form 8594* reports certain information about the purchase price allocation. Penalties for failure to file this form can be extremely large. Needless to say, the information on your *Form 8594* and that of the seller's should be identical, or you both will be inviting IRS audits.

In most cases, whatever value of an asset you and the seller agree on is binding for tax purposes. So, it is very important from a tax standpoint to negotiate the best possible allocation of the purchase price among the assets you acquire and have that allocation reflected in the contract of sale.[4]

3.6 Closing the Deal

The legal procedures involved in buying an existing business are rather complex. To ensure you are protected as fully as possible from liabilities you have not agreed to assume, have your attorney take the steps described below.

Legal Steps in Buying a Business

In many states, the purchaser of a retail or wholesale establishment or certain other types of businesses must prepare a notice to creditors of bulk transfer and file it in counties where the business operates and publish it in a general circulation newspaper before the purchase of the business. If this is not properly done, the seller's unsecured creditors may be able to attach the property that you thought you were buying free and clear. Since 1989, however, more than half the states have decided that their bulk sale or bulk transfer laws were a nineteenth-century anachronism and an unnecessary burden on commerce; these states have repealed such laws outright. See Section 9.14 for more details regarding the increasing number of bulk sale law repeals.

File Bulk Transfer Notice

Before closing the purchase, your attorney should check with the secretary of state's office to determine whether anyone has recorded a security interest — a lien or chattel mortgage — against the personal property of the seller's business. Naturally, if the transaction involves a purchase of real property, you should also have a title search performed to see if the seller has good title and if there are any recorded mortgages or other claims against the property that the seller has not disclosed to you.

Check Security Interests

For a fee, the secretary of state's office (or its equivalent) will provide a listing of any security interests that have been recorded as a lien against the assets of the business you are buying.

As a condition of the sale, have the seller obtain the necessary form that certifies all state employment taxes have been paid by the seller from the appropriate state agency. If you fail to withhold enough of the purchase price to cover any of the seller's unpaid employment taxes, you may be liable to the state for those taxes. See Section 11.3 for specifics on state requirements.

Get Tax Releases

Similarly, require the seller to obtain and provide you with a sales and use tax certification showing that all outstanding sales and use tax payments due have been made by the seller. You do not want to end up paying for the seller's unpaid sales or use taxes.

File *Form 8594* with the IRS regarding the purchase price allocation and other information in connection with the transaction. The penalty for intentional disregard of this filing requirement is 10% of the amount that was not correctly reported, which could mean up to 10% of the entire purchase price. Don't forget to file *Form 8594*.

File with IRS

Retain a Lawyer

Do not attempt to buy or sell a business without the assistance of an attorney to review and structure the deal. Preferably, the attorney should be one who specializes in business law practice rather than a litigation specialist or general practitioner. Obtain competent tax advice, either from your attorney or from an accountant, when negotiating and structuring aspects of the deal, such as the allocation of the purchase price and the disposition of any employee benefit plans carried on by the seller for the employees of the business.

Use an Escrow

In general, both you and the seller will be protected — from the time the sales agreement is signed until the deal closes — if an escrow is used to handle the sale of the business. The escrow holder, which is usually an escrow company or escrow department of a financial institution, will hold the agreement, escrow instructions, funds, and important documents until all conditions for closing the deal or releasing the funds or documents are fulfilled.

When the deal closes, the escrow holder will disburse the funds to the seller and deliver the documents of title to you. If the deal is not completed, the escrow instructions will specify how the items held in escrow are to be distributed to the parties.

Your attorney or the seller's attorney may also act as escrow holder, but you probably will not want the seller's attorney to act in that role in most cases, for obvious reasons.

Build in Holdbacks

If the seller has made misrepresentations to you in the contract of sale regarding assets that do not exist, or the like, you may always seek satisfaction by suing for damages. In view of the cost, delay, and uncertainty in bringing a lawsuit, however, you would generally be far better off if there were some simple way you could merely offset any such overstated asset or understated liability against the purchase price, retroactively.

To make this possible, seek to structure the deal so part of the purchase price is held back for some period, say a year, just in case such a contingency arises. Then, if you discover false representations as to assets or liabilities, it will be relatively simple — compared to bringing a lawsuit against a seller who may have skipped town — to have your claim deducted from the amount held back. Discuss with your attorney the possibilities of structuring the transaction so you either:

- Give the seller a note as part of the purchase price, with a right to reduce the principal amount of the note if certain contingencies occur; or
- Have part of the cash payment price held in escrow for six months or more after the sale occurs.

3.7 Summary Checklist for Buying an Existing Business

☐ Why does the present owner want to sell the business?

Investigation

☐ Will the reputation of the business be helpful or harmful if you take it over?

☐ Obtain tax returns, bank deposit records, and other financial records.

☐ If the business is not currently very profitable, why do you think you can run it more profitably than the present owner?

☐ Thoroughly investigate the business' financial records and history, its reputation, and any factors that might unfavorably impact on its future. You may need the help of an accountant or other experts.

☐ Review or have reviewed the provisions of key contracts, leases, franchise agreements, or any other legal arrangements which have a significant effect on the business. Be sure you are not assuming an unfavorable lease or contract or losing the benefits of a favorable one.

☐ Make sure that the purchase price is fair. Even if it is, can you afford it? Will you have enough working capital to run the business properly after you pay the purchase price?

Negotiations

☐ Insist on getting accurate financial information and access to the supporting data, early in the negotiations.

☐ Push for an allocation of the purchase price to specific assets in the sales agreement. Seek to maximize the amounts allocable to depreciable assets and any noncompetition covenant. Seek to minimize allocations to goodwill or land purchased.

☐ Look for hidden liabilities, such as pending lawsuits, accrued vacation liabilities, unfunded pension plan liabilities, or potential exposure to environmental clean-up costs.

☐ Retain an attorney to participate in drawing up the sales agreement.

Closing the Transaction

☐ If your state still has a bulk sales law, comply with the requirements of the Bulk Transfer Act, if it applies to the particular type of business being acquired.

☐ Be sure that the acquired property is not subject to any recorded security interests or other liens beyond those disclosed by the seller.

☐ Have the seller obtain and furnish a certification that all employment taxes due have been paid.

☐ Have the seller obtain and furnish a certification that all sales and use taxes due have been paid.

☐ Seek to hold back part of the purchase price as security to reimburse yourself for any misrepresentations as to assets or liabilities by the seller.

☐ Prepare *Form 8594*, and file it with the IRS.

☐ See Section 11.3 for state law considerations.

Other Tax Considerations

☐ Determine whether the sale of the business will result in a sales tax liability with respect to part or all of the purchase price. If so, is there a way to reshape the transaction to reduce or avoid sales tax? For example, allocate more of the purchase price to assets not subject to sales tax and less to assets that are.

☐ If you are buying a corporation that has not been paying income taxes because it has carryovers of net operating losses or investment tax credits, be aware you may be able to use only a small portion of those carryovers to shelter the income of the business once you become the owner.

☐ If the seller has a favorable experience rating for unemployment tax purposes, make sure you act promptly so that you can succeed to that rating as a successor employer.

☐ If you are acquiring intangible assets, including previously non-deductible intangibles, such as goodwill or going concern value, you may now amortize the cost of most such intangible assets over 15 years, under recent tax legislation.

Endnotes

1. I.R.C. §197.

2. I.R.C. §167(f)(1).

3. Temp. Treas. Regs. 1.1060-1T(h)(2).

4. I.R.C. §1060(a).

Checklist for Evaluating a Franchise

The Franchise

YES NO

☐ ☐ After studying it paragraph by paragraph, did your lawyer approve the franchise contract you are considering?

☐ ☐ Does the franchise call upon you to take any steps which are, according to your lawyer, unwise or illegal in your state, county, or city? If yes, what are the steps? _____

_____

_____

☐ ☐ Does the franchise give you an exclusive territory for the length of the franchise? or

☐ ☐ Can the franchisor sell a second or third franchise in your territory?

☐ ☐ Is the franchisor connected in any way with another franchise company handling similar merchandise or services? If yes, what is your protection against this second franchisor organization?

_____

_____

☐ ☐ Can you terminate the franchise contract? Under what circumstances can you do it and at what cost to you, if you decide for any reason at all that you wish to cancel it?

_____

_____

☐ ☐ If you sell your franchise, will you be compensated for the goodwill you have built into the business?

The Franchisor

How many years has the firm offering you a franchise been in operation? _____

☐ ☐ Does the firm have a reputation for honesty and fair dealing among the local firms holding its franchise?

☐ ☐ Has the franchisor shown you any certified figures indicating exact net profits of one or more going firms?

☐ ☐ Have you personally checked these certified figures with the franchisor?

☐ ☐ Will the firm assist you in the following areas?

YES NO

☐ ☐ A management training program?   ☐ ☐ Capital?

☐ ☐ An employee training program?   ☐ ☐ Credit?

☐ ☐ A public relations program?   ☐ ☐ Merchandising ideas?

☐ ☐ Will the firm help you find a good location for your new business?

☐ ☐ Is the franchising firm adequately financed so it can carry out its stated plan of financial assistance and expansion?

Checklist for Evaluating a Franchise (continued)

YES NO

☐ ☐ Is the franchisor a one-person company? or

☐ ☐ Is the franchisor a corporation with an experienced management trained in-depth (so that there would always be an experienced person at its head)?

Exactly what can the franchisor do for you which you cannot do for yourself? _____

_____

_____

☐ ☐ Has the franchisor investigated you carefully enough to assure itself that you can successfully operate one of the franchises at a profit both to the franchisor and to you?

☐ ☐ Does your state have a law regulating the sale of franchises? and

☐ ☐ Has the franchisor complied with that law?

You – The Franchisee

How much equity capital will you have to have to purchase the franchise and operate it until your income equals your expenses? _____

Where are you going to get the capital? _____

_____

☐ ☐ Are you prepared to give up some independence of action to secure the advantages offered by the franchise?

☐ ☐ Do you really believe you have the innate ability, training, and experience to work smoothly and profitably with the franchisor, your employees, and your customers?

☐ ☐ Are you ready to spend much or all of the remainder of your business life with this franchisor, offering its product or service to your public?

Your Market

☐ ☐ Have you made any study to determine whether the product or service which you propose to sell under franchise has a market in your territory at the prices you will have to charge?

Will the population in the territory given you increase ☐, remain static ☐, or decrease ☐ over the next five years?

Will the product or service you are considering be in greater demand ☐, about the same ☐, or in less demand ☐ five years from today?

What competition already exists in your territory for the product or service you contemplate selling:

From nonfranchise firms? _____

From franchise firms? _____

Source: *Franchise Opportunities Handbook*, U.S. Department of Commerce, Washington, D.C., 1982.

Starting the Business

Chapter 4

A Trip through the Red Tape Jungle: Requirements that Apply to Nearly All New Businesses

The difference between a taxidermist and a tax collector is that the taxidermist leaves the skin.

— Old American proverb

4.1 General Considerations

This chapter outlines the most common governmental requirements and other red tape that virtually everyone starting a new business must attend to. The requirements discussed will also generally apply if you have bought an existing business, unless you have acquired the stock of an incorporated business. Items covered in this chapter will generally apply even if your business has no employees. If you expect to have one or more employees, a large number of additional legal requirements will affect your business immediately. Chapter 5 covers the additional requirements that apply to new businesses that have employees. This chapter does not discuss the special licenses that many types of businesses are required to have. If you do not know whether the type of business you are considering going into requires a special license or licenses from federal, state, or local government agencies, refer to Chapter 6 and Section 11.6.

4.2 Choosing a Name for the Business

The name you choose for your business can be important from a business image standpoint and also in communicating to the public what you have to offer. Most small businesses should select a name that, at least in part, clearly describes the product or service provided. If you ignore this basic common-sense rule, you run the risk of losing many potential customers for the simple reason they will pass right by without realizing what you do. A fanciful or whimsical name is fine from an image standpoint, but it should also give the public a clear idea of what it is your business provides in the way of goods or services. For example, if you call your restaurant "The Comestible Emporium," a lot of hungry people will probably drive right by without realizing that you serve food.

It is advisable, however, from the standpoint of protecting your business' name as a trademark or service mark under federal or state law, to adopt a name that is also partially arbitrary or nondescriptive, in conjunction with a name that is descriptive of the services or goods provided. An example would be the "21 Club Restaurant." The reason for selecting a name that is partially whimsical or arbitrary is that trademarks or service marks that are merely descriptive of the goods or services cannot be legally protected from use by others unless it can be proven that the name has acquired a secondary meaning, which is very difficult to establish for a new small business.[1]

You also need to think of the possible consequences of putting your name out before the public. You may want to consider using some sort of fictitious name (see Section 4.10) for your business, rather than your name. There is nothing illegal or shady about using a fictitious business name. If you put your name on the business and the venture goes belly up, as some new businesses do, many people in the community will automatically associate your name with the defunct or bankrupt business. This may make it very difficult if you try to start another business or to obtain credit in the same community in the future.

Once you have settled on a name for your business, you or preferably your attorney, should find out whether the same name, or a confusingly similar name, has already been preempted by someone else. This involves making an inquiry with the state's secretary of state's office to find out whether the name is already being used in the state. Inquiry should also be made of the county clerk, in each county where you will do business, to see if another business is already using the same or a confusingly similar name in the county and has filed a fictitious business name statement. If so, you may have to choose a different name. See Section 9.5 for more information on trademark protection.

4.3 Local Business Licenses

Almost every business will need city or county business licenses, or both. These licenses can be obtained at the local city hall or county offices. Failure to obtain a license when you start business will usually result in a penalty when the local government eventually catches up with you; therefore, obtaining the necessary licenses should be among the first steps taken when you start a business.

Some cities and counties impose a gross receipts, income, or payroll tax on most businesses. Certain types of businesses, such as restaurants, may also be required to obtain special permits from local health authorities and fire or police departments.

If your business will construct its own building, it will be necessary to consult your local city or county zoning ordinances. A building permit must be obtained for both new construction and remodeling in most areas.

In addition, whether or not you plan to carry on any construction activity or do any remodeling, you will need to make certain that the business activity you intend to carry on does not violate any zoning regulations or any ordinances regarding hazardous activities. You may also be required to obtain a use permit from the city or county planning commission.

4.4 State Licenses

Most states impose license fees or taxes on a wide range of businesses, occupations, and professions. The fees often vary widely among the different types of businesses and occupations, ranging from relatively nominal to substantial amounts or rates, depending upon the activity. The many different types of licenses and permits are usually granted based on some combination of requirements such as registration, bonding, education, experience, and passage of licensing examinations.

Since you may not legally operate any of these regulated businesses or professions without being licensed, you should find out whether there is a state licensing requirement for the business you plan to start. If so, determine whether and how you will be able to comply with the licensing requirements.

See Section 11.6 for a partial listing of businesses, occupations, and professions that must be licensed under the laws of this state.

4.5 Federal Licenses

Most new small businesses are unlikely to require any type of federal permit or license to operate, unless they are engaged in rendering investment advice, making alcohol or tobacco products, preparing meat products, or making or dealing in firearms. Federal permits or licenses would also be necessary to commence certain large-scale operations, such as a radio or television station or a common carrier and the production of drugs or biological products. If you wish to engage in any of the foregoing activities, all of which are heavily regulated, consult an attorney regarding regulatory requirements well in advance.

4.6 Estimated Taxes

Individual

As a sole proprietor or partner in a partnership, you will have to make advance payments of estimated federal — and possibly state — income taxes and federal self-employment tax once your business begins to turn a taxable profit. Individual estimated tax payments are due in four annual installments on April 15, June 15, September 15, and January 15 of the following year for an individual whose tax year is the calendar year. Any remaining unpaid federal tax is due with your tax return on April 15 of the following year — which is also the date when the first estimated tax installment is due for that year. You will file *Form 1040-ES* with your federal estimated tax payments. During a year, you must make estimated tax payments equal to 90% of the current year's tax or 100% of the prior year's tax, whichever is less.

Certain high-income taxpayers, however, are not allowed to base their payments on the prior year's tax. Starting in 1994, taxpayers with more than $150,000 of adjusted gross income in the prior year may base their payments on 110% of the prior year's tax.[2]

Corporate

If your business is incorporated, the corporation will generally have to make corporate estimated tax payments, if it has taxable income, as early as the fourth month of its first tax year. For tax years beginning after December 31, 1993, your corporation must pay estimated tax equal to 100% of its current year tax or 100% of its tax for the prior year, whichever is less. A large corporation — one which had one million dollars or more of taxable income in one of the three preceding years — may not base its estimates on the prior year's tax. Estimated tax installments are due on April 15, June 15, September 15, and December 15, for a corporation with a calendar year for its taxable year.

Federal estimated tax payments should be computed on *Form 1120-W* — which can be obtained, along with other federal tax forms, from any IRS office — and must be deposited in a bank that is authorized to accept federal tax deposits. The corporate estimated tax deposits must be accompanied by federal tax deposit coupons. Your corporation will be issued one coupon book that contains coupons with your corporate tax identification number already preprinted on them. These coupons can be used for deposits of all types of federal taxes. On each coupon, you must indicate, by checking the applicable box, the kind of tax being deposited and the calendar quarter to which payroll tax deposits are to be applied. The boxes on the coupon indicate the form name for the type of tax being paid.

Type of Tax	Box to Darken on Coupon
Payroll tax deposits	941
Federal unemployment tax	940 (or 940-EZ)
Corporate income tax estimates (and year-end payments)	1120

Federal Tax Deposits

The tax deposit coupon instructions also require you to darken an appropriate quarterly box (1st, 2nd, 3rd, or 4th quarter). While this is fairly straightforward for payroll tax deposits (simply darken the box for the appropriate calendar quarter), the requirements are somewhat less logical in the case of corporate estimated income tax deposits.

For income tax deposits (*Form 1120*), darken the first quarter box for all current year estimated income tax deposits, regardless of the quarter to which the deposit relates. However, when making income tax deposits that relate to the prior taxable year (such as a payment made with extension request *Form 7004* or the final tax payment that is made at the time of filing the *Form 1120* corporation income tax return), darken the fourth quarter box instead.

The coupon books will be sent to you automatically when you file *Form SS-4*, which requests a tax identification number for the corporation. When you receive your coupon book, a reorder form, *Form 8109A*, will be provided so you can request additional coupon books for the current year, if needed.

A penalty may be imposed for failure to make deposits directly to an authorized government depository bank. In the past, when tax deposit cards were unavailable, it was common practice to mail payments to the Internal Revenue Service accompanied by a letter indicating the nature of the tax payment and requesting additional tax deposit cards. This method of paying business taxes is no longer acceptable. Thus, it is important to mail the reorder form in time to receive additional coupon books before you run out; however, the IRS will sometimes send you blank coupons for temporary use. Refer to Section 11.4 regarding state filing requirements for individual and corporate estimated income taxes.

4.7 Miscellaneous Tax Information Returns

As a general rule, every person engaged in a trade or business must report to the IRS any payments of $600 or more made to any person during the calendar year, for items such as rent, compensation for services, commissions, interest, and annuities, plus other items of fixed or determinable

Reporting Payments to Individuals

income.[3] To make these filings, you will use a series of 1099 forms. A number of additional tax reporting requirements are listed below. Be aware there are stiff new penalties for failure to comply with them.

Obtaining Social Security Numbers

It is necessary to obtain the name and Social Security number or other tax identification number of any person to whom you make payments of $600 or more. There is a $50 penalty for failure to obtain their tax identification number — unless you have a reasonable excuse, such as their refusal to give you the number.[4] If they do refuse to give you the number, you must withhold 31% of whatever amount you owe them and deposit it with the IRS, or you will be subject to a penalty for failure to withhold.[5]

Reporting Sales to Direct Sellers

In addition, you must report sales of $5,000 or more of consumer products to any individual who is engaged in direct selling — that is, selling in any way other than through a permanent retail establishment.[6] This will mainly apply to sales made to people in direct sales organizations, such as Tupperware, Amway, or Shaklee. It would also apply in many other situations, such as where the person you sell to sells the goods by mail order. Use *Form 1099-MISC* to report these sales.

1099 Forms

Reportable payments you make that are in excess of $600 per year are usually filed for each payee on *Form 1099-MISC* (information return) or *Form 1099-INT* (for interest); a duplicate must be sent to the payee. In addition, you must prepare and file a *Form 1096* return summarizing all the information on the 1099-MISC forms and on the other forms in the 1099 series. Each of these forms is due by February 28 each year, for the prior calendar year, and a copy must also be sent to the recipient of the payment by January 31.

Be aware that instructions for *Form 1099* say you should use your personal Social Security number rather than your business' employer identification number on the form. Putting down the wrong taxpayer identification number in such a case will subject you to a penalty.

Payments of compensation in excess of $600 made to nonemployees — independent contractors — are also reportable on *Form 1099-MISC*. Businesses must also report royalty payments of $10 or more made to any person.

Penalties

There are stiff IRS penalties for not filing the above 1099 forms. The penalty for not filing or not giving a 1099 to a payee is $50 per failure. Since there is a separate penalty for not giving a copy of the 1099 to the payee, as well as for not filing a copy with the IRS, it can cost you $100 for each person for whom you fail to prepare 1099s.[7] The $50 penalty for late-filed 1099s, and certain other information returns, can be reduced to $30, if you file more than 30 days late but before August 1 of the year the filing is due. Or, if you file within 30 days after the due date, the penalty can be reduced to only $15.

In addition, if you erroneously, but in good faith, treat a person as an independent contractor, and it is later shown that the person was actually an employee, you will only be liable as an employer for 20% of the employee's Social Security tax that should have been withheld and for income tax withholding equal to 1.5% of what you paid the individual provided that you properly filed *Form 1099-MISC* with the IRS.[8] If you failed to file *Form 1099-MISC* for that person, the amount of withholding tax you are liable for is doubled.[9]

Exemptions for 1099 Filings

Fortunately, a number of important exemptions from the 1099 filing requirements will eliminate most of the people or companies to whom you are likely to make payments of $600 or more. You do not have to report:

- Payments to corporations — except certain corporations in the medical field;[10]
- Payments of compensation to employees that are already reported on their W-2s;[11]
- Payments of bills for merchandise, telegrams, telephone, freight, storage, and similar charges;[12]
- Payments of rent made to real estate agents;[13]
- Expense advances or reimbursements to employees that the employees must account to you (the employer) for;[14] and
- Payments to a governmental unit.[15]

Reporting Dividends and Interest

If your business is incorporated, your corporation will have to file a *Form 1099-DIV* for each person to whom it pays dividends of $10 or more each year.[16] You must also file *Form 1099-INT* for each person to whom you pay $10 or more in interest on bonds, debentures, or notes issued by the corporation in registered form.[17] *Form 1099-DIV* or *Form 1099-INT* is also required for any other payment of dividends or interest on which you are required to withhold tax. Payments reported on *Form 1099-DIV* and *Form 1099-INT* must also be reported on the *Form 1096* summary. *Form 1099-S* must be given to recipients of the proceeds from the sales of real estate, in general.

Reporting Large Cash Transactions

Any business that receives a payment of more than $10,000 in cash, in cash equivalents — such as cashier's checks or traveler's checks — or in foreign currency in one transaction, or in two or more related transactions, is required to report the details of the transactions within 15 days to the IRS[18] and to furnish a similar statement to the payor by January 31 of the following year.[19] The form for reporting such "suitcase" transactions is *Form 8300*.

The penalties for noncompliance are generally the same as for not filing 1099s, except that in cases of intentional failure to file, there is an additional penalty equal to the higher of $25,000 or the amount of the cash or cash equivalent received in the transaction, up to $100,000.[20] In addition to the requirement that you file 1099s with the IRS, you may have to file similar forms with the state.

Reporting Mortgage Interest Received

Federal law requires that you give *Form 1098* to any individual from whom you receive $600 or more in mortgage interest during the year, in the course of your trade or business. *Form 1098* has the same filing requirements as *Form 1099*.[21]

Reporting on Magnetic Media

Note that the IRS permits you to file *Form 1098* and *Form 1099*, as well as certain other information returns, on magnetic media (computer tapes or disks) rather than the actual paper forms, if very specific formats for the computer tape or disk are met. The IRS requires that certain information returns be filed on magnetic media, if your business files 250 or more such returns for a calendar year.[22] These include *Form 1098*, all of the 1099 series and W-2 series of information returns, and various others, such as *Form 5498* and *Form 8027*.

A "hardship waiver" to excuse you from having to file in magnetic media format may be granted under certain circumstances, if you file a request on *Form 8508* at least 90 days in advance of the due date.

Failure of a taxpayer to file an information return on magnetic media — or on a machine-readable form where magnetic media filing is not required — when required to do so is treated as a failure-to-file and can result in the imposition of applicable penalties for failure to file, as noted earlier.

If your business finds it will be required to file information returns on magnetic media, there are many data processing firms and computer programs you can buy that will encode the data for you, at a relatively small cost, in a way that meets the IRS's highly technical specifications.

4.8 Sales and Use Tax Permits

With a limited number of exceptions, every business that sells tangible personal property, such as merchandise, to customers must obtain a seller's permit from the state sales tax agency. Usually, a separate permit must be obtained for each place of business where property subject to tax is sold. See Section 11.4 for a discussion of the state's sales and use tax laws and permit requirements. Some states have a gross income or a gross receipts tax rather than a sales tax.

In general, as a wholesaler or manufacturer, you will not have to collect sales tax on goods you sell to a retailer for resale, if the retailer holds a valid seller's permit and provides you with a resale certificate in connection with the transaction. Likewise, if your business, as a retailer, buys goods for resale, you need not pay sales tax to the wholesalers if you provide them with resale certificates. You may buy blank resale certificate forms at most stationery stores in states where such certificates are required.

The sales and use tax laws typically require a business that sells or leases tangible personal property to keep complete records of the gross receipts from sales or rentals whether or not the receipts are believed to be taxable. You must also keep adequate and complete records to substantiate all deductions claimed on sales and use tax returns and of the total purchase price of all tangible personal property bought for sale, lease, or consumption in the state.

4.9 Real Estate Taxes

Property Taxes

As a rule, you do not need to worry about contacting the county tax assessor's office regarding payment of any real property taxes on real property acquired for your business. They will usually contact you by mailing a property tax bill to the owner of record. See Section 11.4 for a general description of how state or local real property and personal property taxes are assessed and collected.

FIRPTA Withholding Tax on Purchase of Real Property

In addition to local property taxes, U.S. citizens and residents who acquire U.S. real estate from foreign persons — including partnership interests or stock in certain firms owning U.S. real property — must withhold up to 10% of the purchase price and remit it to the IRS under the Foreign Investment in Real Property Tax Act (FIRPTA). If you fail to withhold the tax, you are liable for it. This is a potentially dangerous tax trap for unsuspecting American buyers of real estate, since it is often difficult to determine whether a seller is a foreign person.

While there is an exception for residences costing $300,000 or less — if you will live in it for at least 50% of the time for two years — it is far safer to obtain a certificate of nonforeign status from the seller if there is any possibility that the seller is a nonresident alien or a foreign company.

To protect yourself when purchasing real estate — or your client, if you are in the real estate business — you should require, as a condition of closing the transaction, that the seller provide you with an affidavit certifying whether or not the seller is a nonresident alien or a foreign company.

If the seller refuses to sign the affidavit and provide the required information, you should withhold 10% of the gross purchase price and transmit it to the IRS within ten days of the sale along with IRS *Form 8288* and *Form 8288-A*. This can be a real problem in a highly leveraged deal where less than 10% of the purchase price is paid in cash at the closing.

Some states have adopted similar withholding provisions with regard to purchases of real estate within such states where the seller is a nonresident of the state.

In short, if the seller is a foreign person, you will owe the IRS 10% of the purchase price if you fail to withhold the tax, unless you received a certificate of nonforeign status from the seller.

4.10 Fictitious Business Name Statement

Almost every state has laws requiring any person who regularly transacts business in the state for profit under a fictitious business name to file and publish a fictitious business name statement. For a sole proprietorship or partnership, a business name is generally considered fictitious unless it contains the surname of the owner or all of the general partners and does not suggest the existence of additional owners. Use of a name that includes words like "company," "associates," "group," "brothers," or "sons" will suggest additional owners and will make it necessary for a business to file and publish a fictitious business name statement.

Putting a name that would be considered fictitious on your company letterhead, on your business cards, in advertising, or on your products will be considered a use of the name.

Many newspapers will provide the form for filing, publish the notice, and file the required affidavit. See Section 11.4 regarding specific requirements for filing a fictitious business name statement in this state.

4.11 Insurance — A Practical Necessity for Businesses

Insurance, like death and taxes, is an inevitable necessity for the owner of any small business. For almost any business, even one that has no employees, insurance coverage for general liability, product liability, fire and similar disasters, robbery, theft, and interruption of business should be considered.

If your business will have employees, workers' compensation insurance is usually mandatory under state law. Employee life, health, and disability insurance have also become virtual necessities in many businesses and professions, if you wish to be competitive with other firms in hiring and retaining capable employees.

Fidelity bonding should be considered for employees who will have access to the cash receipts or other funds of the business. If you have an employee pension or profit-sharing plan subject to the Employee Retirement Income Security Act of 1974 (ERISA), employees involved in administering the plan or handling its funds are required to be covered by a fidelity bond.[23] See Section 5.5 for further information.

Insurance Agents

Since it isn't realistic to expect you to become a sophisticated comparison shopper for insurance while you are trying to get a business off the ground, seek out a good insurance agent whom you can trust and rely upon to give you good advice. There is no easy way to find such an agent, just as there is no sure way of finding a good lawyer or accountant. In general, the best approach will be to ask friends, lawyers, accountants, or other businesspeople you know to refer you to a topflight insurance agent.

Agents who have earned the Chartered Life Underwriter (CLU) designation will, as a rule, be more experienced and capable than those without the CLU credential. This can be an additional factor to consider when selecting your insurance agent.

Agents who deal primarily in property and casualty insurance will not usually have CLU on their business cards. Instead, they may have the initials CPCU — Chartered Property/Casualty Underwriter — after their name, which is a similar mark of distinction in the field of property/casualty insurance.

Another good tip in finding an insurance agent is to analyze your own insurance needs. There are several how-to books that can help you analyze your risks and compare insurance prices. One such book is the *Buyer's Guide to Business Insurance*, which is available from The Oasis Press for $19.95. Companion software, *The Insurance Assistant*, is also available.

Insurance Consultants

If you cannot find an agent with whom you feel comfortable, call an insurance consultant. Be sure the consultant is a member of the Society of Risk Management Consultants. To belong to the group, the individual or firm cannot be an insurance broker. These consultants are insurance experts and can give you an objective analysis on risk management and insurance.

Society of Risk Management Consultants
300 Park Avenue
New York, NY 10022
(800) 765-SRMC

The usual hourly fees may seem high, but most new businesses probably will not need an excessive amount of time. Most will bill in quarter-hour increments.

You will probably recoup the consultant's fee several times over in premium savings in just the first year alone. Be wary, however, of a consultant who wants to increase the number of hours by offering to create specifications and provide additional services.

Once you have met with an independent consultant and know what is needed, shop for the insurance you need from insurance brokers. Don't let them bid up the amount of coverage or add on additional types of insurance.

Use the insurance consultant as you would an attorney or physician — follow his or her advice.

4.12 Requirements Specific to the Legal Form of the Business

Sole Proprietorships

There are no significant government regulatory requirements that apply specifically to sole proprietorships; although, as a sole proprietor of a business, you will need to attach a form *Schedule C* to your individual federal tax return, on which you will report the income or loss from your business.

If your sole proprietorship shows a profit, you will usually have to pay a self-employment tax equal to 15.3% of your net self-employment income from the business or at least on the first $60,600 of such income, plus an additional 2.9% on self-employment income of more than $60,600 in 1994. The self-employment tax is computed on *Schedule SE*, which must also be attached to your federal income tax return. See Section 11.4 for how to report business profits on your state income tax returns.

Partnerships

Like a sole proprietor, as a partner, you will have to pay a self-employment tax on your share of your partnership's net self-employment income. Net self-employment income usually includes all partnership income less all partnership deductions allowed for income tax purposes. Some types of income, such as interest, may or may not be considered self-employment income. The source of your income and your involvement in the activity from which your income is received will determine whether it is self-employment income.

If your earnings from self-employment is $400 or more for the year, you will have to figure self-employment tax on *Schedule SE* of your federal *Form 1040*. The self-employment tax is a Social Security and Medicare tax for those who work for themselves.

Schedule E of your federal *Form 1040* deals with your personal income tax and includes all other taxable income, such as royalties, rentals, and interest. You report your share of partnership ordinary income or loss on *Schedule E*.

In addition, your partnership must file a partnership information return, federal *Form 1065*, reporting the partnership's income and each partner's share of income and other items. The partnership must also file *Form SS-4* with the IRS to obtain a federal employer identification number, even if it has no employees. See Section 11.4 for state partnership return filing requirements, and the end of this chapter for a sample *Form SS-4*.

When a partner buys, sells, or exchanges a partnership interest, the partnership must file a special information return if the partnership's assets include unrealized receivables or substantially appreciated inventory that might cause the seller to have ordinary gain, rather than all capital gain, on the sale or exchange.[24] Statements also have to be sent to the partners involved in the transaction.[25]

A limited partnership, to qualify as such, is usually required to file a *Certificate of Limited Partnership* with the secretary of state or other state agency. In most states, a limited partnership should also file certified copies in each county where it does business or owns real estate.

Corporations

Corporations are subject to the following requirements. These requirements are not applicable to other legal forms of business organization.

- Filing articles of incorporation;

- Adopting a set of bylaws;

- Observing other corporate formalities on a regular basis, such as the election of directors by shareholders and appointment of officers by action of the board of directors;

- Filing federal income tax returns on *Form 1120* — or *Form 1120-S* for an S corporation — and state income or franchise tax returns in most states where they do business. See Section 11.4 for various filings, taxes, and fees required of corporations that are incorporated or doing business in this state;

- Reporting certain information relating to the transfer of tax-free property under Internal Revenue Code Section 351 on the corporation's income tax return for that year;[26]

- Filing *Form SS-4* with the IRS to obtain an employer identification number, even if there are no employees; and

- Qualifying with the secretary of state to do business, if the corporation was organized under the laws of another state.

Limited Liability Companies

A limited liability company (LLC) must file articles of organization — similar to articles of incorporation — with the secretary of state or other appropriate state agency, and pay any applicable filing fees. See Section 11.2 for filing requirements in this state. In addition, tax treatment of an LLC will generally be the same as for a partnership, if it is properly structured.

4.13 Checklist of Requirements for Nearly All New Businesses

☐ Obtain local business licenses.

☐ Check on local zoning ordinances, regulations, and other land use restrictions.

☐ Determine if your particular business requires a state license to operate.

☐ Determine whether any type of federal permit or license is required.

☐ Be prepared to make estimated income tax payments almost immediately after starting business or incorporating.

☐ Apply for a sales and use tax seller's permit if you will sell tangible personal property.

☐ File sales and use tax returns, if you must collect sales or use tax.

☐ File with the county clerk and publish a fictitious business name statement if the business operates under a fictitious name, and then file an affidavit of publication with the county clerk (in most states).

☐ Locate a good insurance agent or retain and meet with an insurance consultant regarding fire, accident, liability, theft, and other types of commercial insurance. Then obtain the necessary insurance coverage.

☐ If you purchase real estate, you must withhold up to 10% of the purchase price and remit it to the IRS if the seller is a foreign individual or foreign-owned company, under the Foreign Investment in Real Property Tax Act.[27] Otherwise, you should insist upon receiving an affidavit that the seller is not a nonresident alien, with his or her taxpayer identification number, unless you are certain that he or she is a U.S. citizen or resident.

☐ For a sole proprietorship, report any self-employment income on *Schedule SE* of federal *Form 1040*, and report income or loss on *Schedule C* of *Form 1040*.

☐ A partnership files *Form 1065* reporting partnership income. Each partner reports his or her share of self-employment income on *Schedule SE* of *Form 1040* and income or loss from partnership operations on *Schedule E* of *Form 1040*.

☐ For a limited partnership, file a *Certificate of Limited Partnership* with the secretary of state and copies in counties where the partnership has places of business or real estate (in most states).

☐ For an LLC, file articles of organization and, if treated as a partnership, file partnership tax returns and report each owner's share of income or loss on the owners' tax returns. If treated as a corporation, comply with all corporate tax filing requirements.

☐ For a corporation, file articles of incorporation, adopt bylaws, and observe necessary corporate formalities. File federal income tax return *Form 1120*; *Form 1120-S* for an S corporation. If property is transferred to the corporation tax-free under Internal Revenue Code

Section 351, report required information relating to the transfer on the corporation's income tax return for that year.

- ☐ For a corporation, limited liability company, or a partnership, apply for a federal employer identification number on *Form SS-4*, even if the business has no employees. See sample at the end of this chapter.

- ☐ File annual tax information returns, *Form 1096* and the *Form 1099* series, for payments of $600 or more for items such as rent, interest, and compensation for services, and send 1099s to the payees.

- ☐ File *Form 1098* for mortgage interest of $600 or more your business receives in a year from an individual.

- ☐ Also, report any cash payments or cash equivalents of more than $10,000 that you receive to the IRS within 15 days. Such filing may have to be done on computer-readable magnetic media.

- ☐ If your business is a corporation, be sure to obtain an adequate supply of federal tax deposit coupons in time to make your corporate estimated tax payments.

The above requirements apply to any business, whether it has employees or not. There are many additional requirements for businesses that do have employees, and these are covered in the next chapter. See Section 11.4 for a checklist of additional state law requirements that apply to nearly all new businesses.

4.14 Securities Laws

Inherent in the choice of the legal form of the business is the potential application of federal and state securities laws, if the new business is to have more than one owner or should it become necessary to raise capital for an existing business. Because of the potentially dire consequences of violating federal or state securities laws, it is important to consult with your attorney as early as possible when considering issuing or transferring a security. Corporate stock and limited partnership interests generally are considered securities, and even a general partnership interest can be a security in appropriate circumstances, as can certain types of debt instruments.

Registration of Securities

Since the Securities Act of 1933, federal law has required registration as a prior condition to the issuance or transfer of securities. The law exempts various types of securities and certain types of transactions. The most important of these exemptions for small businesses have been the exemption for securities sold to persons residing within a single state and transactions by an issuer not deemed to involve any public offering. The Securities and Exchange Commission (SEC) from time to time has issued regulations exempting small securities issues, attempting to balance the needs of small businesses to raise capital against the public policy of protecting investors. In 1982, the commission adopted Regulation D as its primary method of regulation of securities offerings by small businesses, although not to the exclusion of other exemptions which might apply.

Rule 504 Exemption

Rule 504 under Regulation D exempts the issuance of securities by an entity if the aggregate offering price of all exempt securities sold by the entity during a twelve-month period does not exceed one million dollars — not more than $500,000 of securities can be offered and sold without registration under some states' securities laws.[28] The securities cannot be offered or sold by any form of general solicitation or general advertising, and the securities so acquired cannot be resold without registration or an exemption from registration.

This rule does not require any specific information to be given to the purchasers of the securities; however, since the anti-fraud provisions of the securities laws apply even though the transaction is exempt from registration, it is helpful to memorialize in writing the material information regarding the offering.

Rule 505 Exemption

Rule 505 exempts offers and sales of securities if the offering price for all exempt securities sold over a twelve-month period does not exceed five million dollars.[29] To obtain this exemption, the issuer must reasonably believe that there are not more than 35 purchasers exclusive of accredited investors.

Examples of accredited investors include banks, insurance companies, a natural person whose net worth at the time of purchase exceeds one million dollars, or a person who has individual income in excess of $200,000 — or $300,000 jointly with a spouse — in each of the two most recent years and expects the same in the current year. Exceptions are also made for certain large investors, including corporations, partnerships, or business trusts with total assets in excess of five million dollars, unless formed for the specific purpose of acquiring the securities.

For purposes of Rule 505, the issuer must furnish extensive information and certified financial statements to the investors, unless securities were sold only to accredited investors. The prohibition against advertising and solicitation applies to this rule, as do the anti-fraud provisions of the securities laws.

Rule 506 Exemption

Rule 506 provides exemptions similar to those under Rule 505, including the 35-purchaser limitation, with the same exception for accredited investors described above.[30] However, Rule 506 requires that an issuer of securities must reasonably believe, immediately before making a sale to a nonaccredited investor, that the investor is sufficiently knowledgeable to adequately evaluate the merits and risks of the investment. Alternatively, the issuer can rely on the knowledge and experience of a person who represents the investor. The other main difference between Rule 505 and Rule 506 is that there is no five million dollar or other maximum size limitation on the amount of securities that can be issued in a Rule 506 offering.

Regulation D Filing Requirements

Issuers utilizing any of the above exemptions must file *Form D* with the SEC generally no later than 15 days after the first sale of securities and at other specified times thereafter. Rule 507 disqualifies any issuer found to have violated the *Form D* filing requirement from future use of the Regulation D exemptions, if the issuer has been enjoined by a court for violating the notice filing requirement — but apparently will not disqualify prior issuances of securities merely due to failure to file *Form D*.[31]

The exemptions available under the federal securities laws are more liberal than those available under the securities laws of many states. In connection with any issuance or transfer of securities, it is necessary to consider the possible application of securities laws in the state where the business entity is established or operates, and, if different, the states where purchasers of the securities live. See Section 11.2 for further information concerning state securities laws.

Going Public Easier for Small Businesses

Through its 1993 Regulation S-B, the SEC provides a new set of rules designed to make it easier and simpler for small businesses to raise capital in the public market. Regulation S-B is an integrated system of rules, forms, and reporting requirements designed especially for small firms, which have traditionally found the costs and complexity of "going public" to be prohibitive. To make a public offering of securities that qualifies under the streamlined procedures of Regulation S-B, an issuing company must meet all the following requirements:

- A company must be a U.S. or Canadian company and cannot be an investment company.
- A company's revenues must be less than $25 million per year.
- The aggregate value of a company's outstanding securities (not counting those held by affiliated companies or persons) must not exceed $25 million.
- If the issuer is a majority-owned subsidiary of another corporation, the parent company must also meet the above criteria.

Endnotes

1. *Armstrong Paint and Varnish Works v. New and U-Enamel Corp.* 305 U.S. 315 (1938); *Carter-Wallace, Inc. v. Proctor and Gamble Co.* 434 F.2d 794 (9th Cir. 1970). The author wishes to acknowledge Henry C. Bunsow, esq. of the San Francisco patent and trademark law firm of Townsend and Townsend for alerting him to this important point.
2. I.R.C. § 6654.
3. I.R.C. § 6041(a).
4. I.R.C. § 6724(d)(3).
5. I.R.C. § 3406(a).
6. I.R.C. § 6041A(b).
7. I.R.C. §§ 6721–6722.
8. I.R.C. § 3509(a).
9. I.R.C. § 3509(b).
10. Treas. Regs. § 1.6041-3(c).
11. Treas. Regs. § 1.6041-3(a).
12. Treas. Regs. § 1.6041-3(d).
13. Treas. Regs. § 1.6041-3(e).
14. Treas. Regs. § 1.6041-3(i).
15. I.R.C. § 6041(a) requires filing of information returns for payments made to another "person." As defined in IRC § 7701(a)(1), "person" does not include governmental bodies.
16. I.R.C. § 6042(a).
17. I.R.C. § 6049(a).
18. I.R.C. § 6050I.
19. I.R.C. § 6722.
20. I.R.C. § 6721.
21. I.R.C. § 6050H.
22. Rev. Proc. 93-24, 1993-1 C.B. 555.
23. 29 U.S.C. § 1112 (§ 412 of ERISA).
24. I.R.C. § 6050K(a).
25. I.R.C. § 6050K(b).
26. Treas. Regs. § 1.351-3.
27. I.R.C. § 1445(a).
28. 17 C.F.R. § 230.504.
29. 17 C.F.R. § 230.505.
30. 17 C.F.R. § 230.506.
31. Rule 507, as interpreted in Securities Act Release No. 6825, March 14, 1989 (17 C.F.R. § 230.507).

Form SS-4 – Application for Employer Identification Number: Sample

| Form **SS-4**
(Rev. December 1993)
Department of the Treasury
Internal Revenue Service | **Application for Employer Identification Number**
**(For use by employers, corporations, partnerships, trusts, estates, churches,
government agencies, certain individuals, and others. See instructions.)** | **EIN**
OMB No. 1545-0003
Expires 12-31-96 |

Please type or print clearly.

1 Name of applicant (Legal name) (See instructions.)

| **2** Trade name of business, if different from name in line 1 | **3** Executor, trustee, "care of" name |

| **4a** Mailing address (street address) (room, apt., or suite no.) | **5a** Business address, if different from address in lines 4a and 4b |

| **4b** City, state, and ZIP code | **5b** City, state, and ZIP code |

6 County and state where principal business is located

7 Name of principal officer, general partner, grantor, owner, or trustor—SSN required (See instructions.) ▶

8a Type of entity (Check only one box.) (See instructions.)
- ☐ Sole Proprietor (SSN) _____
- ☐ REMIC   ☐ Personal service corp.
- ☐ State/local government   ☐ National guard
- ☐ Other nonprofit organization (specify) _____
- ☐ Other (specify) ▶ _____
- ☐ Estate (SSN of decedent) _____
- ☐ Plan administrator-SSN _____
- ☐ Other corporation (specify) _____
- ☐ Federal government/military
- (enter GEN if applicable) _____
- ☐ Trust
- ☐ Partnership
- ☐ Farmers' cooperative
- ☐ Church or church controlled organization

8b If a corporation, name the state or foreign country (if applicable) where incorporated ▶

| State | Foreign country |

9 Reason for applying (Check only one box.)
- ☐ Started new business (specify) ▶ _____
- ☐ Hired employees
- ☐ Created a pension plan (specify type) ▶ _____
- ☐ Banking purpose (specify) ▶
- ☐ Changed type of organization (specify) ▶ _____
- ☐ Purchased going business
- ☐ Created a trust (specify) ▶ _____
- ☐ Other (specify) ▶

| **10** Date business started or acquired (Mo., day, year) (See instructions.) | **11** Enter closing month of accounting year. (See instructions.) |

12 First date wages or annuities were paid or will be paid (Mo., day, year). **Note:** *If applicant is a withholding agent, enter date income will first be paid to nonresident alien. (Mo., day, year)* . . . . ▶

13 Enter highest number of employees expected in the next 12 months. **Note:** *If the applicant does not expect to have any employees during the period, enter "0."* . . . . ▶

| Nonagricultural | Agricultural | Household |

14 Principal activity (See instructions.) ▶

15 Is the principal business activity manufacturing? . . . . ☐ **Yes** ☐ **No**
If "Yes," principal product and raw material used ▶

16 To whom are most of the products or services sold? Please check the appropriate box. ☐ Business (wholesale)
☐ Public (retail)   ☐ Other (specify) ▶   ☐ N/A

17a Has the applicant ever applied for an identification number for this or any other business? . . . . ☐ **Yes** ☐ **No**
Note: *If "Yes," please complete lines 17b and 17c.*

17b If you checked the "Yes" box in line 17a, give applicant's legal name and trade name, if different than name shown on prior application.

Legal name ▶   Trade name ▶

17c Enter approximate date, city, and state where the application was filed and the previous employer identification number if known.

| Approximate date when filed (Mo., day, year) | City and state where filed | Previous EIN |

Under penalties of perjury, I declare that I have examined this application, and to the best of my knowledge and belief, it is true, correct, and complete. | Business telephone number (include area code)

Name and title (Please type or print clearly.) ▶

Signature ▶   Date ▶

Note: *Do not write below this line.   For official use only.*

| Please leave blank ▶ | Geo. | Ind. | Class | Size | Reason for applying |

For Paperwork Reduction Act Notice, see attached instructions.   Cat. No. 16055N   Form **SS-4** (Rev. 12-93)

Instructions for Form SS-4: Sample

General Instructions

(Section references are to the Internal Revenue Code unless otherwise noted.)

Purpose

Use Form SS-4 to apply for an employer identification number (EIN). An EIN is a nine-digit number (for example, 12-3456789) assigned to sole proprietors, corporations, partnerships, estates, trusts, and other entities for filing and reporting purposes. The information you provide on this form will establish your filing and reporting requirements.

Who Must File

You must file this form if you have not obtained an EIN before and

● You pay wages to one or more employees.

● You are required to have an EIN to use on any return, statement, or other document, even if you are not an employer.

● You are a withholding agent required to withhold taxes on income, other than wages, paid to a nonresident alien (individual, corporation, partnership, etc.). A withholding agent may be an agent, broker, fiduciary, manager, tenant, or spouse, and is required to file **Form 1042**, Annual Withholding Tax Return for U.S. Source Income of Foreign Persons.

● You file **Schedule C**, Profit or Loss From Business, or **Schedule F**, Profit or Loss From Farming, of **Form 1040**, U.S. Individual Income Tax Return, and have a Keogh plan or are required to file excise, employment, or alcohol, tobacco, or firearms returns.

The following must use EINs even if they do not have any employees:

● Trusts, except the following:

1. Certain grantor-owned revocable trusts (see the Instructions for Form 1040).

2. Individual Retirement Arrangement (IRA) trusts, unless the trust has to file **Form 990-T**, Exempt Organization Business Income Tax Return (See the Instructions for Form 990-T.)

● Estates

● Partnerships

● REMICS (real estate mortgage investment conduits) (See the instructions for **Form 1066**, U.S. Real Estate Mortgage Investment Conduit Income Tax Return.)

● Corporations

● Nonprofit organizations (churches, clubs, etc.)

● Farmers' cooperatives

● Plan administrators (A plan administrator is the person or group of persons specified as the administrator by the instrument under which the plan is operated.)

Note: *Household employers are not required to file Form SS-4 to get an EIN. An EIN may be assigned to you without filing Form SS-4 if your only employees are household employees (domestic workers) in your private home. To have an EIN assigned to you, write "NONE" in the space for the EIN on Form 942, Employer's Quarterly Tax Return for Household Employees, when you file it.*

When To Apply for A New EIN

New Business.—If you become the new owner of an existing business, **DO NOT** use the EIN of the former owner. If you already have an EIN, use that number. If you do not have an EIN, apply for one on this form. If you become the "owner" of a corporation by acquiring its stock, use the corporation's EIN.

Changes in Organization or Ownership.—If you already have an EIN, you may need to get a new one if either the organization or ownership of your business changes. If you incorporate a sole proprietorship or form a partnership, you must get a new EIN. However, **DO NOT** apply for a new EIN if you change only the name of your business.

File Only One Form SS-4.—File only one Form SS-4, regardless of the number of businesses operated or trade names under which a business operates. However, each corporation in an affiliated group must file a separate application.

EIN Applied For, But Not Received.—If you do not have an EIN by the time a return is due, write "Applied for" and the date you applied in the space shown for the number. **DO NOT** show your social security number as an EIN on returns.

If you do not have an EIN by the time a tax deposit is due, send your payment to the Internal Revenue service center for your filing area. (See **Where To Apply** below.) Make your check or money order payable to Internal Revenue Service and show your name (as shown on Form SS-4), address, kind of tax, period covered, and date you applied for an EIN.

For more information about EINs, see **Pub. 583**, Taxpayers Starting a Business and **Pub. 1635**, EINs Made Easy.

How To Apply

You can apply for an EIN either by mail or by telephone. You can get an EIN immediately by calling the Tele-TIN phone number for the service center for your state, or you can send the completed Form SS-4 directly to the service center to receive your EIN in the mail.

Application by Tele-TIN.—Under the Tele-TIN program, you can receive your EIN over the telephone and use it immediately to file a return or make a payment. To receive an EIN by phone, complete Form SS-4, then call the Tele-TIN phone number listed for your state under **Where To Apply.** The person making the call must be authorized to sign the form (see **Signature block** on page 3).

An IRS representative will use the information from the Form SS-4 to establish your account and assign you an EIN. Write the number you are given on the upper right-hand corner of the form, sign and date it.

*You should mail or FAX the signed SS-4 **within 24 hours** to the Tele-TIN Unit at the service center address for your state.* The IRS representative will give you the FAX number. The FAX numbers are also listed in Pub. 1635.

Taxpayer representatives can receive their client's EIN by phone if they first send a facsimile (FAX) of a completed **Form 2848**, Power of Attorney and Declaration of Representative, or **Form 8821**, Tax Information Authorization, to the Tele-TIN unit. The Form 2848 or Form 8821 will be used solely to release the EIN to the representative authorized on the form.

Application by Mail.—Complete Form SS-4 at least 4 to 5 weeks before you will need an EIN. Sign and date the application and mail it to the service center address for your state. You will receive your EIN in the mail in approximately 4 weeks.

Where To Apply

The Tele-TIN phone numbers listed below will involve a long-distance charge to callers outside of the local calling area, and should be used only to apply for an EIN. THE NUMBERS MAY CHANGE WITHOUT NOTICE. Use 1-800-829-1040 to verify a number or to ask about an application by mail or other Federal tax matters.

If your principal business, office or agency, or legal residence in the case of an individual, is located in:	Call the Tele-TIN phone number shown or file with the Internal Revenue Service center at:
Florida, Georgia, South Carolina	Attn: Entity Control Atlanta, GA 39901 (404) 455-2360
New Jersey, New York City and counties of Nassau, Rockland, Suffolk, and Westchester	Attn: Entity Control Holtsville, NY 00501 (516) 447-4955
New York (all other counties), Connecticut, Maine, Massachusetts, New Hampshire, Rhode Island, Vermont	Attn: Entity Control Andover, MA 05501 (508) 474-9717
Illinois, Iowa, Minnesota, Missouri, Wisconsin	Attn: Entity Control Stop 57A 2306 E. Bannister Rd. Kansas City, MO 64131 (816) 926-5999
Delaware, District of Columbia, Maryland, Pennsylvania, Virginia	Attn: Entity Control Philadelphia, PA 19255 (215) 574-2400

Instructions for Form SS-4: Sample (continued)

Form SS-4 (Rev. 12-93) | Page **3**

Indiana, Kentucky, Michigan, Ohio, West Virginia	Attn: Entity Control Cincinnati, OH 45999 (606) 292-5467
Kansas, New Mexico, Oklahoma, Texas	Attn: Entity Control Austin, TX 73301 (512) 462-7843
Alaska, Arizona, California (counties of Alpine, Amador, Butte, Calaveras, Colusa, Contra Costa, Del Norte, El Dorado, Glenn, Humboldt, Lake, Lassen, Marin, Mendocino, Modoc, Napa, Nevada, Placer, Plumas, Sacramento, San Joaquin, Shasta, Sierra, Siskiyou, Solano, Sonoma, Sutter, Tehama, Trinity, Yolo, and Yuba), Colorado, Idaho, Montana, Nebraska, Nevada, North Dakota, Oregon, South Dakota, Utah, Washington, Wyoming	Attn: Entity Control Mail Stop 6271-T P.O. Box 9950 Ogden, UT 84409 (801) 620-7645
California (all other counties), Hawaii	Attn: Entity Control Fresno, CA 93888 (209) 452-4010
Alabama, Arkansas, Louisiana, Mississippi, North Carolina, Tennessee	Attn: Entity Control Memphis, TN 37501 (901) 365-5970

If you have no legal residence, principal place of business, or principal office or agency in any state, file your form with the Internal Revenue Service Center, Philadelphia, PA 19255 or call (215) 574-2400.

Specific Instructions

The instructions that follow are for those items that are not self-explanatory. Enter N/A (nonapplicable) on the lines that do not apply.

Line 1.—Enter the legal name of the entity applying for the EIN exactly as it appears on the social security card, charter, or other applicable legal document.

Individuals.—Enter the first name, middle initial, and last name.

Trusts.—Enter the name of the trust.

Estate of a decedent.—Enter the name of the estate.

Partnerships.—Enter the legal name of the partnership as it appears in the partnership agreement.

Corporations.—Enter the corporate name as set forth in the corporation charter or other legal document creating it.

Plan administrators.—Enter the name of the plan administrator. A plan administrator who already has an EIN should use that number.

Line 2.—Enter the trade name of the business if different from the legal name. The trade name is the "doing business as" name.

Note: *Use the full legal name on line 1 on all tax returns filed for the entity. However, if you enter a trade name on line 2 and choose to use the trade name instead of the legal name, enter the trade name on all returns you file. To prevent processing delays and errors, always use either the legal name only or the trade name only on all tax returns.*

Line 3.—Trusts enter the name of the trustee. Estates enter the name of the executor, administrator, or other fiduciary. If the entity applying has a designated person to receive tax information, enter that person's name as the "care of" person. Print or type the first name, middle initial, and last name.

Line 7.—Enter the first name, middle initial, last name, and social security number (SSN) of a principal officer if the business is a corporation; of a general partner if a partnership; and of a grantor owner, or trustor if a trust.

Line 8a.—Check the box that best describes the type of entity applying for the EIN. If not specifically mentioned, check the "other" box and enter the type of entity. Do not enter N/A.

Sole proprietor.—Check this box if you file Schedule C or F (Form 1040) and have a Keogh plan, or are required to file excise, employment, or alcohol, tobacco, or firearms returns. Enter your SSN (social security number) in the space provided.

Plan administrator.—If the plan administrator is an individual, enter the plan administrator's SSN in the space provided.

Withholding agent.—If you are a withholding agent required to file Form 1042, check the "other" box and enter "withholding agent."

REMICs.—Check this box if the entity has elected to be treated as a real estate mortgage investment conduit (REMIC). See the Instructions for Form 1066 for more information.

Personal service corporations.—Check this box if the entity is a personal service corporation. An entity is a personal service corporation for a tax year only if:

● The principal activity of the entity during the testing period (prior tax year) for the tax year is the performance of personal services substantially by employee-owners.

● The employee-owners own 10 percent of the fair market value of the outstanding stock in the entity on the last day of the testing period.

Personal services include performance of services in such fields as health, law, accounting, consulting, etc. For more information about personal service corporations, see the instructions to **Form 1120,** U.S. Corporation Income Tax Return, and **Pub. 542,** Tax Information on Corporations.

Other corporations.—This box is for any corporation other than a personal service corporation. If you check this box, enter the type of corporation (such as insurance company) in the space provided.

Other nonprofit organizations.—Check this box if the nonprofit organization is

other than a church or church-controlled organization and specify the type of nonprofit organization (for example, an educational organization.)

If the organization also seeks tax-exempt status, you must file either **Package 1023** or **Package 1024,** Application for Recognition of Exemption. Get **Pub. 557,** Tax-Exempt Status for Your Organization, for more information.

Group exemption number (GEN).—If the organization is covered by a group exemption letter, enter the four-digit GEN. (Do not confuse the GEN with the nine-digit EIN.) If you do not know the GEN, contact the parent organization. Get Pub. 557 for more information about group exemption numbers.

Line 9.—Check only **one** box. Do not enter N/A.

Started new business.—Check this box if you are starting a new business that requires an EIN. If you check this box, enter the type of business being started. **DO NOT** apply if you already have an EIN and are only adding another place of business.

Changed type of organization.—Check this box if the business is changing its type of organization, for example, if the business was a sole proprietorship and has been incorporated or has become a partnership. If you check this box, specify in the space provided the type of change made, for example, "from sole proprietorship to partnership."

Purchased going business.—Check this box if you purchased an existing business. DO NOT use the former owner's EIN. Use your own EIN if you already have one.

Hired employees.—Check this box if the existing business is requesting an EIN because it has hired or is hiring employees and is therefore required to file employment tax returns. **DO NOT** apply if you already have an EIN and are only hiring employees. If you are hiring household employees, see **Note** under **Who Must File** on page 2.

Created a trust.—Check this box if you created a trust, and enter the type of trust created.

Note: *DO NOT file this form if you are the individual-grantor/owner of a revocable trust. You must use your SSN for the trust. See the instructions for Form 1040.*

Created a pension plan.—Check this box if you have created a pension plan and need this number for reporting purposes. Also, enter the type of plan created.

Banking purpose.—Check this box if you are requesting an EIN for banking purposes only and enter the banking purpose (for example, a bowling league for depositing dues, an investment club for dividend and interest reporting, etc.).

Instructions for Form SS-4: Sample (continued)

Other (specify).—Check this box if you are requesting an EIN for any reason other than those for which there are checkboxes, and enter the reason.

Line 10.—If you are starting a new business, enter the starting date of the business. If the business you acquired is already operating, enter the date you acquired the business. Trusts should enter the date the trust was legally created. Estates should enter the date of death of the decedent whose name appears on line 1 or the date when the estate was legally funded.

Line 11.—Enter the last month of your accounting year or tax year. An accounting or tax year is usually 12 consecutive months, either a calendar year or a fiscal year (including a period of 52 or 53 weeks). A calendar year is 12 consecutive months ending on December 31. A fiscal year is either 12 consecutive months ending on the last day of any month other than December or a 52-53 week year. For more information on accounting periods, see **Pub. 538,** Accounting Periods and Methods.

Individuals.—Your tax year generally will be a calendar year.

Partnerships.—Partnerships generally must adopt the tax year of either (1) the majority partners; (2) the principal partners; (3) the tax year that results in the least aggregate (total) deferral of income; or (4) some other tax year. (See the Instructions for **Form 1065,** U.S. Partnership Return of Income, for more information.)

REMICs.—Remics must have a calendar year as their tax year.

Personal service corporations.—A personal service corporation generally must adopt a calendar year unless:

● It can establish a business purpose for having a different tax year, or

● It elects under section 444 to have a tax year other than a calendar year.

Trusts.—Generally, a trust must adopt a calendar year except for the following:

● Tax-exempt trusts,

● Charitable trusts, and

● Grantor-owned trusts.

Line 12.—If the business has or will have employees, enter the date on which the business began or will begin to pay wages. If the business does not plan to have employees, enter N/A.

Withholding agent.—Enter the date you began or will begin to pay income to a nonresident alien. This also applies to individuals who are required to file Form 1042 to report alimony paid to a nonresident alien.

Line 14.—Generally, enter the exact type of business being operated (for example, advertising agency, farm, food or beverage establishment, labor union, real estate agency, steam laundry, rental of coin-operated vending machine, investment club, etc.). Also state if the business will involve the sale or distribution of alcoholic beverages.

Governmental.—Enter the type of organization (state, county, school district, or municipality, etc.).

Nonprofit organization (other than governmental).—Enter whether organized for religious, educational, or humane purposes, and the principal activity (for example, religious organization—hospital, charitable).

Mining and quarrying.—Specify the process and the principal product (for example, mining bituminous coal, contract drilling for oil, quarrying dimension stone, etc.).

Contract construction.—Specify whether general contracting or special trade contracting. Also, show the type of work normally performed (for example, general contractor for residential buildings, electrical subcontractor, etc.).

Food or beverage establishments.—Specify the type of establishment and state whether you employ workers who receive tips (for example, lounge—yes).

Trade.—Specify the type of sales and the principal line of goods sold (for example, wholesale dairy products, manufacturer's representative for mining machinery, retail hardware, etc.).

Manufacturing.—Specify the type of establishment operated (for example, sawmill, vegetable cannery, etc.).

Signature block.—The application must be signed by: (1) the individual, if the applicant is an individual, (2) the president, vice president, or other principal officer, if the applicant is a corporation, (3) a responsible and duly authorized member or officer having knowledge of its affairs, if the applicant is a partnership or other unincorporated organization, or (4) the fiduciary, if the applicant is a trust or estate.

Some Useful Publications

You may get the following publications for additional information on the subjects covered on this form. To get these and other free forms and publications, call 1-800-TAX-FORM (1-800-829-3676).

Pub. 1635, EINs Made Easy

Pub. 538, Accounting Periods and Methods

Pub. 541, Tax Information on Partnerships

Pub. 542, Tax Information on Corporations

Pub. 557, Tax-Exempt Status for Your Organization

Pub. 583, Taxpayers Starting A Business

Pub. 937, Employment Taxes and Information Returns

Package 1023, Application for Recognition of Exemption

Package 1024, Application for Recognition of Exemption Under Section 501(a) or for Determination Under Section 120

Paperwork Reduction Act Notice

We ask for the information on this form to carry out the Internal Revenue laws of the United States. You are required to give us the information. We need it to ensure that you are complying with these laws and to allow us to figure and collect the right amount of tax.

The time needed to complete and file this form will vary depending on individual circumstances. The estimated average time is:

Recordkeeping . . . . . . 7 min.

Learning about the law or the form . . . . . . 18 min.

Preparing the form. . . . . 44 min.

Copying, assembling, and sending the form to the IRS . 20 min.

If you have comments concerning the accuracy of these time estimates or suggestions for making this form more simple, we would be happy to hear from you. You can write to both the **Internal Revenue Service,** Attention: Reports Clearance Officer, PC:FP, Washington, DC 20224; and the **Office of Management and Budget,** Paperwork Reduction Project (1545-0003), Washington, DC 20503. **DO NOT** send this form to either of these offices. Instead, see **Where To Apply** on page 2.

Chapter 5

The Thicket Thickens: Additional Requirements for Businesses with Employees

Man is a thinking animal, a talking animal, a tool-making animal, a building animal, a political animal, a fantasizing animal. But in the twilight of a civilization, he is chiefly a taxpaying animal.

— Hugh MacLennan

5.1 General Considerations

As the previous chapter indicated, there is a considerable amount of governmental red tape involved in starting almost any new business. If your business will have any employees — even if it is incorporated and you are the only employee — the level of government regulation and red tape will multiply several times over in a typical case. This chapter outlines the bases you must cover, in addition to those described in Chapter 4, if you start a business that will have employees.

5.2 Social Security and Income Tax Withholding

Once you go into business and begin paying salary or wages to employees, you will find that you have been appointed, as an agent of the government, to collect taxes from your employees. In addition to various payroll taxes, you will also be required to collect income taxes and Social Security (FICA) tax from employees' wages.

The first order of business is to apply for a federal employer identification number (EIN) with the IRS. This number will be used to identify your

Employer Identification Number

business on payroll and income tax returns and for most other federal tax purposes. To apply for an EIN number, you need to file a completed *Form SS-4* at the earliest possible time, especially if you have employees. This will ensure that you will get tax deposit coupons in time for depositing federal payroll taxes or corporate income tax. Corporations and partnerships must file *Form SS-4* even if they have no employees. A sample of this form is located at the end of Chapter 4.

The IRS can provide you with a business tax kit that is specifically put together for new employers. You can also obtain *Circular E, Employer's Tax Guide*, an IRS publication that explains federal income tax withholding and Social Security tax requirements for employers. *Circular E* contains up-to-date withholding tables that you must use to determine how much federal income tax and Social Security tax is to be withheld from each employee's paycheck.

Employer Social Security Tax

In addition to withholding Social Security tax from an employee's paycheck — at the rate of 7.65% on gross wages up to $60,600, 1.45% on wages in excess of $60,600 in 1994 — the employer must also pay an equal amount of employer's Social Security tax. The withheld federal income tax, withheld employee Social Security tax, and employer's Social Security tax are lumped together and paid to the IRS at the same time. In some cases, these taxes can simply be mailed in with your payroll tax return (*Form 941* series) at the end of the calendar quarter or year; however, if you have significant amounts of these taxes to pay, you will generally be required to deposit the taxes with a federal tax deposit form, a precoded coupon, at an authorized commercial bank or a federal reserve bank. As a rule, the greater the amount of taxes due, the sooner they must be paid.

The complex tax deposit deadlines of previous years have been totally revised and considerably simplified and revised under recent IRS regulations. Rules for how and when federal income and Social Security taxes are to be mailed in or deposited are summarized briefly as follows:

Type of Depositor	Deadline
Small depositor — An employer with less than $500 of combined income and Social Security taxes for the calendar quarter.[1]	Deposit by last day of month following the end of the quarter, or mail with *Form 941* return by then.
Monthly depositor — An employer, who for the 12-month period ending June 30th of the preceding calendar year, reported $50,000 or less of employment taxes.[2]	Deposit by 15th day of the following month.
Semi-weekly depositor — All other employers:[3]	
For Wednesday–Friday semi-weekly period:	Deposit on or before next Wednesday.
For Saturday–Tuesday semi-weekly period:	Deposit on or before next Friday.

Some exceptions to the above tax deposit schedules do exist. For example, any employer with $100,000 of employment taxes accumulated at the end of any day — for the current month or semi-weekly period only, whichever applies — must deposit those taxes in an authorized bank by the end of the next banking day, subsequently becoming a semi-weekly depositor.[4] Shortfalls in required deposits will result in underpayment penalties. No penalty, however, will be imposed if the shortfall does not exceed 2% of the required deposit (or $100, if greater) provided the shortfall is made up within specified periods. For a more detailed explanation of federal tax deposits, see IRS *Notice 109*. Deposits of payroll and withholding taxes may be mailed to a depository bank, if postmarked at least two days prior to the tax deposit due date. But tax deposits of $20,000 or more by employers making more than one deposit a month must reach the bank by the due date, regardless of the postmark date.[5]

New Employees

When a new employee is hired, give the employee a federal *Form W-4*. He or she must then complete and return the form to you. When completed, *Form W-4* provides the employee's Social Security number and the number of withholding exemptions the employee is claiming. The number of exemptions is used to determine how much income tax you must withhold from his or her wages. You keep *Form W-4*. Neither it nor the information on it is filed with the IRS, except in the case of an employee who claims more than ten withholding exemptions, or who claims exemption from income tax withholding.

By January 31 of each year, you must furnish each employee with copies of *Form W-2, Annual Wage and Tax Statement*, showing the taxable wages paid to an employee during the preceding calendar year and the taxes withheld, including state income tax. By February 28, the original of *Form W-2* and a summary form, *Form W-3*, should be filed with the IRS.

Independent Contractors

A person who performs services for your business does not necessarily have to be your employee. In many cases, you can structure your legal relationships with persons who provide services to you so they are considered independent contractors for tax and other legal purposes. From an employer standpoint, it is preferable to treat someone as an independent contractor rather than as an employee of your business because you do not have to pay Social Security tax or federal or state unemployment taxes on his or her compensation. An independent contractor is considered to be self-employed for tax purposes and pays self-employment tax.

In addition, you don't have to withhold income and payroll taxes from compensation paid to independent contractors or file payroll tax returns with respect to their compensation. You must, however, file a *Form 1099-MISC* for each independent contractor to whom you make payments of $600 or more during a calendar year (with certain exceptions) or, in the case of a direct seller of consumer goods, for each such direct seller to whom you sell $5,000 of goods during a year.

Because of the obvious advantages employers obtain by treating their employees as independent contractors, the IRS has been very aggressive in attempting to reclassify so-called independent contractors as employees where they perform functions in a manner that is more typical of an employer/employee relationship. Requiring businesses to file *Form 1099-MISC* is an attempt by the IRS to identify those businesses that may be improperly treating employees as independent contractors.

Before you decide to treat anyone who works for you as an independent contractor, consult your tax adviser because there can be serious consequences if those individuals are reclassified as employees by the IRS. See Section 9.11 for a discussion of the risks involved.

Each state has its own withholding taxes. For information on the withholding tax requirements for this state, see Section 11.5.

5.3 Unemployment Taxes

With relatively few exceptions, all businesses with employees must pay both federal and state unemployment taxes. These taxes are imposed entirely on you, the employer. Theoretically, the federal unemployment tax is 6.2% of the first $7,000 of annual wages per employee.[6] In actuality, however, the rate is usually only 0.8% because a credit for up to 5.4% is given for state unemployment taxes paid and for a favorable experience rating for state unemployment tax purposes.[7]

The state unemployment tax rate for an employer can be either more or less than the basic rate, depending upon the amount of unemployment claims by former employees. The more unemployment benefits claimed by your former employees, the higher your unemployment tax rate will be, within certain limits.

Federal Unemployment Tax

Your business will be required to pay federal unemployment tax (FUTA) for any calendar year in which it pays wages of $1,500 or more[8] or if it has one or more employees for at least a portion of the day during any 20 different calendar weeks during the year.[9] Needless to say, this will cover almost any business that has one employee, even if that employee is part-time.

If the FUTA liability during any of the first three calendar quarters is more than $100, you must deposit the tax with a federal tax deposit coupon, *Form 8109*, at an authorized bank during the month following the end of the quarter. If the tax is $100 or less, you are not required to make a deposit, but you must add it to the taxes for the next quarter. For the fourth quarter, if the undeposited FUTA tax for the year is more than $100, deposit the tax with a tax deposit coupon at an authorized bank by January 31. If the balance due is $100 or less, either deposit it with the coupon or mail it to the IRS with your federal unemployment tax return, *Form 940*, by January 31. *Form 940* is not due until February 10 if all of the FUTA tax for the prior year has already been deposited when due.

The IRS also provides *Form 940-EZ*, a greatly simplified FUTA return for certain small employers. In general, the small employers who can use *Form 940-EZ* are those:

- Who pay unemployment tax to only one state;
- Who pay state unemployment taxes by the *Form 940-EZ* due date; and
- Whose wages subject to FUTA are also taxable for state unemployment tax purposes.

The state also imposes an unemployment tax which meshes closely with the federal unemployment tax. Refer to Section 11.5 for details on state unemployment taxes, rates, returns, and registration as an employer.

5.4 Workers' Compensation Insurance

A business is generally required by state law to obtain workers' compensation insurance for its employees. This means that you, as an employer, may have to immediately seek out and obtain a workers' compensation insurance policy covering all your employees, or you will be subject to possible legal sanctions. Workers' compensation insurance coverage provides various benefits to an employee who suffers a job-related injury or illness.

Many insurance companies offer workers' compensation coverage, though many may be reluctant to write a policy that covers only one or a few employees, unless it is tied to other types of insurance policies. See Section 11.5 for a description of other formal requirements applicable to employers under the workers' compensation laws.

5.5 Compliance with ERISA — Employee Benefit Plans

If you have employees and provide them with fringe benefits, such as group insurance — other than workers' compensation — or other types of employee welfare plan benefits, or if you adopt a pension or profit-sharing retirement plan, you will almost certainly have to comply with at least some aspects of the Employee Retirement Income Security Act of 1974 (ERISA).

There are criminal penalties for willful failure to comply with two types of ERISA requirements: 1) reporting to government agencies, and 2) disclosure to employees.[10] In addition, there are a number of different types of civil penalties, which are incredibly numerous and complex, for unintentional failures to comply with ERISA requirements.[11] In short, compliance with ERISA is not a simple matter.

This section lays down some relatively simple and straightforward guidelines you, as a layperson, can follow in trying to recognize when you might have an ERISA compliance obligation. If you recognize your need to be in compliance, call your attorney, accountant, or benefit consultant for help. ERISA deals with two kinds of employee benefit plans: pension plans and welfare plans.

Pension Plans

Pension plans under ERISA are pretty much what you might expect — tax qualified retirement plans including both pension and profit-sharing plans (including Keogh plans), plus other types of benefit programs that defer payments until after employment has terminated.[12]

Because these compliance requirements are so very complex and are constantly in a state of flux, no attempt to spell them out in detail is made here. Instead, the basic ERISA compliance requirements for most pension and profit-sharing plans are summarized in the table on page 22.

If your business maintains a pension or profit-sharing plan, it should be obvious from this summary of basic ERISA compliance requirements that you need some expert help from an attorney, accountant, or pension consulting firm — or all of them — if you are going to be able to properly comply with the requirements of ERISA and avoid potential fines and other civil and criminal penalties.

The cost of maintaining these plans has unfortunately multiplied several times over since the passage of ERISA in 1974, followed by a labyrinth of ERISA regulations issued by several different federal agencies. In short, unless you make substantial contributions to and obtain significant tax savings from an employee retirement plan, it may not be worth having because of the heavy costs of compliance with ERISA.

Welfare Plans

Welfare plans under ERISA include most other types of employee benefit plans that are not considered pension plans.[13] These include typical fringe benefit plans adopted by small firms, such as health insurance, long-term disability, group-term life insurance, and accidental death insurance plans. ERISA compliance for welfare plans is usually less of a burden than for pension plans, but is required for almost every business that provides any kind of benefits for employees of the type mentioned above.

A number of so-called fringe benefits that are in the nature of payroll practices, such as paid holidays, vacation pay, bonuses, overtime premium pay, and most kinds of severance pay arrangements, are usually not considered to be either pension or welfare plans under ERISA.[14] Thus, these kinds of payroll practices are not subject to ERISA at all. Compliance requirements for reporting and disclosure under ERISA are briefly discussed below.

Summary Plan Descriptions

The one ERISA compliance requirement that applies to most small businesses is the requirement for you to prepare a summary plan description

(SPD) for distribution to all employees covered by any type of welfare plan you sponsor, such as typical health, accident, life, or disability insurance plans.[15] An SPD must contain more than 20 specific items of information listed in the U.S. Department of Labor Regulations,[16] including an ERISA rights statement which must be copied more or less verbatim from the regulations.

An SPD must be prepared for each plan and distributed to covered employees within 120 days after the plan is first adopted.[17] Each new employee must be given a copy of the SPD within 90 days after becoming a participant in the plan.[18] Since an SPD must be prepared for each employee plan subject to ERISA, even a very small business may find that it has to produce three or four of these documents, each of which must meet detailed technical requirements.

One important consideration in taking out insurance coverage for employees should be a firm commitment from the insurance company or brokers that they will prepare the necessary SPDs for the insurance plans they are selling you. Otherwise, you may need to have your attorney or benefit consultant prepare the SPDs, which can result in substantial professional fees.

Other than the need for you to prepare SPDs and distribute them to employees, there are no significant ERISA requirements that apply to most kinds of insured-type welfare plans that cover fewer than 100 employees.[19] You must, however, make available the insurance policies and other plan documents for inspection by your employees and you must furnish copies to them upon request.[20]

Additional ERISA Requirements

If your business should grow to have 100 or more employees who are covered by a plan, or if you adopt any type of uninsured funded welfare plan, you will suddenly become subject to a whole array of additional ERISA requirements, including:

- Filing a copy of the SPD with the U.S. Department of Labor;[21]
- Filing an annual return/report or registration (*Form 5500* series) with the IRS each year;[22]
- Preparing and distributing a summary annual report to covered employees each year;[23]
- Preparing a summary of material modifications of the plan, if necessary, and filing it with the U.S. Department of Labor and distributing it to covered employees;[24] and
- Filing a terminal report if the plan is terminated.[25]

Bonding and Withholding Requirements

Besides the ERISA reporting and disclosure requirements listed in the summary on page 22, you should be aware of two other points regarding ERISA: the bonding requirement and withholding requirements on pension or profit-sharing plan distributions. If any of your employees are deemed to handle assets of an employee benefit plan that is subject to

ERISA, they must be covered by a fidelity bond.[26] Consult your attorney or benefit consultant to see if any required bonding needs to be paid regarding any benefit plans you maintain for your employees. This is particularly important if you have a pension or profit-sharing plan.

Secondly, withholding is mandatory on distributions of pension, profit-sharing, and IRA benefits.[27] There is an exception for certain periodic distributions on which the recipient elects, in advance, not to have any tax withheld.

In addition to reporting and disclosure requirements under ERISA, there are other federal reporting and recordkeeping requirements for certain types of fringe benefit plans.[28] For example, employers maintaining educational assistance programs, group legal services plans, and so-called cafeteria plans are currently required to file annual reports with the IRS on *Form 5500* or *Form 5500-C/R* and, if needed, to maintain records to show that those plans qualified for tax purposes for each year after 1984.[29]

5.6 Employee Safety and Health Regulations

As has been discussed in Section 5.4, employers are required by state law in many states to carry workers' compensation insurance for the protection of employees who develop job-related illnesses or who are injured on the job. In addition, there are comprehensive and far-reaching federal laws that set safety standards designed to prevent injuries arising from unsafe or unhealthy working conditions. The primary federal law regulating job safety, the Occupational Safety and Health Act of 1970 (OSHA), imposes several reporting and recordkeeping obligations for employers.

Federal OSHA

Over the years, the Occupational Safety and Health Administration has issued reams of regulations and standards for workplace safety. If you have employees, you will need to consult an attorney, preferably one with OSHA expertise, to determine what, if any, steps you must take to comply with federal and state safety standards at your place of business. Otherwise, you may be subject to fines and other legal sanctions if any employee is injured on the job or OSHA inspectors find that you are not in compliance with applicable safety standards at your place of business.

You should also contact the nearest regional U.S. Department of Labor – OSHA office and request information on any free consultative services or publications the office may have available. Many state occupational safety and health agencies provide confidential, on-site consultations for no charge. These consultations point out state compliance issues at your place of business without fining or penalizing you for any discovered violations.

OSHA requires that you post a permanent notice to employees regarding job safety.[30]

Under OSHA, it is necessary to keep a log of industrial injuries and illnesses.[31] Records maintained under an approved state OSHA plan can be used to satisfy this federal requirement.[32] The information in the log must also be summarized and posted prominently in your workplace from February 1 to March 1.[33] This requirement has been eliminated for most retail, financial, insurance, and service firms,[34] but not for:

- Building material and garden supply stores;
- General merchandise stores;
- Food stores;
- Hotels and other lodging places;
- Repair, amusement, and recreation services; and
- Health services.[35]

Under OSHA, a supplementary record must be prepared after a recordable injury or illness occurs, using federal *Form 101* or any of the substitutes state law permits to be used for this purpose.[36]

Neither of the above recordkeeping forms are ordinarily filed with the government. Instead, these records must be retained and kept available for inspection for five years.[37] In addition, special recordkeeping requirements will generally apply if your employees are exposed to toxic substances, asbestos, radiation, or carcinogens on the job.

You can obtain more detailed information on OSHA recordkeeping requirements by calling the nearest OSHA office (usually listed in the phone book under U. S. Government – Department of Labor) and asking for the booklet entitled, *Recordkeeping Requirements for Occupational Injuries and Illnesses.*

OSHA exempts any employer with ten or fewer employees from most of its reporting and recordkeeping requirements;[38] however, these small employers are not exempt from keeping a log of all injuries and accidents or reporting job-related fatalities and multiple injuries.

Federal OSHA reporting requirements include:

- The Bureau of Labor Statistics may require certain selected employers, including small employers, to report certain summary information on job-related injuries and illnesses annually on an occupational injuries and illness survey form.[39]
- In the event of a fatality or an accident resulting in the hospitalization of three or more employees, you must notify the area OSHA director within eight hours, describing the circumstances of the accident, the extent of any injuries, the number of fatalities, and other information.[40] There are penalties in the event you fail to give notice as required.[41]

See Section 11.5 for a discussion of laws this state may have that govern employee safety and health.

5.7 Employee Wage-Hour and Child Labor Laws

Not all businesses nor all employees of a given business are covered by federal and state wage-hour and child labor laws. The coverage of these laws is a crazy quilt patchwork of exceptions. Thus, there is no simple way to tell you whether your business will be subject to one or more of the federal and state laws relating to minimum wage, overtime pay, and child labor, or, if it is, which employees are covered and which are not. To find out which laws apply to your business, contact your attorney or the local wage-hour office.

Federal Wage-Hour Laws

The Federal Fair Labor Standards Act (FLSA) includes a number of requirements regarding compensation of employees covered under the act. There are two major requirements you need to know about — the minimum wage and overtime requirements.

Minimum Wage Requirement

The minimum wage provisions of the FLSA set an hourly minimum wage that you must pay to an employee. The current federal minimum wage is $4.25 per hour.[42] Certain states provide for a minimum wage in excess of the federal requirement or that applies to some employees who are not covered under the federal minimum wage law. Refer to Section 11.5 for the requirements in this state.

Overtime Pay Requirement

The overtime pay requirement rule states you must pay a covered employee at one and one-half times the employee's regular hourly rate for any hours worked in excess of 40 in a week.[43] The regular hourly rate cannot be less than the minimum wage. For the overtime pay requirement, the FLSA takes a single workweek as its measuring period and does not permit averaging of hours over two or more weeks. For example, if an employee works 30 hours one week and 50 hours during the next, he or she must receive overtime compensation (time and one-half) for the 10 overtime hours worked in the second week, even though the average number of hours worked in the two weeks is 40.

Note that the FLSA only requires overtime pay based on the number of hours worked during a week and not for working long hours on a particular day.

The above rules generally apply to salaried workers as well as to those paid on an hourly basis. To determine the regular hourly rate for a salaried employee, it is necessary to divide the employee's weekly salary by the number of hours in his or her regular workweek (40 or less).

Employee Exemptions

Executives, administrators, professionals, and outside salespeople are not covered by federal wage-hour laws and thus are not entitled by law to a minimum wage or to any pay for overtime hours worked.[44] The theory behind this exemption is apparently the view that these types of employees are independent and sophisticated enough to take care of themselves and do not need to be protected by the government from possible exploitation by their employers.

Under the Code of Federal Regulations, Title 29, Section 541.5, an employee qualifying for the exemption as an outside salesperson must meet the two requirements listed below.

- The employee customarily and regularly works away from the employer's place of business while making sales or obtaining orders or contracts for services or for the use of facilities for which a consideration will be paid by the client or customer.
- The employee cannot do any other kind of work for the company, besides that of selling, for more than 20% of the usual workweek put in by the company's nonexempt employees; for example, the outside salesperson or exempted employee could do receptionist work for only 8 hours of each 40-hour workweek.

Various indicators of an employee's bona fide status as an outside salesperson include:

- A contractual designation or job title that reflects involvement in sales;
- Significant compensation on a commission basis;
- Special sales training; and
- Little or no direct or constant supervision in carrying out daily tasks.

Small Enterprise Exemption

Employees of certain small companies, other than those enterprises engaged in commerce, are exempt from coverage under the wage-hour laws. Translated from the legalese, this means certain smaller businesses that do not significantly affect the flow of goods and services in interstate commerce are exempted from FLSA overtime and minimum wage requirements.

An "enterprise engaged in commerce" is one that "has employees engaged in commerce or in the production of goods for commerce, or that has employees handling, selling, or otherwise working on goods or materials that have been moved in commerce or produced for commerce by any person," and "is an enterprise whose annual gross volume of sales made or business done is not less than $500,000."[45]

All of which means that, if your firm does less than a half million dollars in sales a year, it will generally be exempt from FLSA overtime and minimum wage requirements.[46]

Even if you are exempt from the FLSA wage-hour rules, state wage-hour laws may apply and may be more stringent than federal laws in many states.

Numerous other exemptions from the wage-hour laws are based on the type of business, the nature of the work performed by the employee, where the work is done, and other factors.[47] Before you assume your employees are covered by the FLSA, consult your attorney, or at least call the local wage-hour office on an anonymous basis and ask for an informal and nonbinding opinion over the phone.

Detailed Records Required

Possibly, the most important thing you should be aware of, if you have employees subject to FLSA standards, is the need to keep detailed records of hours worked, the type of work, and wages or salary paid.

Under the law, if an employee files a claim against you for alleged failure to pay required wages in the past, you will need to be able to produce proof that you met the statutory requirements. Keeping detailed pay and work records for each employee is the only way to protect yourself against such claims for back pay. In addition, the FLSA requires employers to preserve such records for up to three years.

Poster Requirement

If you have employees whose wages, hours, and working conditions are subject to FLSA regulations, you will need to post the official wage- hour poster that is provided by the U.S. Department of Labor. In addition, you will most likely be required to post an official wage-hour poster for this state. For a discussion of the basic wage-hour and other significant labor law requirements under the law, refer to Section 11.5.

Child Labor Laws

Both the FLSA and various state laws regulate or prohibit the employment of children in businesses, with very few exceptions. If you intend to hire children to work in your business — other than hiring your own children, which is usually permitted, except in hazardous situations — you need to be aware of the following basic child labor law provisions.

As a general rule, the FLSA prohibits the employment of children under 16 years of age;[48] however, there are a number of exceptions to this rule.[49] In addition, all children under age 18 are excluded from certain occupations that are designated as hazardous by the secretary of labor.[50] Children under 16 years of age cannot be hired under any of the following circumstances:

- To work in any workplace where mining, manufacturing, or processing operations take place;
- To operate power machinery, other than office equipment;
- To operate or serve as a helper on motor vehicles — with certain exceptions for vehicles not exceeding 6,000 pounds gross weight, during daylight hours;
- To work in public messenger services; and
- To work in the following occupations: transportation, warehousing or storage, communications or public utilities, or construction — except in sales or office work.[51]

Children 14 or 15 years of age can be hired in other occupations not considered to be hazardous, but there are numerous limitations on the hours and times when they may work, particularly when schools are in session.

A few occupations, such as delivering newspapers and doing theatrical work, are exempt from the federal child labor laws, even for children under 14 years of age.[52]

Most states also strictly regulate the employment of children. See Section 11.5 regarding state child labor laws in this state. Thus, if you intend to employ children under 18 years of age in a business, you will probably need legal guidance as to the conditions under which they may work, if at all, under federal and state child labor laws.

5.8 Fair Employment Practices

As an employer, you will also need to be alert to your obligations under a number of federal and state laws that prohibit discrimination in employment on the basis of sex, age, race, color, national origin, religion, or on account of mental or physical handicaps. These anti-discrimination laws are not just limited to hiring practices, but relate to almost every aspect of the relationship between an employer and employee, including compensation, promotions, type of work assigned, and working conditions.

In addition to outlawing discrimination in employment, companies contracting for business with the federal government are generally required to adopt affirmative action programs in the employment of minorities, women, people with disabilities, and Vietnam veterans.

Affirmative action programs are employment programs that go beyond elimination of discrimination. Under such programs, employers consciously make an effort to hire more women and minority group members and to upgrade the pay and responsibility levels of women and other groups that have historically been subject to patterns of discrimination.

Affirmative action programs are generally required for businesses that are government contractors. On the other hand, most other businesses are only required to refrain from discriminating in employment.

Federal Anti-Discrimination Laws

If your small business employs fewer than 15 employees and is not working on government contracts or subcontracts, the federal anti-discrimination laws listed on the following page will generally not apply to you. The one exception to this would be the Equal Pay Act of 1963, which requires equal pay for equal work for women and men. This act is applicable to employers with two or more employees.

Employers Subject to Federal Anti-Discrimination Laws

Name of Law	Employers Who Are Covered	What the Law Requires
Title VII of the Civil Rights Act of 1964 and Americans with Disabilities Act (ADA)	Employers with 15 or more employees during 20 weeks of a calendar year	No discrimination in employment practices based on race, religion, disability or national origin
Pregnancy Discrimination Act	Same as for Title VII above	Equal treatment for pregnant women and new mothers for all employment-related purposes, including fringe benefits
Executive Order 11246 as amended	Employers with federal contracts or subcontracts of $10,000 or more	No discrimination in employment practices based on race, sex, color, religion, or national origin
Equal Pay Act of 1963	Nearly all employers with two or more employees	Equal pay for women and men doing similar work
Age Discrimination in Employment Act of 1967, as amended	Employers with 20 or more employees during 20 or more weeks in a calendar year	No discrimination in hiring or firing on account of age, for persons age 40 or older
Rehabilitation Act of 1973	Employers with federal contracts or subcontracts of $2,500 or more	No discrimination in employment practices on account of mental health or physical handicaps
Vietnam-Era Veteran Readjustment Assistance Act of 1974	Employers with federal contracts or subcontracts of $10,000 or more	Affirmative action programs for certain disabled veterans

Employers who violate any of the above laws may be sued by either the complaining individuals or by the various government enforcement agencies, or both.

Formal Compliance Requirements

Small businesses are not required to do a lot of paperwork or filling out of forms when it comes to federal anti-discrimination laws. An employer with more than 100 employees, however, must file *Form EEO-1* with the Equal Employment Opportunity Commission (EEOC) each year.[53]

As an employer you are required to keep detailed records — and should, for your own protection — as to the reasons for hiring or not hiring, promoting or not promoting, any employee or job applicant. In the event it is ever necessary to demonstrate that your firm has not discriminated against any group or individual member of a group in violation of federal laws, these records will provide the needed documentation.

Besides these requirements, there are a number of official posters you may be required to post in your place of business. These may include:

Type of Poster	Who Must Post	Source of Poster	Display Posters
Civil rights poster regarding sexual, racial, religious, and ethnic discrimination or because of physical or mental disability (*WH Publication 1088*)	Employers with 15 or more employees during 20 weeks of the year or with federal contracts or subcontracts of $10,000 or more[54]	EEOC offices, the nearest Office of Compliance	
Age discrimination poster	Employers with 20 or more employees who work 20 or more weeks a year[55]	EEOC offices	
Notice to employees working on government contracts (*WH Publication 1313*)	Any employer performing government contract work subject to the Service Contract Act or the Public Contracts Act	U.S. Department of Labor, Employment Standards Division	
Poster required under the Vietnam Era Veterans Readjustment Assistance Act	Employers with federal contracts or subcontracts of $10,000 or more	From the federal contracting officer administering the contract	
Poster explaining the Family and Medical Leave Act of 1993	Employers with 50 or more employees during 20 weeks of the year	U.S. Department of Labor, Wage and Hour Division	

To obtain these posters, contact each of the appropriate federal agencies and request a copy of their required poster.

Sexual Harassment

You need to be keenly aware of your potential liability for sexual harassment in the workplace, another increasingly significant area of the anti-discrimination laws under Title VII of the Civil Rights Act. While the federal Civil Rights Act does not specifically refer to sexual harassment as a form of discrimination, the courts and the EEOC have long accepted it as such. There are two types of sexual harassment under Title VII, as it has been interpreted over the years.

One type of sexual harassment is where tangible job benefits are granted or withheld based on an employee's receptiveness to unwelcome requests or conduct. For example, a male supervisor tells a female employee to meet him in the hot tub of his mountain chalet on a Saturday afternoon to discuss a business contract. She refuses to meet him at his place and later receives a bad rating from him for a "poor attitude and unwillingness to work overtime," which costs her a raise or promotion. The female employee in such a case has been denied a tangible job benefit due to sexual harassment.

The second type of sexual harassment involves a hostile work environment; that is, a situation in which the work environment is oppressive and hostile to members of one sex. This occurs when such conditions either unreasonably interfere with the individual's work performance or create an intimidating, hostile, or offensive environment. This type of harassment may not have any economic effects on the individual, and management or supervisory personnel may not be involved. Nevertheless, an employer who allows such a condition to persist may still be liable if management was aware of the harassment by co-workers — or even by customers — and fails to take appropriate actions to remedy the situation.

Merely having a company policy that prohibits sexual harassment at your company won't automatically stop such activity or protect the firm from liability if harassment occurs, but the absence of such a policy makes such conduct somewhat more likely to occur and will also tend to strengthen an employee's claim against you if your firm is sued for allowing such acts to occur. Adopt a sexual harassment policy that not only prohibits such conduct, but which sets up a grievance mechanism for employees who are victims of any such harassment, and communicate this company policy strongly and clearly to your employees.

In addition to federal civil rights case law, the statutes of many states, or the regulations of many state civil rights commissions, now specifically prohibit sexual harassment in the workplace. Some of these laws go well beyond the protections afforded under federal law. For a more detailed discussion of anti-discrimination laws in this state, refer to Section 11.5.

5.9 Immigration Law Restrictions on Hiring

The Immigration Reform and Control Act of 1986 represents a major governmental requirement regarding the relationship between an employer and employee. Under this law, you are prohibited from hiring illegal aliens, and depending on the number of any prior violations, you are subject to fines of $250 to $20,000 for each illegal alien hired after November 6, 1986. At the same time, the act also prohibits employment discrimination on the basis of citizenship status and national origin; you may not fire or fail to hire anyone on the basis of foreign appearance, language, or name.

For all employees hired after November 6, 1986, you are required to verify their eligibility for employment within three business days of each new hire. As an employer, you will need to fill out and retain *Form I-9*. The employee fills out the top portion of the form, indicating whether he or she is a citizen or national of the United States; an alien lawfully admitted for permanent residence; or an alien authorized by the U.S. Immigration and Naturalization Service (INS) to work in the United States.

On the back portion of *Form I-9*, there are three separate lists of various forms of identification and employment eligibility documents the employee must provide for you. In Section 2 of the form, you must record the documents you have examined, such as a passport or certificate of naturalization. These papers must include either one document in List A or one each in lists B and C. Both you and the employee must sign the form under penalty of perjury, and you must retain the completed form and make it available if the INS or U.S. Department of Labor requests it during an inspection.

You may obtain copies of *Form I-9* and a related *Employer's Handbook* from the nearest office of the U.S. Immigration and Naturalization Service. A sample *Form I-9* is also included at the end of this chapter. For more information on employer responsibilities, call:

U.S. Immigration and Naturalization Service
(800) 755-0777

The U.S. Department of Justice also has a hotline number you can call to hear prerecorded taped messages regarding the type of documents you can request to establish identity and work eligibility. The messages also offer tips on how to avoid discrimination when completing *Form I-9*. To hear these messages, call:

Office of Special Counsel for Immigration-Related
Unfair Employment Practices (OSC)
U.S. Department of Justice
(800) 255-8155

5.10 Restrictions on Layoffs of Employees

The WARN Act

If your business grows to where you have 100 or more full-time employees — or the equivalent, based on 40-hour workweeks — at a single location, you may be subject to the potentially onerous provisions of the plant closing law called the Worker Adjustment and Retraining Notification Act, or WARN Act.[56] This act would affect you if you laid off 50 or more employees, or one-third of the work force, in a 30-day period. It applies to virtually any plant closing or major layoff for any reason, with a few obvious exceptions, such as due to an earthquake or flood, or due to a labor dispute, such as a strike or lockout for which no notice need be given.

A "layoff" under this act includes any of the following:

- A permanent termination of employment;
- A layoff of an employee for more than six months; or
- A loss of half the employees' working hours for six consecutive months.

In case of any major layoff or shutdown, the law requires you to give at least 60 days advance notice. If you give less than that, you are required to pay the laid-off workers for 60 days minus the actual number of days' notice you gave. The law requires you to notify the labor union that represents the employees, or, if none, the individual employees by mailing the notice to their last known address or including it in their pay envelope. You must also notify the local city or county government and state labor agency of the planned shutdown or cutback.

The WARN Act doesn't generally prohibit a company from making lay-offs or shutting down a money-losing plant, but it makes it more costly for the employer to do so, and also gives local unions and politicians time to find some way to attempt to coerce or persuade a company into maintaining its operations, even if it is no longer economically viable.

The WARN law does impose stiff restrictions on a firm's ability to sell off, reorganize, merge, or consolidate operations, if such a decision would adversely affect the jobs of 50 or more employees. In other words, if your foreign competition renders your plant obsolete, you will not be allowed to sell it off to a competitor, if doing so would cost 50 or more employees their jobs. The act has made it much more costly to take a risk on building a plant in the United States — if it fails, you may have to close shop rather than restructure or sell.

As a result, there is considerable litigation over what does and does not constitute a mass layoff or shutdown under the WARN Act.

5.11 The Americans with Disabilities Act

In 1990, Congress enacted a revolutionary and wide-reaching piece of legislation, the Americans with Disabilities Act (ADA), which is designed to make both the workplace and most public facilities much more accessible to disabled persons.

The ADA and related regulations, which are being phased in over several years, will have a significant impact on a great many businesses, both in terms of employment practices and in terms of removing architectural barriers and other physical features that have limiting effects on the lives of disabled persons.[57]

Anti-Discrimination Rules Regarding the Disabled

Title I of the ADA prohibits discrimination against any "qualified individual with a disability" in all aspects of employment, including hiring and discharging of workers, compensation, and benefits. Title I applies to employers who employ 15 or more employees during 20 weeks of any calendar year. In addition, you must reasonably accommodate employees' or applicants' disabilities, which may mean modifying facilities, restructuring work schedules, or transferring disabled workers to vacant positions for which they are qualified, in appropriate circumstances. You are not required to accommodate a disabled worker, however, if doing so would impose an "undue hardship" on your business.

One area that is now significantly affected in the hiring process is the limitation on medical screening of applicants. Under the ADA, companies can no longer screen out prospective employees with disabilities because the applicant has an elevated risk of an on-the-job injury or a medical condition that might be aggravated because of job demands. The law specifically bans questions about a job applicant's physical or mental condition either on an employment application form or during a job interview. This would include general questions such as, "Do you have any mental or physical conditions that would prevent you from performing your job functions?"

Medical exams are still allowed, but they are greatly restricted. Pre-offer exams are prohibited, but an offer may be conditioned upon the satisfactory results of a medical examination. Results, however, cannot be used to withdraw an offer, unless they show that the individual in question is not able to perform the tasks required by the position.

The definition of "disabled" under the ADA includes people with AIDS, those who test positive for the HIV virus, and rehabilitated drug abusers and alcoholics; however, the ADA does not:

- Prohibit voluntary tests, such as employer-sponsored cholesterol or blood pressure tests; or
- Require employers to hire persons who are drug users or who have contagious diseases.

The ADA is neutral on the issue of drug testing of employees, in effect leaving that up to regulation by the states.

Medical Screening Tests

Title III of the ADA requires practically all businesses to make their facilities accessible to disabled employees and customers. Examples of various accessibility requirements with regard to public accommodations include:

- One designated parking space for the disabled must be provided for every 25 or fewer spaces. A lesser ratio applies if there are more than 100 total spaces.
- Hotels and motels must have 5% of their rooms accessible to wheelchairs and another 5% must be equipped with devices such as visual alarms for the hearing-impaired.
- Access ramps must be in place where the floor level changes more than one-half of an inch.
- Elevators must be provided in three-story or taller buildings and in those with more than 3,000 square feet per story.
- In retail or grocery stores, checkout aisles must be at least 36 inches wide. This is wide enough for wheelchairs.
- Theaters and similar places of assembly for 50 or more persons must have at least three wheelchair spaces dispersed throughout the seating area.

Public Accommodations for the Disabled

Tax Incentives

Companies spending money to remove architectural and transportation barriers to the disabled can deduct up to $15,000 a year of such expenses.[58] In addition, small firms — those with gross receipts under one million dollars or fewer than 30 full-time employees — who spend between $250 and $10,250 a year on access for the disabled, can claim a tax credit for up to 50% of the cost of such expenditures, a maximum annual credit of $5,000.[59]

For more information on the ADA, contact:

Equal Employment Opportunity Commission   or   **Civil Rights Division**
2401 E Street   **U.S. Department of Justice**
Washington, DC 20506   (800) 514-0301
(202) 663-4900 or
(800) 669-4000 (information)
(800) 669-3362 (publications)

5.12 Mandatory Family and Medical Leave Requirements

The Family and Medical Leave Act of 1993 became effective on August 5, 1993. This new law applies to all companies — as well as nonprofit entities — that have 50 or more employees during 20 or more calendar workweeks during the current or preceding calendar year.[60] As a result, many companies, who employ roughly half of all employees in the United States, are now subject to the family leave law's requirements.

The new act requires covered employers to:

- Offer their employees twelve weeks of unpaid leave after the birth or adoption of a child; to care for a seriously ill child, spouse, or parent; or for an employee's own serious illness.

- Maintain health care coverage for an employee who is on a leave of absence as described above; and

- Guarantee that employees will be able to return to either the same job or to a comparable position after the leave.

- Post a notice, which may be obtained from the U.S. Department of Labor – Wage and Hour Division, explaining the rights of employees under the Family and Medical Leave Act of 1993.[61]

A serious illness must be verified by a physician's certification, and as the employer, you may require a second medical opinion if desired. An employee is required to provide you with 30 days notice for foreseeable leaves of absence for a birth, adoption, or planned medical treatment.

One major exception to the law's coverage is a provision that exempts certain "key employees" from coverage. Key employees are defined as the highest-paid 10% of the employer's workforce and those whose leave of absence would cause significant economic harm to the employer. Also exempted from the law's provisions are employees who haven't worked at least one year for the employer and who haven't worked at least 1,250 hours, or 25 hours a week, in the preceding twelve months. In addition, you are given the option of substituting an employee's accrued paid leave, if any, for any part of the twelve-week period of family leave.

A number of states, such as California and Hawaii, have also enacted similar family leave laws. Refer to Chapter 11 for information on any such laws that have been adopted in this state.

Endnotes

1. Treas. Regs. §31.6302-1(f)(4).
2. Treas. Regs. §31.6302-1(b)(2).
3. Treas. Regs. §31.6302-1(b)(3).
4. Treas. Regs. §31.6302-1(c)(3).
5. I.R.C. §7502(e)(3).
6. I.R.C. §§3301(1) and 3306(b)(1).
7. I.R.C. §§3301(1) and 3302(b).
8. I.R.C. §3306(a)(1)(A).
9. I.R.C. §3306(a)(1)(B).
10. 29 U.S.C. §1131.
11. 29 U.S.C. §1132; I.R.C. §§4971, 4975, 6057–6059, and 6652.
12. 29 U.S.C. §1002(2); 29 C.F.R. §2510.3-2.
13. 29 U.S.C. §1002(1); 29 C.F.R. §2510.3-1.
14. 29 C.F.R. §2510.3-1(b), 29 C.F.R. §2510.3-2(b).
15. 29 C.F.R. §2520.104b-2.
16. 29 C.F.R. §2520.102-3.
17. 29 C.F.R. §2520.104b-2(a)(2).
18. 29 C.F.R. §2520.104b-2(a)(1).
19. 29 C.F.R. §2520.104-20.
20. 29 U.S.C. §1024(b)(4); 29 C.F.R. §2520.104b-1.
21. 29 C.F.R. §2520.104a-3.
22. 29 C.F.R. §2520.104a-5.
23. 29 C.F.R. §2520.104b-10.
24. 29 C.F.R. §§2520.104a-4 and 2520.104b-3.
25. 29 U.S.C. §1021(c).
26. 29 U.S.C. §1112.
27. I.R.C. §3405(a).
28. I.R.C. §6039 D.
29. Announcement 86-20, I.R.B. 1986–87, 34.
30. 29 C.F.R. §1903.2.
31. 29 C.F.R. §1904.2.
32. 29 C.F.R. §1904.10.
33. 29 C.F.R. §1904.5.
34. 29 C.F.R. §1904.16.
35. 29 C.F.R. §1904.12.
36. 29 C.F.R. §1904.4.
37. 29 C.F.R. §1904.6.
38. 29 C.F.R. §1904.15.
39. 29 C.F.R. §§1904.15 and 1904.21.
40. 29 C.F.R. §1904.8 as amended, April 1, 1994.
41. 29 C.F.R. §1904.9.
42. 29 U.S.C. §206(a)(1).
43. 29 U.S.C. §207(a)(1).
44. 29 U.S.C. §213(a)(1).
45. 29 U.S.C. §203(s).
46. 29 U.S.C. §207(a)(1).
47. 29 U.S.C. §213.
48. 29 U.S.C. §§203(1) and 212.
49. 29 U.S.C. §213.
50. 29 C.F.R. §570.50–570.71.
51. 29 C.F.R. §570.33.
52. 29 U.S.C. §213(c) and (d).
53. 29 C.F.R. §1602.7.
54. 29 C.F.R. §1601.30.
55. 29 U.S.C. §627 and 29 C.F.R. §1627.10.
56. 29 U.S.C. §§2101–2109.
57. 42 U.S.C. §§12101 *et seq.* and 29 C.F.R. §1630.
58. I.R.C. §190.
59. I.R.C. §44.
60. 29 C.F.R. §825.104(a).
61. 29 C.F.R. §825.300(a).

Summary of Basic ERISA Compliance Requirements for Pension Plans

Item	Provided to
Summary plan description.	U.S. Department of Labor; participants; beneficiaries
Annual return/report (*Form 5500, 5500-EZ,* or *5500-C/R*).	IRS (now required even for a simple one-person Keogh plan)
Schedule A, Form 5500 series (insurance information).	IRS
Schedule B, Form 5500 series (actuarial information prepared and signed by an enrolled actuary for "defined benefit" plans only).	IRS
Schedule SSA, Form 5500 series (registration statement).	IRS
Form W-2P (report of periodic plan benefit payments made during the year).	IRS; recipient of distribution
Form 1099-R (report of total distribution of benefits during the year).	IRS; recipient of distribution
Form W-3 or *W-3G* (transmittal of *Form W-2P* and *Form 1099-R*).	IRS
Form PBGC-1 (premium payment of required plan termination insurance — for "defined benefit" plans only).	Pension Benefit Guaranty Corporation (a government agency that insures pension plans of corporate employers)
Summary annual report.	Participants; beneficiaries
Individual deferred vested benefit statement to separated employee.	Former participant in plan
Summary of material modifications to a plan.	U.S. Department of Labor; participants; beneficiaries
Terminal report (when plan is terminated).	U.S. Department of Labor; participants; beneficiaries
Written explanation of joint and survivor annuity and financial effect of not electing to receive it (if plan provides benefits in the form of an annuity).	Participants
Written explanation of reasons for denying benefit claim and description of appeal procedures.	Person claiming entitlement to plan benefits
Various documents and information to be provided on request.	U.S. Department of Labor; participants
Various formal notices upon occurrence of certain events.	IRS; U.S. Department of Labor; Pension Benefit Guaranty Corporation; participants

Form I-9 – Employment Eligibility Verification: Sample

EMPLOYMENT ELIGIBILITY VERIFICATION (Form I-9)

1 EMPLOYEE INFORMATION AND VERIFICATION: (To be completed and signed by employee.)

Name: (Print or Type) Last	First	Middle	Birth Name

Address: Street Name and Number	City	State	ZIP Code

Date of Birth (Month/Day/Year)	Social Security Number

I attest, under penalty of perjury, that I am (check a box):

☐ 1. A citizen or national of the United States.

☐ 2. An alien lawfully admitted for permanent residence (Alien Number A _____).

☐ 3. An alien authorized by the Immigration and Naturalization Service to work in the United States (Alien Number A _____ ,
or Admission Number _____ , expiration of employment authorization, if any _____).

I attest, under penalty of perjury, the documents that I have presented as evidence of identity and employment eligibility are genuine and relate to me. I am aware that federal law provides for imprisonment and/or fine for any false statements or use of false documents in connection with this certificate.

Signature	Date (Month/Day/Year)

PREPARER/TRANSLATOR CERTIFICATION (To be completed if prepared by person other than the employee). I attest, under penalty of perjury, that the above was prepared by me at the request of the named individual and is based on all information of which I have any knowledge.

Signature	Name (Print or Type)		
Address (Street Name and Number)	City	State	Zip Code

2 EMPLOYER REVIEW AND VERIFICATION: (To be completed and signed by employer.)

Instructions:

Examine one document from List A and check the appropriate box, _OR_ examine one document from List B _and_ one from List C and check the appropriate boxes. Provide the *Document Identification Number* and *Expiration Date* for the document checked.

List A Documents that Establish Identity and Employment Eligibility	List B Documents that Establish Identity and	List C Documents that Establish Employment Eligibility
☐ 1. United States Passport	☐ 1. A State-issued driver's license or a State-issued I.D. card with a photograph, or information, including name, sex, date of birth, height, weight, and color of eyes. (Specify State)_____	☐ 1. Original Social Security Number Card (other than a card stating it is not valid for employment)
☐ 2. Certificate of United States Citizenship		☐ 2. A birth certificate issued by State, county, or municipal authority bearing a seal or other certification
☐ 3. Certificate of Naturalization	☐ 2. U.S. Military Card	
☐ 4. Unexpired foreign passport with attached Employment Authorization	☐ 3. Other (Specify document and issuing authority) _____	☐ 3. Unexpired INS Employment Authorization Specify form # _____
☐ 5. Alien Registration Card with photograph		
Document Identification # _____	*Document Identification* # _____	*Document Identification* # _____
Expiration Date (if any) _____	*Expiration Date (if any)* _____	*Expiration Date (if any)* _____

CERTIFICATION: I attest, under penalty of perjury, that I have examined the documents presented by the above individual, that they appear to be genuine and to relate to the individual named, and that the individual, to the best of my knowledge, is eligible to work in the United States.

Signature	Name (Print or Type)	Title
Employer Name	Address	Date

Form I-9 (05/07/87)
OMB No. 1115-0136

U.S. Department of Justice
Immigration and Naturalization Service

Form I-9 – Employment Eligibility Verification: Sample (continued)

Employment Eligibility Verification

> NOTICE: Authority for collecting the information on this form is in Title 8, United States Code, Section 1324A, which requires employers to verify employment eligibility of individuals on a form approved by the Attorney General. This form will be used to verify the individual's eligibility for employment in the United States. Failure to present this form for inspection to officers of the Immigration and Naturalization Service or Department of Labor within the time period specified by regulation, or improper completion or retention of this form, may be a violation of the above law and may result in a civil money penalty.

Section 1. Instructions to Employee/Preparer for completing this form

Instructions for the employee.

All employees, upon being hired, must complete Section 1 of this form. Any person hired after November 6, 1986 must complete this form. (For the purpose of completion of this form the term "hired" applies to those employed, recruited or referred for a fee.)

All employees must print or type their complete name, address, date of birth, and Social Security Number. The block which correctly indicates the employee's immigration status must be checked. If the second block is checked, the employee's Alien Registration Number must be provided. If the third block is checked, the employee's Alien Registration Number *or* Admission Number must be provided, as well as the date of expiration of that status, if it expires.

All employees whose present names differ from birth names, because of marriage or other reasons, must print or type their birth names in the appropriate space of Section 1. Also, employees whose names change after employment verification should report these changes to their employer.

All employees must sign and date the form.

Instructions for the preparer of the form, if not the employee.

If a person assists the employee with completing this form, the preparer must certify the form by signing it and printing or typing his or her complete name and address.

Section 2. Instructions to Employer for completing this form

(For the purpose of completion of this form, the term "employer" applies to employers and those who recruit or refer for a fee.)

Employers must complete this section by examining evidence of identity and employment eligibility, and:

- checking the appropriate box in List A *or* boxes in both Lists B and C;
- recording the document identification number and expiration date (if any);
- recording the type of form if not specifically identified in the list;
- signing the certification section.

NOTE: Employers are responsible for reverifying employment eligibility of employees whose employment eligibility documents carry an expiration date.

Copies of documentation presented by an individual for the purpose of establishing identity and employment eligibility may be copied and retained for the purpose of complying with the requirements of this form and no other purpose. Any copies of documentation made for this purpose should be maintained with this form.

Name changes of employees which occur after preparation of this form should be recorded on the form by lining through the old name, printing the new name and the reason (such as marriage), and dating and initialing the changes. Employers should not attempt to delete or erase the old name in any fashion.

RETENTION OF RECORDS.

The completed form must be retained by the employer for:

- three years after the date of hiring; or
- one year after the date the employment is terminated, whichever is later.

> Employers may photocopy or reprint this form as necessary.

U.S. Department of Justice
Immigration and Naturalization Service

OMB #1115-0136
Form I-9 (05/07 87)
☆ U.S.G.P.O. 1987- 183-918/69085

For sale by the Superintendent of Documents, U.S. Government Printing Office
Washington, D.C. 20402

Chapter 6

Businesses that Require Licenses to Operate

The bureaucrat who smiles when something serious has gone wrong
has already found someone to blame it on.

— Anonymous

6.1 General Licensing

Almost any kind of business activity you engage in will require a city or
county business license, which is usually fairly simple to obtain. In addition, some types of businesses will have to obtain licenses from the federal government to operate, while other businesses, occupations, and professions are also licensed and regulated by the state.

Even though there are tremendous variations regarding the requirements
for obtaining necessary federal and state licenses, these requirements
generally relate to educational attainments, experience in the particular
field, passage of examinations, submission of detailed applications, meeting financial or bonding requirements, or some combination of the foregoing, plus payment of a licensing fee or tax.

In addition to the federal and state licensing requirements, certain local
city or county permits may have to be obtained. For example, if you will
be in the food business, you may have to get a license from the county
health department; or, if your business would like to do any construction
or remodeling, you might have to get approval from your local planning
commission.

Before you begin to operate any kind of business, find out whether you
will be required to obtain any special government licenses or permits,
since in most cases, you must obtain the particular license before com-
mencing operation.

This chapter and Section 11.6, respectively, provide a partial listing of the federal and state licensing requirements you are most likely to encounter as a small business owner. Because the number of activities that may require federal or state licenses is so large, no attempt has been made to try to list all of them in this book.

Thus, the lists of licensing agencies and businesses that require licenses found in this chapter and in Chapter 11 should be helpful in alerting you, as a small business owner, to possible licensing needs, but you should remember that these lists are not complete and are not a substitute for individualized legal advice.

6.2 Federal Licenses

If you are starting a small business, it is relatively unlikely that you will need any type of license or permit from the federal government; however, the following is a list of the federal licensing requirements you might possibly encounter:

Federal Licensing Requirements

Activity	Federal Agency
Rendering investment advice	Securities and Exchange Commission
Providing ground transportation as a common carrier	Interstate Commerce Commission
Preparation of meat products	Food and Drug Administration
Production of drugs or biological products	Food and Drug Administration
Making tobacco products or alcohol	Treasury Department, Bureau of Alcohol, Tobacco, and Firearms
Making or dealing in firearms	Treasury Department, Bureau of Alcohol, Tobacco, and Firearms
Radio or television broadcasting	Federal Communications Commission

For a partial listing of businesses and professions required to be licensed in this state, see Section 11.6.

Operating the Business

Chapter 7

Excise Taxes

Taxation without representation is tyranny.

— Patrick Henry

Taxation with representation is worse.

— Will Rogers

7.1 General Considerations

Both federal and state tax laws impose excise or similar taxes on a number of different types of businesses, products, services, and occupations. These taxes are usually imposed without any assessment or notice to the taxpayer. Thus, it is up to you to find out if you are subject to any of these taxes and, if so, to obtain the proper tax return forms and pay the tax on time.

It is not uncommon for a small business to operate for several years without the owner ever being aware of the need to pay excise taxes. Then comes the day of reckoning, when a formal notice is received from the government demanding immediate payment of several years' worth of back taxes on some particular item subject to excise tax, plus interest and penalties for not filing the returns and not paying the tax. This can be a disastrous surprise, especially since the business owner has not factored the cost of paying the excise into the price of his or her goods or services.

This chapter is designed to alert you in advance to the types of federal and state excise — and similar — taxes that you may need to know about. Some excise taxes, such as those on telephone service and insurance companies, are not discussed below since they are passed along or absorbed by the telephone company, insurance company, or other large institution with which your business may deal, and you have no obligation to file any returns or make any direct payment to the government of such taxes.

See Section 11.7 for a summary of various state excise taxes that may affect your business.

7.2 Federal Excise Taxes

Federal excise taxes on many products and transactions have been repealed over the last 20 years, so these taxes are much less pervasive now than in the past. The excise tax that the largest number of small businesses are likely to be subject to is the motor vehicle highway use tax on vehicles of more than 55,000 pounds gross weight.[1] *Form 2290* must be filed by owners of trucks and buses subject to the highway use tax. If you want information about the highway use tax, request a copy of IRS *Publication 349* from any IRS office.

The federal government imposes a number of excise taxes on various types of business activities. Some excise taxes are on the production or sale of certain goods. Some are on services or the use of certain products or facilities. Still others are imposed on businesses of a certain type.

Most federal excise taxes are reported on *Form 720, Quarterly Federal Excise Tax Return*, the most common excise tax form. Environmental taxes on petroleum and 42 designated chemical substances are reported on *Form 6627* and attached to *Form 720*. Federal excise taxes can be broken down into several major categories:

- The motor vehicle highway use tax — This tax is imposed on vehicles of more than 55,000 pounds gross weight.[2]

- Retailer taxes on certain fuels[3] — The federal gasoline tax is $0.183 (18.3 cents) per gallon on gasoline, and the tax on diesel is $0.243 (24.3 cents) per gallon.

  In addition, both of the taxes are increased by $0.01 (one-tenth of one cent) per gallon by the Leaking Underground Storage Tank Trust Fund Tax. A reduced tax rate applies to qualified methane and ethanol fuel.

Other retail excise taxes are imposed on sales of:
- Heavy trucks and trailers;[4]
- Tires and tubes;[5]
- Recreation equipment, such as bows, arrows, fishing rods, reels, lures, and creels;[6] and
- Firearms and ammunition.[7]

Other excise taxes exist on the following as well:

- Air transportation — If you are in the business of transporting people by air, you may have to collect an excise tax;[8]
- Telephone and teletype services;[9]
- Wagering;[10]
- Coal mined in the United States;[11]
- Alcohol and tobacco products;[12] and
- Manufacturers of certain vaccines — Certain vaccines manufactured or imported into the United States are subject to an excise tax in order to create a Vaccine Injury Compensation Trust Fund, a no-fault program for compensating persons who are injured by, or die from, certain vaccines.[13]

There are also several environmental excise taxes, such as:

- An excise tax on ozone-depleting chemicals;
- An oil spill liability excise tax of $0.05 (5 cents) a barrel;[14] and
- Environmental taxes on petroleum products, various chemicals, and hazardous wastes.[15]

Luxury Taxes

A luxury tax applies to retail purchases of passenger automobiles costing more than $30,000.[16] The tax is equal to 10% of the amount by which the purchase price exceeds $30,000. For example, the luxury tax on a new $35,000 automobile would be 10% of $5,000 — the excess of $35,000 over $30,000, or $500. The $30,000 threshold amount is indexed for inflation that has occurred since December 31, 1990, and is set at $32,000 in 1994.

The luxury tax does not apply to:

- Vehicles of more than 6,000 pounds unloaded gross weight; or
- Any vehicle, such as a taxicab, that is used exclusively in the active conduct of a trade or business of transporting people or property for compensation or hire.

The luxury tax on automobiles is collected by the retailer who sells the item. This luxury tax only applies to the first retail sale of an item. For example, if you buy a used $50,000 automobile, there is no luxury tax on the purchase.

Other luxury taxes on boats, aircraft, furs, and jewelry were repealed on August 10, 1993, retroactive to January 1, 1993. If you paid luxury taxes on any of those items in 1993, you are entitled to a refund of the tax from the retailer who collected it from you.

For further information on excise taxes and other federal taxes, you may wish to obtain IRS *Publication 334, Tax Guide for Small Business*, or for more detailed information on excise taxes, IRS *Publication 510, Excise Taxes*.

Endnotes

1. I.R.C. § 4481(a).
2. Id.
3. I.R.C. §§ 4041, 4081, and 4091.
4. I.R.C. § 4051.
5. I.R.C. § 4071(a).
6. I.R.C. § 4161(a) and (b).
7. I.R.C. § 4181.
8. I.R.C. §§ 4261(a) and 4271(a).
9. I.R.C. § 4251.
10. I.R.C. §§ 4401 and 4411.
11. I.R.C. § 4121(a).
12. I.R.C. §§ 5001, 5041(b), 5701, and 5801–5822.
13. I.R.C. §§ 4131–4132.
14. I.R.C. §§ 4611(c)(2) and 4681.
15. I.R.C. §§ 4611 and 4661.
16. I.R.C. §§ 4001–4012.

Chapter 8

Planning for Tax Savings in a Business

*The words of such an act as the income tax merely dance before
my eyes in a meaningless procession: cross-reference to cross-
reference, exception upon exception — couched in abstract terms
that offer no handle to seize hold of — leave in my mind only
a confused sense of some vitally important, but successfully
concealed, purport, which it is my duty to extract, but which
is within my power, if at all, only after the most inordinate
expenditure of time. I know that these monsters are the result of
fabulous industry and ingenuity, plugging up this hole and
casting out that net against all possible evasion; yet at times
I cannot help recalling a saying of William James' about certain
passages of Hegel: that they were no doubt written with a
passion of rationality; but that one cannot help wondering
whether to the reader they have any significance save that the
words are strung together with syntactical correctness.*

— Judge Learned Hand

referring to the 1939 Internal Revenue Code, a statute which was almost
childlike in its simplicity compared to our current tax law.

8.1 General Considerations

One of the most shocking and unpleasant realizations of many successful small business owners comes when they realize they have acquired
an unwanted silent partner — a partner who contributes nothing to the
business but who often lays claim to half or more of the owner's hard-
earned profits. That silent partner, of course, is the government income

tax collector, and this chapter is a summary of many of the best and most effective legal ways to reduce that silent partner's share of the profits from your business.

This chapter is not intended to be a substitute for professional tax advice regarding your individual situation. Because the tax laws are so enormously complex, a technique that may work brilliantly in most cases might be useless or even disastrous in your particular tax situation. This chapter will provide you with a working understanding of some of the key ways to plan for tax savings and to avoid tax pitfalls in your business.

After you have read this chapter, you may want to talk to your tax adviser about one or more of the ideas discussed, if you feel they might be useful for applying to your business. Your tax adviser should be able to tell you whether a particular idea will work in your situation. If it will, he or she can help you implement it.

Tax attorneys and accountants often have a very heavy workload and a large number of clients to serve. An unfortunate result of this situation is your tax adviser may tend to spend most of the time responding to inquiries by clients and meeting tax deadlines rather than taking the initiative in seeking out ways to minimize your taxes. Thus, by having some understanding of what you would like to do in the way of reducing taxes on your business income, you can propose ideas to your tax advisers and maximize the effectiveness of their expert knowledge and advice. In tax planning, as in so many areas of life, it pays to be assertive. "The wheel that squeaks is the one that gets the grease."

8.2 Using a Corporation as a Tax Shelter

One of the most effective ways to reduce your taxes, in many cases, is to incorporate your business. Incorporation is most likely to be advantageous if the business is generating about $75,000 or less in annual profits and salary for the owner — or per owner, if there is more than one. There are three basic ways, other than the adoption of employee fringe benefit plans, that incorporation can reduce your taxes on business income:

- Leaving profits in the corporation
- Income-splitting
- Investing in stock

Leaving Profits in the Corporation

If you are able to leave your first $75,000 of annual profits in your corporation, the profits will generally be taxed at corporate rates that are lower than your individual income tax rates. This provides a strong incentive for you to leave at least that much taxable income in the corporation rather than pay it all out to yourself as salary. At taxable income levels above $75,000, corporate income is taxed at roughly the same rates as individual income, except at very high income levels of $335,000 or more. Refer to the table of corporate income tax rates in Section 2.4 and compare those rates with the personal income tax rates for your filing status. Be careful about leaving too much profit in your corporation. Sections 8.5 and 8.9 discuss the potential benefits and risks of having your profits accumulate in your corporation.

By using a corporation, it is also possible to split your overall profit between two or more taxpayers, so that none of the income gets taxed in the highest tax brackets. For example, with an overall economic profit of $100,000, an incorporated business may be able to reduce its taxable income to $50,000 by paying (and deducting) a $50,000 salary to its owner, as an officer/employee of the corporation. The corporation would pay tax only on the remaining $50,000 profit, at a maximum federal tax rate of only 15%, while the owner would pay tax on the $50,000 salary received.

Income Splitting

Because of the progressive tax rate structure under the federal income tax laws, the tax on the $100,000 income divided between the owner and his or her corporation would typically be much less than if the whole $100,000 were taxable to the owner. In 1993, for example, a single individual would pay $26,522 in federal income taxes on $100,000 of taxable income, while if the income were split evenly between the owner and his or her corporation, the corporation's tax would be $7,500 and the owner's $11,127, a savings of $7,895 — assuming the corporation is not a personal services corporation subject to a 35% flat rate of tax.

Another way to split the income of a business between multiple taxpayers is for you to make your children part owners of the business. Ideally, the children should be given an interest in the business when it is started, since the value of the gifts to them will often be minimal for gift tax purposes at that time.

It is frequently more feasible to split corporate income with your children by giving them some of the corporation's stock. This approach, however, will work only if your corporation has filed for an S corporation election on *Form 2553* with the IRS. The taxable income of a corporation that qualifies as an S corporation is taxable to its shareholders — in proportion to the stock they own in the corporation — and is generally not taxed to the corporation.

By giving a number of shares of stock in such an S corporation to one or more of your children, part of the taxable income of the business can often be shifted to the children[1] and taxed at their low tax brackets — assuming, as is usually the case, that the children do not have a lot of taxable income from other sources.

If, however, the parents attempt to shift too much income to the children by drawing no salary or too little salary from the corporation, the IRS has the power to reallocate the corporation's income to the parents to reflect the value of services rendered to the corporation. Shifting significant income to your children will not work if the children are under 14 years of age.[2]

Investing in Stocks

By investing accumulated corporate funds in dividend-paying stocks of other corporations, you can take advantage of the 70% deduction that corporations are entitled to on the dividends they receive.[3] Because this special deduction makes most dividends received by a corporation — other than those received by an S corporation — practically tax-free to the recipient corporation, your incorporated business can be an excellent place to hold stocks you wish to invest in, if you do not need the dividend income to live on.

Before you get too excited about putting your whole stock portfolio into your incorporated business, take these potential drawbacks into account:

- If you decide to later withdraw your corporate dividends or the stocks themselves, the withdrawal will usually be taxable to you as ordinary income[4] or perhaps, if you liquidate the corporation, as capital gains.[5] Capital gains are taxed at a maximum rate of 28% for individuals.[6]

- If you should accumulate more than $250,000 — $150,000 for professional and certain personal service firms — in after-tax earnings in your corporation, including the 70% of dividends that the corporation doesn't pay income tax on, and invest part of those earnings in liquid, nonbusiness investment assets like stocks, you may be inviting an IRS audit and a potential penalty tax for unreasonably accumulating earnings and profits in the corporation.[7] See the discussion of the accumulated earnings tax in Section 8.9.

- If too much of your corporation's income is in the form of dividends and other passive types of investment income, the corporation may be classified as a personal holding company for tax purposes, and this can have drastic tax consequences, as outlined in Section 8.9.[8] As long as more than 40% of your corporation's gross income is from sales of goods and services, however, as a general rule, you should not have to be concerned about personal holding company taxes.[9]

- Putting your personal assets that are not needed in the business into your corporation will subject those assets to the risk of the business. That is, anything you put into the corporation will be subject to the claims of the corporation's creditors if it goes bankrupt. If you put all of your assets into the corporation, you will in effect have given up the benefits of limited liability.

- If your corporation borrows money to invest in or carry stock investments, the 70% dividend exclusion will be reduced in part by the interest paid on the borrowed funds.[10]

Your accountant will probably be the best person to consult for determining how and whether you can use a corporation to reduce taxes on your business profits.

8.3 Retirement Plans and Other Fringe Benefits

One advantage of being your own boss, either as a sole proprietor, a partner, or a shareholder of a closely held corporation, is the opportunity to be able to set up a Keogh plan or corporate retirement plan. In a C corporation, you can also obtain insurance and other important fringe benefits as an officer and employee of the corporation on a tax-favored basis. Some of the ways you can benefit from using retirement plans and other tax-favored fringe benefits are outlined in this section.

There are three types of tax-favored retirement plans:

Tax Advantages of Retirement Plans

- Corporate pension and profit-sharing plans;
- Keogh pension and profit-sharing plans for unincorporated business; and
- Individual Retirement Accounts (IRAs), which may be set up by any individual who has earned income, including an employee.

IRAs are of limited interest to most business owners, since the maximum annual contribution to an IRA is $2,000 a year — $2,250 if you have a nonworking spouse. Even these small deductions may not be available if you are a participant in a Keogh or corporate retirement plan and your adjusted gross income is over $50,000 — $35,000 if you are a single person. Accordingly, the discussion below focuses on corporate and Keogh retirement plans.

The primary tax advantages of the three types of tax-qualified retirement plans — corporate, self-employed (Keogh), and IRA — are these:

- Amounts contributed, up to certain limits, are deductible from the income of the corporation or individual taxpayer.[11] This deduction can be as much as 25% of the individual's compensation for the year (not counting the plan contribution) or $30,000, whichever is less. Even larger contributions can be made by so-called defined benefit plans.
- Contributed funds can be invested by pension or profit-sharing plans on a tax-free basis.[12] The qualified retirement trust that is usually set up to hold the retirement funds is exempt from state and federal income taxes on its income or capital gains from investments in stocks, bonds, savings accounts, gold, silver, real estate, and other passive investments. Note, however, that gold, silver, and other collectibles can no longer be purchased as investments by individually directed retirement plans or by an IRA. The only exception is for certain gold and silver coins minted by the United States.[13]
- When trust funds are paid out to you at retirement, you may be in a lower tax bracket than when you made the contributions to the plan. Thus, not only do you get to defer payment of any tax on amounts contributed to the plan until you retire, but the tax you finally pay at retirement is apt to be at a lower rate than you would have paid when you were working.

- Receipt of all your retirement plan funds in a lump sum at retirement, or in certain other circumstances, may often qualify for special low tax rates if the distribution is from a corporate or Keogh plan but not from an IRA.

Corporate and noncorporate Keogh retirement plans are almost identical under the tax law in all major respects, except for the ability to borrow one's retirement funds from the plan, which will be subject to an excise or penalty tax in the case of a Keogh. It does not pay to incorporate your business just for pension and profit-sharing plan purposes. If you decide to establish a retirement plan, there are several practical points you should consider before reaching a decision.

Model SEP Plans from Financial Institutions

If you are setting up a Simplified Employee Pension (SEP) plan for yourself, or a Keogh plan, consider obtaining a "canned" plan from a bank, savings and loan, insurance company, or mutual fund. Usually, these preapproved plans will be suitable for you unless you have a significant number of employees to cover under your Keogh, in which case, you probably should be incorporated anyway. The great advantages of getting a canned SEP or Keogh plan from a financial institution are cost and simplicity. Most such institutions will charge you only $10–$25 to adopt their plan. Their profit comes from investing your funds for a management fee, in the case of a mutual fund; or maintaining your deposits in interest-bearing accounts, in the case of a bank or savings and loan.

By contrast, hiring a lawyer or benefit consultant to draw up a customized SEP or Keogh plan for you could cost anywhere from a few hundred to a few thousand dollars in fees. In addition, since the pension laws seem to be rewritten every time Congress meets, you may find yourself paying hundreds or even thousands of dollars each year to your attorney or benefit consultant to revise or amend a custom-designed plan, just to keep it in compliance with the never-ending changes in the tax and other laws affecting pension plans.

Model SEP and Keogh Plans from Stockbrokerages

If you are not content to invest your SEP or Keogh funds in or with a financial institution, you can still participate in a canned plan offered by some stockbrokerage firms. These plans usually permit you to direct your own stock and bond investments.

Model Corporate Plans

If you are setting up a corporate retirement plan, it is also possible to obtain canned prototype plans from banks, if you allow them to act as trustee — or from insurance companies, if you buy their insurance or managed fund accounts through the plan. These plans usually have variable terms that can be tailored somewhat to suit your needs, unless you want to do something out of the ordinary, such as allow each participant to direct the investment of his or her portion of the plan's funds. Other institutions, such as stockbrokerages and mutual funds, also offer corporate plans.

Even if you do need something unusual that requires a customized retirement plan for your corporation, you will probably find it more cost-effective to have a benefit consulting firm draw up the plan for you. This way, your attorney would only be involved in reviewing the plan and obtaining approval of the plan from the IRS. Typically, benefit consultants or pension consultants will charge only a fraction of what a law firm would charge to draw up the plan, and the larger benefit consulting firms are generally quite competent. Most of their fees come from helping you administer the plan under ERISA after it is set up — a service you will need anyway.

Customized Plans

Simplified Employee Pension (SEP) plans have gotten very little use since they were created by Congress several years ago; however, they now offer most of the attractive features of typical Keogh and corporate plans with virtually no administrative costs. This is in contrast to a Keogh or corporate plan that may cost up to $2,000 or $3,000 a year to maintain for only five or ten employees.

Saving with SEPs

A SEP is basically a glorified individual retirement account (IRA), but it is one where you contribute to each employee's IRA account an amount of up to 15% of an employee's compensation with a maximum of $30,000 — $22,500, as a practical matter.

The amount contributed is not taxed to the employee and can be invested in any type of IRA account the employee chooses. SEPs can be set up by corporations, partnerships, or sole proprietorships. Participants can still contribute up to $2,000 a year to their SEP/IRA or to another IRA plan.

SEP participants with taxable income in excess of $25,000 (single) or $40,000 (married filing jointly), however, will have their IRA deductions reduced or eliminated.

The main existing drawback of an SEP is that any distributions from the plan at retirement are taxed as ordinary income. The special five-year averaging — which can result in a lower tax rate — for lump sum distributions from a Keogh or corporate qualified plan is not available for IRAs or SEPs. Even so, they strongly merit consideration as an alternative to Keogh or corporate retirement plans, due to their relative simplicity.

An increasingly popular form of qualified retirement plan is the Section 401(k) plan. This type of plan generally permits employees to elect to have a percentage of their salary — with various limitations — deducted from their paychecks, free of income tax, and deposited on their behalf in a profit-sharing-type plan. In many cases, as an additional incentive to employees to make such tax-favored savings, you, as an employer, may provide some degree of matching contribution to the plan on behalf of the employee.

Section 401(k) Plans

For example, a typical situation would be where you contribute $0.50 (50 cents) for every dollar the employee elects to have withheld from his or her pay. Your contribution is placed in the 401(k) plan and is tax-free to the employee.

Various Nonretirement Fringe Benefit Plans

The federal tax laws are replete with a whole host of tax-favored employee fringe benefits, which are characterized as being deductible to you and nontaxable to the employee. Some of the most common and important nontaxable fringes are discussed below.

Medical Insurance Plans

The corporation that maintains a medical insurance plan, such as Blue Cross or a prepaid health care plan, is permitted to deduct the premiums it pays to the insurer. In addition, the employee is not required to include either the cost of the premiums or the benefits provided by the insurer in his or her taxable income, as a general rule.[14]

Self-Insured Medical Reimbursement Plans

A corporation can set up a plan under which the corporation directly reimburses employees for medical expenses or even for such expenses as dental care, orthodontic work, and prescription eyeglasses or contact lenses.[15] If the plan satisfies tax law requirements prohibiting discrimination in favor of highly paid employees, the reimbursements paid can be deducted by the corporation and are not taxable to the recipients.[16]

Such plans are often set up in addition to medical insurance plans, either to cover deductibles that the insurance does not pay or to cover particular types of medical or dental costs that the insurance plan does not provide for. The costs of cosmetic surgery are no longer deductible as medical expenses.

Disability Insurance

Payment by a corporation of disability insurance premiums is deductible by the corporation and is not taxed to the employees covered by the insurance — except in the case of an S corporation.[17]

If an employee becomes disabled and receives disability benefits under a policy that the employer has paid the premiums for, the benefits will be included in the employee's income for tax purposes. On the other hand, if an individual, such as a sole proprietor or partner, has paid his or her own premiums for disability insurance, any disability benefits received are tax-free.[18]

Group-Term Life Insurance

Your corporation may set up a group-term life insurance plan and deduct the insurance premiums it pays on behalf of employees. To the extent the life insurance coverage on an employee does not exceed $50,000 under the plan during the taxable year, the premiums paid by you are not taxable income to the employee.[19]

Even to the extent an employee's coverage exceeds $50,000, the amount the employee must include in taxable income from the additional insurance premiums paid by you for the excess coverage is sometimes considerably less than the premium actually paid and deducted.

Unless your business is a C corporation, it cannot deduct the premiums for your own coverage under a group life insurance plan because you are not considered an employee of the business for tax purposes.

The following fringe benefits are excludable both from income and employment taxes (FUTA and FICA) for you and the employee:

Section 132 Excludable Fringe Benefits

- No-additional-cost services provided to an employee — These services consist of benefits such as free airline, rail, or bus transportation provided by companies in those industries; rooms for hotel employees; or free phone service for telephone company employees.
- Employee discounts — Service companies can provide their services to employees at up to a 20% discount. For companies selling goods, the discount may not exceed the employer's gross profit percentage multiplied by the usual selling price of the item to customers.
- Working condition fringes — These fringe benefits are tax-free, up to the amounts that would have been deductible if paid by the employee. Benefits include such items as a company car or plane used for business purposes; subscriptions to trade or professional publications; on-the-job training; business travel; and others.
- Qualified transportation fringes — These benefits include employer-provided transit passes and commuter transportation worth up to $60 a month and parking provided to employees worth up to $155 a month. Parking fringes are not available to self-employed individuals.
- Minor fringes — These benefits are items that are considered to be minimal to justify the administrative costs for them, such as using the company's copier machine or having a secretary type a personal letter.
- On-premises athletic facilities — Providing and operating facilities such as gyms, pools, tennis or golf courses on the business premises, for employees, their spouses, and dependents is a nontaxable fringe benefit.[20]

Meals on Premises

If meals are provided on-premises to employees, for your convenience as the employer, the value of such meals is usually not taxable to the employee for income tax purposes;[21] however, you can deduct 50% of the cost of furnishing such meals.

Educational Assistance Plans

You may pay educational expenses on behalf of an employee — free of employment taxes or income tax to the employee — if the purpose of such education meets one of the two following tests: 1) the education maintains or improves skills required by the job, and 2) the education meets requirements set by you or applicable laws, where such requirements are imposed as a condition of the retention of employment or rate of compensation.

You may also set up tax-qualified educational assistance plans to provide other — not necessarily job-related — educational benefits for employees, in amounts up to $5,250 a year per employee.[22] To qualify, such a plan must be in writing, disclosed to employees, and no more than 5% of benefits paid under the plan can go to 5% owners of the firm or their spouses or dependents. This tax benefit expired on June 30, 1992, but has been retroactively extended again for the period from June 30, 1992 through December 31, 1994.

Dependent Care Plans

Dependent care plans are one of the most popular and rapidly growing types of employee fringe benefit plans in recent years, providing up to $5,000 a year of dependent care benefits for children or elderly dependents per employee. Not more than 25% of benefits provided, however, can be on behalf of 5% owners of the employer company, and other technical nondiscrimination rules also apply.[23]

Stock Option Plans

Companies have devised, or Congress has provided, a number of different stock option plans with various tax advantages, all of which are designed to encourage employees to acquire a proprietary stake in the companies they work for. Major types of such plans include:

- Nonqualified stock options — In this plan, you usually grant favored employees options to acquire stock of the company at a bargain price during a period of several years. Such an option is usually not a taxable event; although, the excess of the value over the option price of the stock received, when the option is eventually exercised, is then taxed as ordinary compensation income in most cases — unless the stock is restricted or forfeitable.

- Incentive stock options (ISOs) — ISOs are options granted under a plan that meets IRS requirements, where the term of the option is limited and the option price is not less than the value of the stock at the day the option is granted. That is, with an ISO, there is no bargain element built into the option. If the stock is worth $20 a share the day the option is granted to the employee, the option must be at an exercise price of no less than $20. Thus, the employee will not stand to profit from exercising the option unless the value of the stock subsequently rises to above $20 a share — which is good incentive for the employee to help make the company as profitable as possible. If certain requirements are met, the employee does not recognize taxable income when he or she exercises an ISO and may qualify for subsequent capital gains treatment if the stock received from exercise of the option is sold at a gain.[24]

- Employee stock purchase plans — Under a tax-qualified employee stock purchase plan, a company may allow employees to purchase its stock, directly from the company, for up to a 15% discount from the fair market value of the stock. The employee is not taxed when exercising the right to purchase stock under such a plan and may receive capital gain treatment when the stock is eventually sold at a gain.[25]

Flexible Spending Plans

In the last few years, the flexible spending plan, or flex plan, has become another increasingly popular type of tax-favored employee benefit plan.

Each of the three flex plans below are designed to permit employees to choose how much to spend on a tax-free basis for various employee benefits, such as health care or dependent care. Flex plans are for employees only and cannot cover sole proprietors, partners in a partnership, or 2% shareholders in an S corporation.

Premium-Conversion Accounts

Premium-conversion accounts are the simplest kind of flex account. They primarily are set up to allow employees to pay for their share of health, disability, or group-term life insurance premiums with untaxed dollars by deducting specified amounts out of their regular paychecks to pay for such coverage. The amounts the employees agree to have withheld from their salaries or wages to pay such insurance premiums are excluded from their taxable income, but deductible by the corporation or unincorporated employer. Such plans, in effect, convert part of wages directly into insurance payments, without having the government first remove a slice for taxes. Premium-conversion accounts are practical for even the smallest companies with only one or two employees.

Flexible Reimbursement Accounts

Flexible reimbursement accounts are accounts where an employee may agree to contribute a specified amount to each year and draw on the account to pay for health care expenses not covered by the company. Health care expenses could include medical insurance deductibles, vision care, dental coverage, or for up to $5,000 a year for dependent care expenses.

Here is how these accounts work: Before the start of each year, the employees must estimate their medical and dependent care costs for the coming year that they want paid out of their accounts. The amount designated by an employee is withheld from his or her paycheck during the year (tax-free). As expenses are incurred during the year for health and dependent care, the employee submits requests for reimbursement out of the account to the plan administrator, up to the specified maximum. Employers may choose to supplement or match amounts employees choose to have withheld from their pay, as an additional tax-free benefit to the employee.

Flexible reimbursement accounts may stand alone, or may be combined with premium-conversion accounts. They are feasible for fairly small employers as well; although, administrative costs may tend to be greater than for premium-conversion accounts.

Cafeteria Plans

Cafeteria plans are more complex and are rarely adopted by companies with fewer than 50 employees. Under a cafeteria plan, a company gives employees a menu of benefit choices, provides a fixed number of tax-free dollars per employee each year, and allows the employees to each select or buy the particular benefits desired, such as:

- 401(k) contributions
- Health insurance

- Life insurance
- Disability insurance
- Vision or dental care, or both
- Vacation time

If the costs of the benefits selected exceeds the dollar amount provided by you, the employee may fund the balance with salary reduction amounts through premium-conversion or reimbursement accounts, or both, also on an untaxed basis.

Under flex plans, the golden rule is "use it or lose it." Any amount in an employee's account that is not utilized by the employee during the year is forfeited, and reverts back to you at the end of the year. Flex plans are required to meet nondiscrimination tests to ensure that highly compensated employees do not receive a disproportionate share of the benefits provided.[26] For more information on flex plans, contact:

Employers Council on Flexible Compensation
927 15th Street NW, Suite 1000
Washington, DC 20005
(202) 659-4300

8.4 Sheltering Profits on Export Sales

Many small and large American businesses have an unfortunate tendency to look at the United States as their only market and to ignore the vast potential markets for their products or services that lie outside the borders of this country. One way in which Congress has taken constructive steps to encourage more exports and to make American goods and services more competitive in foreign markets is to provide a form of indirect tax subsidy to American firms that export.

While this export subsidy has not succeeded in stemming the unfavorable trend in the balance of trade the United States has experienced in recent years, it does provide a very attractive tax benefit for U.S. companies that export. If your business is one of the many small firms that does sell its goods or services overseas, you may be able to qualify for this tax incentive by setting up either a Domestic International Sales Corporation (DISC) or a Foreign Sales Corporation (FSC).

In general, a DISC will allow you to accumulate profits earned from export sales in a specially treated corporation, free of U.S. taxes until you eventually choose to distribute the deferred income. An FSC will allow you to accumulate such income, whether or not distributed, free (in part) of U.S. corporate taxes. For an FSC, the exempt foreign trade income will not even be taxed when paid out as a dividend, if the shareholder is a corporation.[27] For small companies, DISCs may often be much simpler to operate and preferable to the FSCs, at least for the first few years of operation.

A DISC is usually just a separate dummy corporation that has no employees and does not carry on any sort of business, except on paper.

The tax law allows a U.S. firm that has qualified export receipts to set aside part of its profits on the export transactions by paying a so-called sales commission to a DISC.[28] As a corporation without any employees, the DISC does not actually do anything to earn the commissions; your firm pays the DISC the largest commission permitted by the tax law on each qualifying export sale. It is usually advisable to have a written commission agreement between your firm and the DISC for legal purposes, although this is not required for tax purposes.

The commission that can be paid to the DISC on an export sale is the larger of 4% of the gross sales price or 50% of the profit on the sale[29] — so long as the commission does not create a loss on the sale for your firm.[30] In addition, the DISC's commission income can be increased by 10% of certain export promotion expenses, if any, incurred by the DISC.[31] As you might suspect, some fairly elaborate tax accounting rules determine how much profit you have on an export sale, for purposes of computing the DISC's maximum commission.[32]

The tax benefits for your business arise because you or your business owns the DISC stock, and the commissions your business pays to the DISC are deducted from the business taxable income, while the DISC pays no tax on income it receives.

However, about 6% (or $1/17$) of the DISC's income each year is taxed to its corporate (but not individual) shareholders,[33] so the DISC will usually pay about 6% of its income back as a dividend to the business that owns the stock of the DISC — which is usually, but not necessarily — your corporation that paid the DISC the commissions. Thus, 94% (or $16/17$) of the income that is shifted to the DISC as export sales commissions escapes federal income tax indefinitely, until the DISC either pays out the accumulated income as dividends or is disqualified and loses its status as a DISC.[34]

For deferred DISC income that accumulates after 1984, however, each DISC shareholder must compute the amount of additional tax it would pay each year if all the deferred DISC income were taxed and pay the IRS interest on the deferred tax.[35] This interest will apparently be tax-deductible if paid by a corporation. The interest rate is based on the going rate for one-year T-bills.

Conceptually, having a DISC can be thought of as taking $100 of pre-tax income out of your left-hand pocket and putting it in your right-hand pocket, then putting $6 back into the left-hand pocket. You do not have to pay tax on the $94 that remains in the right-hand pocket as long as you leave it there. In fact, there are even legal ways in which you can borrow the $94 and put it back in the left-hand pocket (your business) without paying tax on it — another example of having your cake and eating it too.[36] But as long as you keep the $94 in the right-hand pocket, you pay interest on the tax saved.

DISCs — In a Nutshell

Another advantage of having a DISC is that the DISC can continue to accumulate its undistributed profits year after year without fear of incurring an accumulated earnings tax, since a DISC is exempt from the accumulated earnings tax as well as the regular federal income tax.[37]

FSCs — In a Nutshell

A Foreign Sales Corporation (FSC) is somewhat similar to a DISC, but it will probably be too great of an administrative burden for it to be worthwhile for your small business to consider. Unlike a DISC, an FSC cannot be a dummy or paper corporation set up in the United States. Instead, it must meet all of the following requirements:

- It must be a foreign corporation, incorporated in a U.S. possession or in a foreign country that, in general, has arrangements to swap tax information with the IRS.
- There can be no more than 25 shareholders in an FSC.
- An FSC cannot issue preferred stock.
- An FSC must maintain a foreign office, at which there is a permanent set of tax records, including invoices.
- The FSC's board of directors must include at least one person who is not a resident of the United States — although the nonresident member can apparently be a U.S. citizen.
- An FSC cannot be part of a controlled group of corporations that also includes a DISC. That is, you can set up either an FSC or a DISC, but not both.[38]

Summary

Here is a brief summary of this section on DISC and FSC tax benefits.

- If your business will be engaged or is engaged in selling goods or services abroad, consult your tax adviser as to the advisability of establishing a DISC or FSC to shelter a large portion of your export profits.
- Both DISCs and FSCs are extremely complex entities to establish and administer, although a DISC will probably be much less of a headache for a small business to operate than an FSC. In either case, you will need to hire some very sophisticated accounting talent, so unless you earn some fairly substantial export profits, the administrative costs of having a DISC or FSC may well exceed any tax savings you will generate.
- State tax treatment of DISCs and FSCs is discussed in Section 11.8.

8.5 Planning for Withdrawal of Corporate Funds with Minimum Tax Cost

Because of the many tax and other advantages of operating a corporation, there is a good chance you will choose, either initially or later on, to incorporate your business. If you do, and your business becomes profitable to the extent that it has significant profits even after paying you the largest salary that can be justified as "reasonable compensation" under the circumstances, you will eventually be faced with the problem of how to remove the accumulated profits from the corporation without excessive tax costs. That is, unless you decide to liquidate the corporation at some point and operate as an unincorporated business or decide to sell your stock to someone else. The proceeds you receive from liquidation or selling your stock would probably result in capital gains tax in most cases, in addition to a tax at the corporate level upon liquidation. For a definition of unreasonable compensation, see Section 8.9.

If the corporation simply pays dividends to you, this activity will normally be a tax disaster because the dividends you receive will probably be taxable to you as ordinary income at federal income tax rates up to 39.6% or somewhat more. Since the corporation will have already paid tax on the money it distributes to you as dividends, double taxation will result. If both you and the corporation are in the maximum tax brackets, the result can be an effective tax rate of approximately 60% (federal corporate and individual taxes) on the income that is paid out as dividends and an even higher rate if there are also state income taxes. There are better ways to get the money out of the corporation.

Personal Loans from the Corporation

Your corporation can often serve as a bank for your short-term financial needs; however, if you continually borrow from your corporation, the IRS can in some cases treat the loans as dividends to you, which is just what you want to avoid. Or, if your corporation has an accumulated earnings problem, as described in Section 8.9, the existence of loans to shareholders can make it very difficult to argue that the corporation is accumulating earnings for the reasonable needs of the business. So, while a loan from your corporation can be a very good way to tap its funds on a temporary basis, it is not a long-term solution.

If you do borrow, you should normally pay interest if the loan is greater than $10,000. The interest rate should not be less than the applicable federal rate established by the IRS.[39] This rate is announced by the IRS each month of the year for transactions that occur during the following month.

Preliminary Structuring

A number of different ways of structuring your corporation at its inception can give you a great deal of potential flexibility in getting money out of the corporation for yourself or family members later at no tax cost or, at worst, as only partially taxable. Some of these approaches can also make it possible to keep a great deal of the value of the corporation's stock out of your taxable estate for estate tax and inheritance tax purposes. Discuss the structuring of your corporation with your tax adviser before you form the corporation. Here are some of the strategies you might explore.

Putting Stock in Names of Spouse and Children

When the corporation is formed, consider putting a substantial part of the stock in the name of your spouse or children, or both. Later, when or if the business has prospered and the stock has become valuable, it may be possible to bail out a large chunk of the corporation's accumulated profits at a child's lower tax rates by having the corporation redeem (purchase) all of the stock of your spouse or child.

The redemption will usually be treated as a sale for a capital gain if your spouse or child agrees to notify the IRS if he or she reacquires any interest in the corporation within ten years after the redemption.[40] Working as an employee of the corporation would be an "interest" that would prevent the spouse or child from receiving favorable capital gains treatment. So if you want your son or daughter to work for you in the business, do not count on being able to redeem his or her stock as a capital gain.

Note that while capital gains are taxed at only slightly lower rates than ordinary income, it is still very desirable to have a stock redemption qualify for capital gains treatment, because part of the money received will be a nontaxable recovery of the shareholder's tax basis in the stock that is being redeemed. This is usually not the case if the redemption payment is treated as an ordinary income dividend.

Such redemption of stock as a capital gain could even be made on an installment basis.[41] For example, if your daughter had all her stock redeemed by the corporation for $150,000, the corporation could pay the $150,000 price, plus interest, in 15 annual installments of $10,000 each, so that your daughter would not have a "bunching" of all the capital gain on the sale in one tax year. Instead, the capital gains tax would be spread over a 15-year period, and the corporation should be able to deduct interest paid on the note held by the daughter.

Constraints in Community Property States

Unfortunately, this tactic does not work as well in community property states if you attempt to redeem your spouse's stock. Under the community property laws, half of your stock will generally be treated as owned by your spouse. This makes it difficult to completely terminate his or her interest, unless all of the stock that is community property is first split in half between you by agreement, so that you each own your shares as separate property.

Even in that case, your spouse may be considered to have reacquired a community property interest in your separately owned stock if you continue to work for the corporation and the value of the stock increases on account of your efforts. Thus, if you live in a community property state, you probably should not count on trying to redeem your spouse's interest in the corporation as a capital gain. The states that have community property laws are Arizona, California, Idaho, Louisiana, Nevada, New Mexico, Texas, Washington, and Wisconsin.

Gifts of Stock to Children

Even if the corporation never redeems your children's stock, it is useful to put some of the stock in their names when you form the corporation — especially at a time when a gift to them of the stock will be subject to little or no gift tax because of its low value. When you die many years later, the stock owned by your children may then be very valuable and will not be included in your estate in most instances, which could save your children a great deal in estate and inheritance taxes. The federal gift tax laws now permit you to make gifts worth up to $10,000 per child per year free of federal gift tax. If you are married, you and your spouse can jointly make gifts of up to $20,000 per year per child; however, you may be subject to state gift taxes in some states.

Debt Capitalization Pitfall

Until the Revenue Reconciliation Act of 1989 was passed, it was considered astute tax planning — when setting up a new corporation — to capitalize the company with both equity capital (stock) and debt capital (an interest-bearing note from the corporation to you); however, such a tactic can now be a tax trap.

This type of structuring can still be done without adverse tax consequences, but only if the assets you are transferring to the corporation are cash or other assets on which you would not have a taxable gain if sold at current fair market value. Otherwise, under the 1989 law, any notes or other debt capital you take back from the corporation will cause you to pay tax on appreciated assets (land, equipment, etc.) that you transfer to the corporation in return for the stock and debt instruments.

Debt Capitalization Still Can Be Advantageous

If, however, the only asset you are putting in the corporation to start it up is, for example, cash, you will not be affected by the 1989 tax law change mentioned in the preceding paragraph. As an illustration, if you plan to put $10,000 in the corporation to get the business started, you might take back stock for $5,000 and a $5,000 note when the corporation is set up, rather than having the corporation issue you stock for the whole $10,000. While the note is outstanding, you will be able to siphon off some funds from the corporation as interest on the note, which the corporation can deduct. By contrast, if the corporation distributed profits to you as dividends on its stock, it would result in double taxation of those profits, since, unlike interest, the corporation cannot deduct dividends it pays.

More importantly, when the note becomes due, the corporation will repay you the $5,000 principal of the note; if things have been handled properly, you should pay no tax on that $5,000. In contrast, if the corporation attempted to return part of your investment in the stock, whatever you received would probably be fully taxable to you as a dividend, even if you surrendered some of your stock in a redemption. Lending the corporation part of its start-up capital allows you to withdraw part of your investment without paying tax.

Thus, there are considerable advantages in partially capitalizing your corporation with debt in the form of a note or notes that you will hold from the corporation. You will need competent tax advice before you do so, however, since there are hundreds of court cases that have tried to define when debt instruments will be considered debt and when they will be considered stock. For example, if you capitalize your corporation with more than $3 of debt for each $1 of stock — say a $6,000 note and $2,000 of stock — the note (debt) may be treated as though it were stock for tax purposes. Thus, if the corporation paid you interest or principal on the note, whatever payments you received would be treated as dividends to you, and the corporation's deduction for the interest payments would be disallowed. So tread very lightly in lending money to your corporation. See Section 8.9 for more on the distinction between debt and equity for tax purposes.

Post-Incorporation Planning

Whether or not you take advantage of the above planning suggestions at the time you incorporate, there are a number of other ways you can get cash out of your corporation at a low tax cost later on.

Leasing to the Corporation

Instead of putting your own money into the corporation so it can buy property it needs, keep the money outside the corporation, and buy the property yourself and lease it all at a reasonable rental to the corporation. This way, you will be able to directly obtain the tax depreciation and other benefits of owning the property. At the same time, by keeping the property out of the corporation, you will be putting less of your assets at risk in the business, especially if the corporation goes broke. Also, if the leased property is real estate, it will probably appreciate in value.

You can personally and directly benefit from that appreciation, including the increased rent you will be able to charge the corporation as inflation continues. Furthermore, if you have used straight-line depreciation and sell the property at a gain, all of the gain will be capital gain. By contrast, if the corporation sells real property at a gain, 20% of the straight-line depreciation is recaptured as ordinary income.[42] Although a corporation's capital gains are currently taxed at the same rate as ordinary income, Congress restored preferential tax rates for individuals' capital gains in 1990, and it may do the same for corporations in the future.

Trusts for Your Children

You could make a gift of business property — or the funds to buy it — to a trust and have a bank or other independent trustee negotiate a reasonable lease of the property to the business, with the rental income going to the trust for distribution to your children. Upon the trust's termination, or earlier, such as when your children reach specified ages, the property and accumulated income can be distributed to the children, or if a child does not live until age 21, revert to you at his or her death.

This can be a useful way of taking cash out of the corporation for the benefit of your children, who have lower tax brackets; however, since the IRS regularly attempts to attack these types of arrangements, you should go into this only with the help of an astute tax adviser. Be aware that the Tax Reform Act of 1986 eliminated nearly all the tax advantages of trusts for children under 14 years of age.

DISC Deferrals

Consider setting up a DISC corporation if your corporation has foreign sales. You can then hold the DISC stock yourself or give it to your children.

This will not only enable you to indefinitely defer federal income taxes on part of the profits from export sales, it will also, in effect, allow you or your children to siphon off part of the profits on export sales — dividends paid by the DISC — in a manner that allows your corporation to deduct those dividends, thereby avoiding double taxation.

Benefit Plans

Consider adopting corporate pension or profit-sharing plans and various corporate fringe benefit plans. These types of benefit plans, in appropriate circumstances, can provide deferred retirement benefits or current insurance benefits to you tax-free — or on a tax-deferred basis, in the case of retirement plans — while reducing the corporation's current taxable income. See the discussion of these kinds of employee benefit plans in Section 8.3.

8.6 Deducting Expenses Related to Your Business

One major advantage of operating your own business is the opportunity it may give you to deduct the costs of certain activities or luxuries as business expenses. Some of these deductions are discussed below.

Some of the tax benefits that were available in the past, however, such as costs of attending foreign conventions[43] and treating part of your home as a business office[44] have been severely curtailed, and there are strict recordkeeping requirements for others.[45] For instance, deductions for attending foreign conventions are now completely disallowed, unless you can show that:

- It is just as reasonable for the convention to be held abroad as it would be to hold it in North America; and
- The meeting is directly related to your trade or business.

If these two requirements are met, you must then meet the general requirements for traveling outside the United States. Deductions for conventions or seminars on cruise ships are limited to $2,000, and other travel by "luxury water transportation" is deductible only up to certain per diem amounts.[46] For more on office-in-the-home expenses, refer to Section 8.14.

Travel, Entertainment, and Meal Expenses

It is still possible to deduct business travel expenses, entertainment of your clients or customers, and business-related meals; however, you can only deduct 50% of qualifying business meals and entertainment. Consequently, this 50% rule considerably complicates recordkeeping for these types of expenses.

For instance, if you stay in a hotel on a business trip and charge your meals to your room, you are required to separately break out your meal expenses for tax purposes because your meal expenses are only 50% deductible.

If you are an employee of your business, the 50% disallowance of meal and entertainment expenses does not apply to you individually, if your company reimburses you for the expenses; it applies only at the company level.

Detailed Records Required

To claim any of these kinds of deductions, you must keep daily, detailed records of such expenditures, including bills, receipts, and the following information for each expense:

- The relationship of the expenditure to the business;
- The time when the expense was incurred;
- Where the money was spent, and to whom it was paid;
- The amount of the expenditure; and
- The identities of the persons involved, including persons entertained.[47]

The law requires that taxpayers keep "adequate records or . . . sufficient evidence corroborating the taxpayer's own statement."[48] It is strongly recommended that you pick up a daily expense record book or diary and enter all expenses for travel, meals, and entertainment you think should be deductible. Include the above information for each item.

Not All Expenses Deductible

Not all expenses for entertaining clients or customers will be deductible, even if you keep meticulous records. As a general rule, your records must show that you were engaged in a substantial and bona fide business discussion during or immediately before or after the entertainment.[49] Expenses of entertaining people just to create a good impression on them, in the hope they might send some business your way in the future, are classified as goodwill entertainment, and you cannot deduct them for tax purposes.

The rule allowing quiet business meals with clients or potential customers to be deductible, even if no business is discussed, has been repealed.[50] For more information on business-related expenses you can deduct, contact your local IRS office and request *Publication 463, Travel, Entertainment, and Gift Expenses.*

Automobile Expenses

If you use an automobile more than 50% of the time for business purposes, you will generally be able to deduct a percentage of the costs of owning and operating the car, if you can substantiate the business mileage. The expenses of using the car for commuting to and from work and for personal travel are not deductible.[51]

For example, if your business purchases a new car for your use as a business car, and 80% of the mileage on the car can be shown to be for business trips, and only 20% for commuting to work and other personal use, you should be able to deduct 80% of the gas, oil, insurance, and maintenance costs relating to the car. You can also depreciate the cost of the car, less 20% for personal use.

Rules are even more drastic for any automobile, airplane, boat or computer not kept in your place of business if you can't establish a business-use percentage in excess of 50%. Automobile depreciation is stretched out over at least six years, straight-line: 10% the first year; 20% a year thereafter, for four years; and 10% the final year. For boats, planes, or computers, it can be stretched out for longer periods.[52] There are also strict dollar limits on maximum annual depreciation deductions for so-called luxury automobiles costing more than about $15,000. For luxury automobiles, the maximum annual depreciation deduction allowed is limited to the amounts below.

Luxury Automobile Depreciation

1993 Acquisitions	1994 Acquisitions
$2,860 for the first year	$2,960 for the first year
$4,600 for the second year	$4,700 for the second year
$2,750 for the third year	$2,850 for the third year
$1,675 for each succeeding year	$1,675 for each succeeding year

Exemptions

These restrictions don't apply to business vehicles such as ambulances, hearses, taxis, delivery vans, or heavy trucks.[53]

Mileage Deduction

If you drive an inexpensive economy car on business, it may be simpler and more advantageous to elect to deduct a flat $0.29 (29 cents) per mile for 1994[54] for your business mileage rather than keep records of your various kinds of automobile expenses. If you use this method, you can still deduct tolls and parking incurred on business trips. If you drive an expensive car, you will probably get much larger tax deductions by reporting your actual operating expenses, plus depreciation, than by electing the mileage allowance. Be sure to keep an accurate record of your business mileage so you can substantiate the car was used for business purposes.

Form 4562 of your annual tax return requires you to answer a number of detailed questions if you claim an automobile deduction.

8.7 Choosing the Best Taxable Year for a Corporation

If your business is an S corporation or is considered a personal service corporation, you will generally have no choice but to operate on a calendar-year basis, and you can skip over the following discussion of how to select a taxable year. If, however, your business is incorporated and is neither an S corporation or a personal service corporation in which the services performed are "substantially performed" by owner/employees,[55] you will have an opportunity to choose any tax fiscal-year period you desire during your initial year of operation as a corporation. There are significant tax deferral and savings opportunities in selecting the right year end.

Unfortunately, in some cases, it will be necessary to be able to project with some accuracy how much your corporation will earn or lose each month for several months to a year ahead. If you expect to have start-up losses and show an overall net profit for your first year as an incorporated business, one good rule is to cut off your first taxable year at the end of the month in which you first get back to break even for the year-to-date.

For example, assume your first tax year starts on January 1, 1995, and you show a cumulative tax loss of $20,000 at the end of June. You then have taxable income of $10,000 a month in July, August, and September, and expect profits to continue. If you chose June 30 as your tax year end, you would have a $20,000 loss for your first tax period ending June 30, 1995. For federal income tax purposes, it is no problem, since you can carry over the loss and use it to offset $20,000 of taxable income during the next tax year. Some states, however, do not allow a carryover of losses.

Another approach would be to choose an August 31 year end, so that you would show no taxable income for your first year, assuming the corporation continued to net $10,000 a month.

If you do not mind paying some tax earlier, it might pay, in the above example, to wait until the end of October, November, or even December to cut off the first tax year. This would enable the corporation to isolate $20,000 to $40,000 or so of profit in a tax period subject to low federal corporate income tax rates, which are only 15% on the first $50,000 of corporate income.

If you do so, however, you are making an assumption that the corporation will be in a higher tax bracket in the following year, which cannot be known with any certainty. In addition, the existence of tax credits would somewhat complicate the simple picture portrayed above. Obviously, your accountant can help you decide which tax year will produce the best result.

Start-up Losses Must Be Capitalized, Not Deducted

Remember, when projecting your start-up losses, you can't immediately deduct preopening expenses; instead, you must capitalize those costs and write them off (straight-line) over 60 months.[56] For example, if you are starting a restaurant and are paying salaries to a manager and to employees being trained before the day the restaurant opens for business, you might well think those expenses are immediately deductible. Not so! All such preopening expenses must be capitalized, and you can't begin to amortize them until opening day.

Another planning approach in adopting a year end, which may sometimes conflict with the above strategy, is to adopt a January 31 year end. If you structure your employment contract with your corporation so that you receive a substantial part of your compensation in January each year, you can, in effect, defer the bonus to your following tax year, while the corporation can deduct it — if paid in January — for its fiscal year ending just after the bonus is paid. Naturally, the corporation will be required to withhold income tax from your bonus, but at reduced rates, compared to regular monthly salary payments. Federal income tax withholding on bonuses is at a flat rate of only 28%.

Benefits of Adopting January 31 Year End

If you have a seasonal business, you may want to defer taxes by selecting a tax year that ends just before your most profitable season begins. For example, if you are in the business of selling Christmas tree ornaments and do most of your business from October through December each year, you might choose a September 30 tax year end.

Seasonal Businesses

Remember, though, that tax considerations are not the only factors to take into account in choosing a fiscal year. If taking an annual inventory is a major task, consider adopting a year end that occurs when inventory is at a low ebb and when business is slow, if possible. You may also find that you will get somewhat quicker and better service from your CPA firm for annual tax returns, audits, etc. if you pick a fiscal year that ends several months before or after December. Most CPAs are at their busiest during their annual tax season from about February to May, preparing 1040s and doing audits for their many clients who have December year ends.

8.8 Selecting Tax Accounting Methods

Rely on your tax accountant's advice when choosing which tax accounting methods you should adopt in your business. This section is provided for your information in case you are not sure whether your accountant has recommended the method that will produce the best results for you.

The two overall tax accounting methods most commonly used are the cash method and the accrual method. There are, however, other special overall methods, plus a number of special kinds of accounting elections a business can make with regard to particular items, such as installment sales, inventory valuations, and deduction of accrued vacation pay.

The cash receipts and disbursements method of accounting, called the cash method, is the simplest accounting method in use. Under this method, you include income only as it is actually or constructively received.

Cash Method

Likewise, you only become entitled to deductions when you actually pay expenses — except for certain special items like depreciation or amortization of certain kinds of expenditures — rather than when you receive bills for the expenses. Thus, you usually do not have to report your year-end accounts receivable in income for the year and cannot deduct your year-end accounts payable. This will normally allow you to defer some taxable income each year if your year-end receivables are larger than accounts payable and other accrued but unpaid expenses. Obviously, this gives you some flexibility, too, if you want to pay off a number of payables at year end to reduce your taxable income for the current year.

The cash method is the method used by most individual taxpayers and by businesses in the real estate, financial, and service fields, where inventories of goods are not material factors in producing income.

Businesses with significant inventories, such as manufacturers and wholesale or retail firms, are usually required to use an accrual method of tax accounting.[57] In some cases, however, it is possible even for those businesses to use a hybrid accounting method — accounting for income and the cost of goods sold on an accrual method — while using the cash method to report selling expenses and administrative expenses.

The Tax Reform Act of 1986 disallowed use of the cash method for C corporations — regular corporations — and for partnerships that have C corporations as partners. One exception is for small firms with an average gross receipts of five million dollars or less during the three preceding years.[58] Another exception is made for larger firms in the farming business and for certain employee-owned qualified personal service corporations in fields such as law, medicine, accounting, architecture, or consulting.

Sole proprietorships, S corporations, and partnerships with no C corporation partners are not affected by these restrictions, unless they are considered tax shelters, and may remain on the cash method if that is a permissible accounting method for their particular type of business. Firms that are forbidden from using the cash method must adopt the more complex accrual method of accounting.

Accrual Method

As noted above, most large corporations and businesses with significant inventories are required to report income on the accrual method of accounting for tax purposes. This method requires you to report income when income is earned rather than when you receive it. Similarly, expenses can be deducted when all events have occurred that fix the amount and the fact of your business' liability for a particular expense, even if it is paid in a subsequent tax year. However, if economic performance required of the other party does not occur until a subsequent tax year, you may not be able to deduct an accrued expense until economic performance occurs.

For example, if you sign a contract with your accountant in 1995 to prepare your tax return in 1996, "economic performance" does not occur until 1996, and you may be unable to accrue the deduction in 1995, unless you meet several requirements, such as recurring expenses or performance occurs within a reasonable time after the end of the tax year.[59]

Even though the accrual method may not be required for your business, you may find it preferable to use, if most or all of your income is from cash sales and you pay a large part of your expenses on a delayed credit basis. In this case, you would have few, if any, receivables at year end but might have substantial accrued payables you could deduct in the current year without having to actually make payment before year end.

Accrual of bonuses to employees, in an incorporated business, is a good example of a deduction that can be accelerated by a business using the accrual method. But expenses owed to you or a related owner of the business can't be deducted until actually paid.[60]

Special Accounting Methods Long-Term Contracts

If your business is engaged in heavy construction work on a long-term contract basis, it may be difficult to tell in advance whether a particular contract will result in a profit or loss, since many unforeseen difficulties may arise. The tax regulations recognize this problem and allow such contractors to utilize special methods of accounting which may delay the time at which profit or loss is recognized on a long-term contract. They are:

- The percentage of completion method; and
- The completed contract method.[61]

The Tax Reform Act of 1986, however, and subsequent legislation has eliminated the use of the completed contract method of accounting for most large companies, except for certain ship contracts and for some home construction and other residential building contractors.

Fortunately, small businesses, whose average annual gross receipts for the three preceding years do not exceed ten million dollars, are still allowed to use completed contract accounting for tax purposes, at least for contracts that are estimated to take no more than two years to complete.[62]

Even those completed contract method deferrals that survive the new restrictions are now mostly considered tax preference items under the alternative minimum tax rules.[63] In other words, heads you lose, tails the tax collector wins.

Installment Sales

If your business makes casual or occasional sales of personal property — other than merchandise held for sale — or makes sales of real estate it owns, the profit on any such sale can, in general, be reported on the installment basis as and when payments are received, rather than in the year of sale.[64] The installment method of reporting, however, is not available for "dealers," such as retailers, in personal or real property, except for certain dealers in real property. This is an election that sellers of residential lots or time-shares may make to use the installment method. The catch is that the dealer making such an election must agree to pay interest on any tax that is deferred by using installment reporting.[65]

In the case of nondealer sales of property for more than $150,000, if the total face amount of all installment notes exceeds five million dollars for the year, at the end of the year, the seller must pay interest on the deferred tax liability.[66] Sales of personal-use property or of farm property, for any amount, are exempt from the interest-on-deferred-tax provisions.[67]

Inventory Valuation Methods

If you maintain substantial inventories, discuss with your accountant the pros and cons of using the last-in-first-out (LIFO) method of valuing year-end inventories[68] versus the more common and simpler first-in-first-out (FIFO) method.

FIFO Method

Under the FIFO method, the cost of ending inventory is calculated under the assumption that the first items of inventory bought were the first ones to be sold, so that only the most recently purchased items are assumed to be left in inventory at the end of each year. This usually means the highest-cost items, in times of inflation. That is, if a company turns all its inventory over every three months each year, FIFO assumes, in effect, that the inventory remaining on hand at December 31 was all bought in the last three months of the year, rather than at some earlier date when prices may have been lower.

Most companies use the FIFO method because:

- FIFO is much simpler to use in terms of maintaining accounting records;
- When prices of goods are generally rising, FIFO has the effect of making a company's net income appear to be greater than if the more conservative LIFO method were used — but it also tends to inflate the amount of a company's taxable income; and
- Their accountants never mention to them that there is an alternative method (LIFO) of inventory accounting that can be used.

LIFO Method

In contrast to FIFO, the LIFO method assumes that the items in your ending inventory are the first or oldest ones that were acquired. Thus, under LIFO, ending inventory values for many of the items of inventory will be based on what that item cost in the very first year in which the business began using the LIFO method. The difference in inventory valuation can be dramatic if, for example, a business using LIFO for ten years was paying $10 each ten years earlier for the widgets it keeps in inventory versus a current price of $75 per widget. Under LIFO, the widgets would still be carried on the accounting records at a cost of $10 apiece versus $75 under FIFO.

Accordingly, the difference in inventory cost, or $65 per widget in the above example — called the LIFO reserve — would be the amount of taxable income per widget that the company has deferred over the ten years. Thus, for a company with large amounts of capital invested in inventories, it is easy to see how LIFO can result in a huge tax saving.

At present, using the LIFO method is extremely complex, and the tax savings may in some cases be offset by increased accounting fees incurred and additional management time spent in attempting to comply with the LIFO tax regulations. The tax requirements for using LIFO, however, are somewhat relaxed for those small businesses with less than five million dollars a year in sales.[69]

Any firm with inventories may elect to use either FIFO or LIFO. If a firm is already using FIFO, it may be able to change over to LIFO, if a number of technical requirements set by the IRS are met. Or, a company using LIFO may also change over to FIFO. Note, however, that if a firm uses LIFO and changes to FIFO for some reason, it will usually have to pay a large amount of tax, when it recaptures the LIFO reserve described above, at the time of the changeover. Any such changes in inventory accounting methods should not be attempted without the assistance of a competent tax adviser. If your C corporation already uses LIFO inventory accounting and elects S corporation status, your corporation will be required to pay tax, in four annual installments, on the LIFO reserve at the time of the changeover to an S corporation.[70]

Regardless of whether a company uses LIFO or FIFO for inventory accounting, it generally must allocate a wide range of its indirect costs to inventory, rather than simply deducting them as expenses, under the IRS's uniform capitalization rules. The practical effect of this is that any such costs that have been absorbed into the cost of inventory on hand at the end of the tax year do not get deducted currently for tax purposes. Manufacturing and processing operations of any size are subject to these complex capitalization rules. Fortunately, the uniform capitalization rules do not apply to a wholesale or retail business in any year when the company's annual gross receipts for the preceding three years have averaged ten million dollars or less.[71]

Vacation Pay Accrual Method

If you accrue employees' vacation pay for internal business purposes, you normally can only deduct your liability for such accruals when an employee actually uses his or her vacation pay. The only exception is for accrual-basis taxpayers, where vacation pay is vested at the end of a tax year and paid within two and a half months afterwards.

8.9 Tax Problems Unique to Corporations

While this book has outlined some of the many tax and other advantages inherent in operating a corporation, you need to be aware of a number of traps in the tax law if you go overboard in trying to take advantage of the tax benefits bestowed on corporations.

As is emphasized in this chapter, the most basic goal in corporate tax planning for many high-income individuals is to leave as much profit in the corporation as possible so it can be taxed at the relatively low corporate tax rates and later withdrawn tax-free or at capital gains rates, such as by selling or having the corporation redeem the stock or by liquidating the corporation.

The government's role is to prevent the taxpayer from reaching these goals except where the corporation has good business reasons — as opposed to the individual's tax and investment reasons — for virtually everything it does. In attempting to plug up all the possible loopholes taxpayers might use to take advantage of low corporate rates, the tax law contains a whole array of penalties for corporations:

- That unreasonably accumulate earnings;[72]
- That are used as "incorporated pocket books" for holding personal investments;[73] or
- That are capitalized too heavily with debt.[74]

These and other operating problems of corporations under the tax law are briefly outlined below to give you a sense of what the limits are and how far you can go in utilizing corporate tax advantages. None of these problems are significant concerns for S corporations.

Penalty Tax on Accumulated Earnings

The accumulated earnings tax might well be called the scourge of the overly successful small corporation.[75] This tax potentially applies to almost every corporation that accumulates more than $250,000[76] in after-tax profits (with certain adjustments),[77] unless the corporation can demonstrate that it needs to retain the profits for use in its business operations.[78]

Your corporation can accumulate up to $250,000 — $150,000 for professional and certain personal service firms — in earnings without having to be concerned about this penalty tax.[79] If additional accumulations cannot be justified as being made for the "reasonable needs of the business," however, the corporation will be faced with the choice of paying out the excess earnings as dividends or paying the accumulated earnings tax. The tax is imposed at the rate of 39.6% on the improperly accumulated earnings.[80] Since this is a tax that is imposed in addition to the corporate income tax, it is one you probably do not ever want to be forced to pay.

As long as you are able to keep plowing profits back into your business; buying more facilities, equipment, and inventory; and maintaining needed working capital, you will not have much cause for worry about the accumulated earnings tax. If, however, you reach a point where the corporation has more liquid funds than it needs, and you are beginning to look for places to invest the surplus cash, like real estate or the stock market, that should serve as a signal to you that there may be a potential accumulated earnings problem. In that case, you will need some good tax advice as to what you can do to protect the corporation from imposition of the penalty tax.

Fortunately, there are a number of acceptable reasons that can justify accumulating funds that are not currently being used in the corporation's business. Some of the more important ones include:

- Setting up a reserve to redeem enough of the stock of a shareholder (yourself, for example) who dies, in order to enable the individual's estate to pay certain expenses related to his or her death — estate and inheritance taxes, funeral expenses, and expenses of administering the estate.[81] This reserve can only be created by the corporation after the death of a shareholder, prior to the repurchase of the shareholder's stock;
- Creating a fund to allow for a bona fide plan to replace facilities or expand the business, including the acquisition of another business;[82]
- Creating a reasonable reserve fund to pay potential uninsured product liability claims;[83]
- Accumulating funds to retire indebtedness created in connection with the business of the corporation;[84] and
- Setting up a defined benefit pension plan with an initial "past service liability" to be funded over a number of years.

A number of ways also exist to reduce the accumulated earnings without paying them out as dividends. Some typical examples would be to redeem part of the stock of the corporation, such as the stock of one of your children. This will not only reduce accumulated earnings but will reduce the amount of excess cash not needed in the business.

Another useful approach is to have the corporation purchase real estate that it might currently be leasing. This can sometimes be particularly advantageous where you are the landlord who is leasing the property to the corporation, as suggested in Section 8.5. This tactic technically will not reduce the corporation's accumulated earnings, but will use up excess cash that would otherwise raise questions by IRS auditors.

Another effective solution if you have an accumulated earnings problem is to convert your C corporation to an S corporation, if that is possible. S corporations are not subject to the accumulated earnings tax because all their earnings are deemed to be distributed to shareholders.

Justifiable Accumulations

If a closely held corporation gets a large proportion of its gross income, usually 60% or more, in the form of personal holding company income,[85] such as dividends, interest, rents, and royalties, it will generally be considered a personal holding company for tax purposes.[86]

Other kinds of income considered personal holding company income include income received by a service business from anyone (other than the corporation) who has the right under a contract to designate a particular individual to perform the contracted services. The person designated, however, must own at least 25% of the corporate stock.[87] Also, payments a corporation receives from a 25% shareholder for use of its property is personal holding company income.[88] This puts a damper on schemes such as having your corporation buy a yacht and charter it to you.

Penalty Tax on Personal Holding Company Income

As a rule, if a corporation comes within the definition of a personal holding company, the tax law imposes a 39.6% penalty tax on any personal holding company income not distributed as a dividend.[89]

Most actively conducted small businesses will not need to be very concerned about being treated as personal holding companies since they will seldom get 60% or more of their gross income from passive sources like dividends and interest.

The kind of small business most likely to have a personal holding company problem is the incorporated personal service business — when the corporation enters into contracts and agrees to provide the services of an employee who is a major shareholder.

The best way to avoid this problem is to specify in the contract that the corporation reserves the right to designate the person who will provide the services. You will need to consult your tax adviser, however, before entering into any such personal service contract since the tax rules in this area are quite subtle and the tax penalty is very heavy if the income under the personal service contract is considered to be personal holding company income.

Another type of operating company that frequently encounters personal holding company tax problems is the developer of computer software that generates much of its income from software licensing agreements.

While the Tax Reform Act of 1986 included a special exemption from the personal holding company provisions for corporations actively engaged in the computer software business, the terms of this exception are quite technical and many software firms will only be able to qualify for this relief with very careful planning.[90]

Possible Treatment of Corporate Debt as Stock

As discussed in Section 8.5, there are two significant advantages to putting part of your investment in an incorporated business into the corporation in the form of debt, rather than all of it in exchange for stock. These advantages are:

- The interest paid to you is normally deductible by the corporation, unlike dividends paid on its stock.
- Repayment of the money you loaned to the corporation allows you to take part of your investment out of the corporation free of tax.

Because the use of debt in structuring a closely held corporation is so advantageous, Congress has taken steps to limit the extent to which you can use debt to capitalize a corporation and still enjoy these advantages.[91]

Over the last two decades, the IRS has proposed several sets of new and complex regulations as to when loans to a corporation by its shareholders will be treated as equivalent to an investment in its stock — in which case interest payments will not be deductible by the corporation and principal payments would be taxable to the recipient.

These regulations raised such a storm of protest each time they were proposed that the IRS finally withdrew them. So, to determine what constitutes debt and stock, guidelines are used from hundreds of different court decisions. Nevertheless, there are a few generally accepted ground rules that you should follow to avoid having corporate debt reclassified by the IRS as equity or stock:

- The loan should not have any equity-type features, such as interest or payments, pegged to the corporation's income.
- The loan should be made at a reasonable interest rate, such as the rate at which the IRS imputes interest between related parties.
- The corporation's total debts — other than trade accounts payable — should not be more than about three times its net worth.
- The loan should be documented by a written note and should have a specified maturity date. All interest and principal payments on the note should be made on time.

If you follow each of the above rules, you will generally avoid the problem of having debt reclassified as stock. If you fail to comply with one or more of those rules when lending money to your corporation, the loan may be treated as a stock investment. This can be a serious tax trap if, when the loan is to be repaid, you are unaware that the repayment to you may constitute taxable income.

The most basic tax problem resulting from incorporating a business is the possibility of double taxation of the business income if it is paid out as dividends. That is, if the corporation has any profit after payment of salaries and other expenses, it must pay tax on those profits, unless it is an S corporation. Then, if those profits left after taxes are distributed to stockholders as dividends, the stockholders must also pay tax on the dividends they receive.

Fortunately, the problem of double taxation is generally quite manageable and most small incorporated businesses never pay dividends. The owners normally are also the officers of the corporation and can take enough income out in the form of salary and fringe benefits to live on, usually leaving some profit in the corporation to be plowed back into the business.

Also, as outlined briefly in Section 8.5, there are a number of better ways to get the accumulated profits out of the corporation than by paying dividends.

If you own an incorporated business or own a portion of its stock and are actively involved in operating the business, you will be an employee of the corporation and will draw a salary. Drawing a large salary from the corporation may enable you to withdraw much of the profits of the business without any problem of double taxation, since the corporation can deduct reasonable compensation it pays to you as your salary.[92]

Thus, taking salary out of the corporation is preferable to taking money out in the form of dividends, since the corporation cannot deduct dividends it pays. The salary you receive, if reasonable, is deductible by the corporation; however, the key word here is reasonable. If you try to take too much income out of the corporation as salary, including bonuses and fringe benefits like pension and profit-sharing contributions, the IRS may try to treat part of your salary as unreasonable compensation. If you are fortunate enough to be worried about the one-million-dollar limitation on executive compensation that went into effect in 1994, you can relax. That limitation will only apply to executives of publicly held corporations. So unless your company has gone public, you don't need to be concerned about this limitation.[93]

There are no hard and fast rules as to how much compensation is reasonable, but if you are taking no more than the officers in similar businesses of the same size are paid, you should not have any problem establishing that your compensation from the corporation is reasonable under the circumstances.

If, however, the IRS does succeed in treating part of your compensation as excessive, there will be two serious tax consequences:

- The deduction by the corporation for the unreasonable portion of your salary will be disallowed.
- Part of your salary will be reclassified as dividend income, and thus pension and profit-sharing plan contributions based on that salary may not be fully deductible, which could even result in disqualification of your pension or profit-sharing plan.

8.10 Estate Planning in Connection with Your Business

As the owner of part or all of even a moderately successful business, you may find that after a few years, the value of your business accounts for a very large portion of your personal net worth. As such, your business will probably be the most important single asset you have to be concerned with for estate planning purposes, both during your lifetime and at the time of your death. No attempt will be made here to go into the intricacies of the estate-planning possibilities that may be available; instead, the fundamental approaches you need to be aware of are outlined below. Discuss how to relate these concepts to your own situation with your tax adviser and attorney.

Income Splitting

A useful method of reducing lifetime income taxes is to split the taxable income from your business between two or more persons or entities. Usually a corporation, particularly an S corporation, is a useful vehicle for doing this; you can split income between you and your children by giving them stock in the corporation. A corporation that has not elected S corporation treatment can also be used to split income between you and the corporation. See Section 8.2.

Reducing Estate and Gift Taxes

Often, the best time to remove potential wealth from your taxable estate at death is by giving your children part of the stock in your incorporated business when the business is formed — when the value of the stock is likely to be negligible. If you wait until the business has become a valuable and profitable enterprise, gifts of stock at that time may result in substantial taxable gifts for gift tax purposes, even though the tax cost of those gifts may not be felt until you die, in some cases. You can currently make gifts of up to $10,000 ($20,000 if married) per year to each of your children completely free of federal gift taxes.

Assuming that you want part of your stock in your incorporated business to pass to your children at your death, it obviously makes sense to give them a portion of the stock — but not enough to affect your control of the corporation — during your lifetime. By doing this, there will be little or no gift tax cost if it is done when the business is started. Thus, they will already own the stock when you die, and that valuable asset will have passed to them free of death taxes in most instances. In addition, as noted above, lifetime gifts of stock to your children may also save on income taxes.

Buy-Sell Agreements

If you have one or more partners or business associates who also own a part of the business, it is very important that you enter into a buy-sell agreement with them that spells out what happens if one of you dies, becomes disabled, or wants to sell his or her interest in the business.

Often, these agreements are funded by life insurance on the owners, so that if you die, the business or the other owners will collect the life insurance proceeds and use those funds to buy out your interest in the business. Otherwise, your surviving family members might find it very difficult to sell the interest in the business they inherit from you, except at a give-away price.

Many small business owners ignore the need for buy-sell agreements or, like having a will drawn up, they keep putting it off. When one of the partners or shareholders dies, the survivors may have a problem in raising enough cash to pay the death taxes. This is only one of the problems that may arise when there is no buy-sell agreement.

The few hundred dollars you may spend in legal fees to have a buy-sell agreement with your business partners or associates drawn up is probably one of the best investments you and your associates will ever make.

Unlimited Estate Tax Marital Deduction

Thanks to the estate tax unlimited marital deduction, enacted by Congress in 1982, any assets you leave to your spouse are treated as a deduction from the amount of your estate that is subject to federal estate tax. Thus, if you leave all of your assets to your spouse when you die, it is generally possible to avoid all federal estate tax at that time. However, those assets will increase the size of your surviving spouse's estate later, when he or she also dies, thus pyramiding the estate tax on the second spouse's death. Keep in mind that estate tax rates go up as the size of a taxable estate increases.

This exemption from the estate tax also applies to pension benefits you leave to your spouse when you die, unless the accrued value of your pension benefits exceeds $750,000 (less in some instances). If so, your estate will have to pay a special 15% excise tax on the amount over $750,000.[95]

If you are married, and if you and your spouse have a combined net worth of more than $600,000, you may be able to save a much as several hundred thousand dollars of estate tax by having wills drawn up that provide for creation of a "bypass trust" (or "credit shelter trust") for the other spouse when one of you dies. No tax will be saved, or need be paid, on the first death; however, up to $600,000 can be left in trust (still tax-free) at that time for the survivor, instead of passing everything under the unlimited marital deduction to the surviving spouse. This $600,000 amount — plus any investment growth — will be entirely excluded from the estate of the other spouse later, when he or she dies.

Because the federal estate tax often takes close to 50% of the net estate on the death of the second spouse, having set aside $600,000 in a trust — plus any appreciation on that amount — at the first death will quite clearly result in a very large estate tax savings, thus greatly increasing the after-tax amount you can leave to your children. For a relatively small expenditure in legal fees to draw up such wills and trust, this is one of the most easily attainable, and yet most substantial tax benefits you will ever be able to achieve, with almost no downside — except that you won't be around to see your heirs enjoy it.

The Oasis Press/PSI Research publishes a software program, *Small Business Expert*, which includes a tax-planning module that allows you to do quick and easy what-if estate tax scenarios. You can instantly calculate and illustrate how much estate tax you could save by using a bypass trust as suggested above, based on assumptions you input about your net worth and several other key factors. *Small Business Expert* is available from:

The Oasis Press
(800) 228-2275

Since not all state inheritance tax laws permit an unlimited marital deduction, it can create inheritance tax problems in those states if you leave too much property to your spouse. Refer to Section 11.8 for details regarding this state's marital deduction rules under its inheritance tax laws.

Wills or trusts executed before September 13, 1981 may not qualify for the unlimited estate tax marital deduction.[96] If you have such a will or trust, you need to have it updated immediately, unless your state has enacted protective legislation to ensure that such older wills of its residents qualify for the federal unlimited marital deduction.

8.11 Targeted Jobs Tax Credit

Are you aware that if you hire members of certain economically disadvantaged groups, the federal government will pay you a subsidy of up to $2,400 in the form of tax credits per employee? Unfortunately, most employers, particularly small businesses, seem to be unaware of this substantial tax subsidy.

Part of the reason so many employers fail to take advantage of this tax incentive appears to be on account of a Catch-22 in the way the program works. To qualify for the targeted jobs tax credit for hiring a disadvantaged category person, he or she must be certified as such by a designated state employment security agency, and the certification must be received by the employer (or requested in writing) at least one day before the employee begins work.[97]

At the same time, state and federal anti-discrimination laws make it very difficult for you as an employer to ask prospective job applicants if they belong to any of the disadvantaged groups that are eligible for the targeted jobs tax credits, since to do so could be considered a discriminatory hiring practice.

Your best bet is to check first with your local state employment department or division to find out how to take advantage of state and federal job credit programs. The department will either refer you to the proper agency or organization that can assist you, or the department itself will help you find an individual who qualifies under this program and matches your specific job requirements.

Targeted Groups

The targeted group individuals for whom you can claim the jobs tax credit are:

- Vocational rehabilitation referrals — These referrals are for certain disabled individuals who have completed rehabilitation programs. Tax credits aside, disabled individuals often are extremely good and conscientious employees.

- Economically disadvantaged youths — These individuals are between 18 and 22 years of age and are certified as members of economically disadvantaged families.

- Economically disadvantaged Vietnam veterans.

- Supplemental Security Income (SSI) recipients — SSI recipients are people who are 65 or older, or blind, or have a disability and who don't own much or have a lot of income. SSI payments are not just for adults; they can also go to disabled and blind children.

- General assistance recipients — These persons receive state or local welfare payments.

- Economically disadvantaged ex-convicts.

- Youths participating in a cooperative education program — Youths in this category are between 16 and 20 years of age and have not finished high school.
- Eligible work incentive program employees.
- Qualified summer youth employees — These economically disadvantaged youths are 16 or 17 years old and are hired to work between May 1 and September 15. They cannot have been previously employed by you.

On the first $6,000 you pay an eligible target group employee, you will earn tax credits of 40% of the wages. This is limited to $3,000 of wages for qualified summer youth employees during the first 90 days they work for you.

Here is how the federal targeted jobs tax credits apply for eligible and certified new employees:

Category of Employee	Federal Tax Credit	Minimum Work Period
All qualified employees as listed above	40% of wages on first $6,000 of wages or a maximum credit of $2,400 per employee	90 days or 120 hours
Qualified summer youth employees	40% of first 90 days' wages for up to $3,000 of wages or maximum credit of $1,200	14 days or 20 hours

Drawbacks

One drawback with all of these tax credits is that you must reduce the wages you can deduct dollar-for-dollar for credits you claim.[98] That is, if you pay someone $1,000 and claim a $400 targeted jobs tax credit, you can only deduct $600 for wage expense, not the full $1,000. The credit is not allowed for wages paid to strikebreakers.

The targeted jobs credit expired on December 31, 1994, but may, once again, be extended by Congress. The Clinton administration, however, appears to oppose extending the targeted jobs credit.

8.12 Hiring a Spouse as an Employee

If you run an unincorporated business and your spouse works with or for you, there are three ways your spouse can be treated for tax purposes:

- As an employee;
- As a partner in the firm; or
- As an unpaid employee in a family business.

Social Security Tax

Congress, by enacting the Omnibus Budget Reconciliation Act of 1987, ended the exemption from Social Security (FICA) taxes for wages paid to a spouse, parent, or minor child — with the exception of a child under 18 years of age. There are, however, still some advantages to having your spouse be a paid employee of your proprietorship, as described below.

If your spouse works for you without pay and has no other income from an outside job, the most the two of you can put into an individual retirement account (IRA) is $2,250. If you start compensating your spouse, even as little as $2,000 a year, you should each qualify for a $2,000 IRA deduction or a total of $4,000 a year, rather than only $2,250. Note that IRA deductions may be limited if either of you is an active participant in another retirement plan.

Individual Retirement Account for Spouse

You can deduct any medical insurance premiums that you pay for employees, but you can only deduct a limited portion, if any, of your own medical insurance premiums. If your spouse works for you, however, you can put your spouse on the payroll and provide a medical expense reimbursement plan or medical insurance for your spouse and his or her family — which includes you — you can then deduct the payments or premiums in full since your spouse is an employee.[99] See Section 11.8 regarding state tax exemptions and other implications of hiring a spouse as an employee.

Medical Insurance

8.13 How to Save on Unemployment Taxes

The unemployment tax rate you pay as an employer is one of the few taxes where you have some control over the rate you pay. The state maintains a reserve account for each employer, in which it monitors the unemployment taxes you pay in and the unemployment benefits it pays out to your former employees. The more benefits the state pays to your former employees, the higher your individual company's tax rate will be and vice versa.

So it pays for you to have as few former employees as possible who are collecting unemployment benefits, since these are charged to your reserve account.

To succeed in keeping down the unemployment claims charged to your account, you need to challenge any former employees' claims that appear to be unjustified. Often, you will be surprised to learn that an employee you had fired for stealing or who had quit on you has filed for benefits and has lied about his or her reasons for leaving. In general, an ex-employee can't collect unemployment from you if he or she left your employment for one of these reasons:

- Refusal to work;
- Voluntarily quitting;
- Inability to continue work due to illness or injury; or
- Misconduct, such as theft, not showing up for work, or the like.

An employee who leaves your employ for virtually any other reason, such as being fired for incompetence, can generally collect benefits, which will cost you money by raising your unemployment tax rate. Here

Reducing Claims

are some tips on how you can keep down the number of unemployment claims filed against your account.

- When you are hiring, be aware of the cost you may have if you lay off these people in the future. You may hire a number of new employees for an expansion or new project with the view that if things don't work out as planned, you will simply lay them off and cancel the project with no further cost. Count the cost. Remember that if you do have to lay them off, you may pay a much higher unemployment tax rate for several years.

- Document in writing your reasons for firing an employee, if for reasons such as theft, insubordination, absence, or intoxication on the job. This will buttress your argument that the fired employee is not entitled to benefits if he or she should file a claim.

- Be aware that if you change an employee's hours of work and he or she quits as a result, it will be considered involuntary dismissal and the employee will probably be eligible for benefits. So it pays to have a written agreement signed by the employee to work any shift or hours that are required, if needed. Then, if the employee quits, it will not be due to a change in job conditions in the eyes of the law.

- If you decide to fire someone for misconduct, do it on the spot. If you keep them on at your convenience until you find a replacement, it will not usually be considered a discharge for misconduct, and the fired employee will most likely be eligible for benefits.

- If new employees do not work out, consider firing them before they have worked three months. In most states, a person has to work for you at least three months before they can earn unemployment benefits that are chargeable to your reserve account.

In general, it pays to keep a close eye on your employer reserve account and be aware of who is filing benefit claims that will cost you money. Contest any claims that you feel are not legitimate.

8.14 Deductions for Office-in-the-Home Expenses

If you use part of your residence for business purposes, you may be able to deduct part of your office-in-the-home expenses; however, the rules are rather stringent, and the general rule is that office-in-the-home expenses are not deductible for tax purposes, unless you meet a number of very technical requirements.

There are several types of situations under which you may be able to claim deductions for part of your rent or expenses related to ownership of your residence, as well as other occupancy expenses, despite the home-office deduction limitations.

If you use part of your residence exclusively for business purposes and on a regular basis, you may be able to claim office-in-the-home deductions, if you also qualify under one of these tests:[100]

- You use a portion of your home as your principal place of business.
- You use your home as a place to meet clients, customers, or patients.
- Your home office is a separate structure that is not attached to your house or living quarters.

The ability to treat a home office as your "principal place of business" has been sharply limited by the U.S. Supreme Court's 1993 decision in the *Soliman* case. Under this holding, even if your home office is your *only* office, it won't qualify if it is not also your *most important* place of work. In *Soliman*, the Supreme Court disallowed home-office deductions of a physician who had no office other than a room in his home, where he kept his business records and made business-related phone calls. Most of his actual work was done at various hospitals where he performed services as an anesthesiologist.

As a result, the rule for determining whether your home office is your principal place of business now depends on two primary considerations:

- The relative importance of the activities performed at each work location; and
- The amount of time spent at each location.

Two special exceptions are made where part of a home is regularly, but not exclusively, used for business purposes.

- Storage of inventory — A wholesaler or retailer who uses part of a home to store inventory that is being held for sale; if the dwelling unit is the taxpayer's sole fixed location of the trade or business; or
- Day care facility — Part of the home is used for day care of children, physically and mentally handicapped persons, or individuals age 65 or older.

If you can show that a portion of your residence qualifies as a home office, you have cleared the first hurdle. But note that even if you don't meet any of the above requirements, these rules will not disallow your deductions that are otherwise allowed for tax purposes, such as interest on your home mortgage, real estate taxes, or casualty losses from damage to your residence. Also, business expenses that are not home-related, such as business supplies, cost of goods sold, wages paid to business employees, and other such operating expenses, are not affected by the limitation on home office-related deductions.

If the business use of your home qualifies under one of the above tests, then you may be able to deduct part of the home office expenses that are allocable to the portion of your home that is used in your business, in addition to home mortgage interest, property taxes, and casualty losses.

For example, if 15% of your home is used exclusively and regularly as your principal place of business, you could possibly deduct up to 15% of your occupancy costs, such as gas, electricity, insurance, repairs, and similar expenses, as well as 15% of your rent or depreciation expense on 15% of the tax basis of your house. The IRS and the tax court don't agree on the deductibility of certain other types of expenses, such as lawn care.

Deductions Limited to Income

Note, however, that the amount of qualifying home office expense you can actually deduct for the year is limited to the gross income from your home business, reduced by regular operating expenses (wages, supplies, etc.) and an allocable portion (15% in the above example) of your mortgage interest, property taxes, and casualty loss deductions. If you still have net business income after taking those deductions, then you may deduct the allocable portion of your home office expenses, up to the amount of such net income.

Any portion of your home office expenses that aren't deducted due to the income limit in one year can be carried over to future years until usable, if ever. Thus, it pays to keep track of any such disallowed expenses, in case your home-based business becomes more profitable in the future, and you are then able to deduct the carried-over expenses from earlier years.

Your federal individual return, *Schedule C*, no longer asks you whether expenses for business use of a home are being deducted. Instead, you must determine a tentative profit or loss on *Schedule C*, without taking into account home use expenses. Home office expenses are now computed separately on *Form 8829*. On this form, you must compute the amount of deductible expenses for business use of the home, which (if any) can then be deducted from the net *Schedule C* income. This will make it impossible, or at least illegal, for taxpayers filing *Schedule C* to simply bury the home office expenses in with other business expenses.

Potential Tax Trap

The downside of taking home office deductions is a potential tax bite when you sell your home. For example, if 15% of your home has been used for business and you sell your home for a gain, you will have to pay tax on 15% of the gain, even if you reinvest in a new house, or even if you qualify for the once-in-a-lifetime $125,000 exclusion of gain — for persons over age 55 — when you sell the house. Thus, a few hundred dollars of home office deductions now, could later result in many thousands of dollars of tax on the "business" part of your house, if you sell it for a gain a few years down the road. For more information on the deductibility of home-office expenses, obtain IRS *Publication 587, Business Use of Your Home.*

Endnotes

1. I.R.C. § 1366(e).
2. I.R.C. § 1(g).
3. I.R.C. § 243(a).
4. I.R.C. §§ 301 and 302(d).
5. I.R.C. § 331.
6. I.R.C. § 1(h).
7. I.R.C. § 531.
8. I.R.C. § 542.
9. I.R.C. § 542(a)(1).
10. I.R.C. § 246A.
11. I.R.C. §§ 219 and 404(a).
12. I.R.C. § 501(a).
13. I.R.C. § 408(m).
14. I.R.C. §§ 105–106.
15. I.R.C. § 105(b).
16. I.R.C. § 105.
17. I.R.C. § 106.
18. I.R.C. § 104(a)(3).
19. I.R.C. § 79(a).
20. I.R.C. § 132.
21. I.R.C. § 119.
22. I.R.C. § 127.
23. I.R.C. § 129.
24. I.R.C. § 422.
25. I.R.C. § 423.
26. I.R.C. § 125.
27. I.R.C. § 245(c)(1).
28. I.R.C. §§ 991–997.
29. I.R.C. § 994(a).
30. Treas. Regs. § 1.994-1(e).
31. I.R.C. § 994(a).
32. Treas. Regs. § 1.994.
33. I.R.C. § 995(b)(1)(F)(i) (as amended by The Tax Reform Act of '86).
34. I.R.C. § 995.
35. I.R.C. § 995(f).
36. Rev. Rul. 75-430, 1975-2 C.B. 313; Rev. Rul. 76-284, 1976-2 C.B. 236.
37. Treas. Regs. § 1.991-1(a).
38. I.R.C. § 922(a)(1).
39. I.R.C. § 7872.
40. I.R.C. § 302(c)(2) permits the complete termination of the interest of a family member in a corporation by means of a stock redemption to qualify for capital gains treatment, if certain conditions are met.
41. I.R.C. § 453(g).
42. I.R.C. § 291(a).
43. I.R.C. § 274(h).
44. I.R.C. § 280A.
45. I.R.C. § 274(d).
46. I.R.C. § 274(m)(1).
47. I.R.C. § 274(d).
48. I.R.C. § 274(d), as amended by Pub. L. No. 99-44.
49. I.R.C. § 274(a)(1)(A).
50. I.R.C. § 274(e)(1). (Repealed as of 1-1-87.)
51. I.R.C. § 262; Treas. Regs. § 1.212-1(f).
52. I.R.C. § 280F(b)(2).
53. I.R.C. § 280F(d)(5)(B).
54. Rev. Proc. 93-51, § 5.01, 1993-42 I.R.B. 30.
55. I.R.C. § 441(i).
56. I.R.C. § 195.
57. Treas. Regs. § 1.446-1(c)(2)(i).
58. I.R.C. § 448.
59. I.R.C. § 461(h).
60. I.R.C. § 267(a)(2).
61. Treas. Regs. § 1.451-3.
62. I.R.C. § 460.
63. I.R.C. § 56(a)(3).
64. I.R.C. § 453(b).
65. I.R.C. §§ 453(1)(2)(B) and 453(1)(3).
66. I.R.C. § 453A(b).
67. I.R.C. § 453A(b)(3).
68. I.R.C. § 472.
69. I.R.C. § 474.
70. I.R.C. § 1363(d).
71. I.R.C. § 263A(b)(2)(B).
72. I.R.C. § 531.
73. I.R.C. § 541.
74. I.R.C. § 385.
75. I.R.C. § 531.
76. I.R.C. § 535(c)(2).
77. I.R.C. § 535(a) and (b).
78. I.R.C. § 537(a).
79. I.R.C. § 535(c)(2).
80. I.R.C. § 531.
81. I.R.C. § 537(a)(2).
82. Treas. Regs. §§ 1.537-1(b)(1) and 1.537-2(b)(2).
83. I.R.C. § 537(b)(4).

84. Treas. Regs. § 1.537-2(b)(3).
85. As defined in I.R.C. § 543.
86. I.R.C. § 542.
87. I.R.C. § 543(a)(7).
88. I.R.C. § 543(a)(6).
89. I.R.C. § 541.
90. I.R.C. § 543(d).
91. I.R.C. § 385.
92. I.R.C. § 162(a)(1).
93. I.R.C. § 162(m).
94. I.R.C. § 2056.
95. I.R.C. § 4980A(d).
96. Economic Recovery Tax Act of 1981, Pub. L. No. 97-34, § 403(e)(3).
97. I.R.C. § 51.
98. I.R.C. § 280C(a).
99. Rev. Rul. 71-588, 1971-2 C.B. 91.
100. I.R.C. § 280A(c)(1).

Chapter 9

Miscellaneous Business Pointers

Money is not the root of all evil. The lack of money is the root of all evil.

— Reverend Ike

9.1 General Considerations

This chapter contains helpful information on a variety of topics of interest to many small businesses, ranging from basic information on accounting, auditing, cash flow management, and sources of financing, to useful tax and business tips and a comprehensive discussion of the very wide range of environmental laws that may affect your business. Also covered are other matters you may have to consider, such as consumer credit laws, the pros and cons of using independent contractors, key areas of pending legislation, and developing legal and economic trends that may have an impact on you in the near future.

9.2 Accounting — Some Basics

Maintaining good accounting records is a must for any small business. Without accurate and up-to-date records, you will be operating your business without vitally important information. Meaningful financial statements can only be prepared if the underlying records of transactions are accurate and current.

Accounting Systems

It may help to think of your accounting system as being like an airplane's radar system. If you are not getting current and correct feedback from either system, you will not have enough time to react to prevent a potential crash.

Single-Entry Method

While most schools and colleges teach only the double-entry method of bookkeeping, which provides a series of checks and balances in recording income and expenditures, some small business owners use a single-entry method of accounting.

If you are not knowledgeable about double-entry bookkeeping and handle most of the funds directly yourself, you may find that a single-entry system is acceptable for your needs and much simpler to use. The single-entry method is only slightly more involved than keeping a checkbook record of cash income and disbursements and usually consists of three basic records:

- A daily cash receipts summary — This summary may come from a cash register tape or sales slips. It will not only give you a total of your daily cash receipts, but it will break down your sales by product, by salesperson, or by store, depending on how much detail you need.
- A monthly cash receipts summary — This is simply a monthly summary of the daily cash receipts.
- A monthly cash disbursements report — This is a report on expenses and other payments, such as debt repayments, purchases of capital assets, or distributions of profits.

A number of simplified write-it-once systems for all different kinds of businesses are available at office supply stores.

Double-Entry Method

While a single-entry system is easy to use, it is not a complete accounting system because it focuses mainly on profit and loss and does not provide a balance sheet. For all but the very smallest of businesses, a single-entry accounting system is likely to be inadequate. Even if your business is very small, but expects to grow, it is usually advisable to start out with a full set of books, using the double-entry method.

You can avoid many future problems if you get a CPA to help you set up the accounting system for your business. He or she will tailor a chart of accounts to your specific needs and build in internal controls to record all transactions and to reduce the possibilities of employee theft or embezzlement that might go undetected with a poorly designed system.

If you use a personal computer in your business, there are any number of general ledger accounting software packages you can buy if your accounting needs are fairly straightforward and if you have a reasonable understanding of how double-entry accounting works. For a very small business, there are adequate software packages available for under $100.

Accounting Firm Services

If you are going to use an outside accounting firm to prepare financial statements, they can provide three different levels of service — compilations, reviews, and audits.

Compilations

Most financial statements prepared for small businesses are compilations because they are far less expensive than an audit or review. In a compilation, the outside accountant has no obligation to do any investigation unless something looks suspicious or misleading. Generally, all an accountant is required to do in preparing compilation statements is to take the financial data you give him or her and present it in a manner that conforms with generally accepted accounting principles (GAAP).

In a compilation, the accountant expresses no opinion on the accuracy of the information presented. The accountant is simply taking what you gave him or her and putting it in a proper financial statement format. It is important for you to remember that regardless of what type of assurance your accountant expresses, you are ultimately the one responsible for ensuring your financial statements are prepared accurately.

Reviews

A review involves some limited analysis or testing of the financial records, but the certified public accountant (CPA) expresses only a very limited opinion as to the accuracy of the information in the financial statements. A review is somewhat less expensive than an audit, but more expensive than a compilation. Most small businesses hire a CPA firm to do a review only if their bankers or other lenders or financial backers insist on a review rather than a compilation.

Audits

An audit is invariably the most involved and most expensive level of service in connection with financial statements. An accounting firm that audits financial statements must not only verify that your financial statements are presented fairly and in accordance with GAAP, but it also checks and verifies some or all of the accounts to satisfy itself that they are real.

To verify accounts, an accounting firm can request confirmations of bank accounts or receivable and payable account balances from banks, customers, and vendors to uncover possible errors or fraud in recordkeeping. Because audits are relatively expensive, many small businesses elect to have review or compilation statements done; however, lenders or bonding companies often insist that you have a certified audit.

Depreciation

The Tax Reform Act of 1986 effectively repealed the highly favorable accelerated cost recovery system (ACRS) tax depreciation system that was in force from 1981 until the end of 1986. In January 1987, taxpayers learned to live with another whole new complex system of depreciation. Unfortunately, it is still necessary to know the former ACRS rules for assets acquired during the 1981–86 period, as well as the old depreciation rules for items acquired before 1981, to compute current depreciation on those assets.

The Modified ACRS System

The modified ACRS (MACRS) law from 1986 does not provide depreciation tables, unlike the previous ACRS system. Instead, all assets (with a few special exceptions) placed in service after 1986 are assigned to 3-, 5-, 7-, 10-, 15-, or 20-year recovery period categories, except for real estate, which must be depreciated over 39 years — 27.5 years for residential rental property.[1]

Under the MACRS system, most personal property is depreciated under the 200% declining balance method over a specified number of years — called a recovery period. The only exceptions are for 15- or 20-year property, for which the 150% declining balance method is used. Real estate may only be depreciated under the straight-line method.

Assets other than real estate are mostly assigned to the various recovery periods that vary from industry to industry and are far too voluminous and technical to reproduce in a book of this nature. MACRS, however, specifically assigns some types of assets to recovery classes. For example, autos and light trucks are five-year property. The MACRS provisions have also reduced the maximum annual depreciation deductions on luxury automobiles as discussed in Section 8.6.

One small ray of sunshine in the MACRS tax depreciation nightmare is a liberalization of the former $10,000 first-year expending election for tangible personal property. You may elect to expense up to $17,500 in cost of furniture and equipment in the year such assets are placed in service.[2] For example, if the only depreciable items you buy in 1994 are $15,000 of office equipment, you may be able to deduct the full $15,000 in 1994. Note, however, that this special deduction is not allowed to the extent that it would create a loss for your trade(s) or business(es) for the year. Also, the deduction is phased out if you acquire more than $200,000 of eligible property during the tax year.

Internal Accounting Controls

Poor internal accounting controls and recordkeeping procedures are a weakness for many small business owners. Lax procedures are frequently to blame when a secretary or bookkeeper departs for Brazil with thousands of dollars of stolen or embezzled funds belonging to his or her employer. Ideally, you would consult a good accountant to set up and review your internal financial controls; however, that will cost you a good deal of money, so before you do so, you may want to do your own review of your internal controls, utilizing the checklist located at the end of this chapter.

9.3 Cash-Flow Management

Cash flow is the lifeblood of any business organization; yet, small business operators are often so concerned with other matters, they don't pay attention to managing their cash resources properly. Good cash management can make a significant contribution to the competitiveness and profitability of your business. Poor cash management is one of the main causes of business failures, particularly among smaller firms, since a cash shortage due to poor planning can set off a chain reaction of disastrous consequences, even in a profitable business.

Cash-flow management has two aspects: 1) projecting future cash flow, and 2) controlling and maximizing the cash available from operations at all times.

Perhaps the most important part of cash-flow management is accurately projecting your business' near- and long-term cash needs and making your business decisions reflect those needs. Often, to project what your sales will be in coming months, it will be necessary to rely on what has happened in the past — what percentage will be credit sales and when your receivables are likely to be collected.

Projecting Cash Flow

Similarly, you have to estimate and project what you will have to pay out in the way of payroll, rent, taxes, servicing debts, purchasing inventory, and paying off existing payables, plus extraordinary outlays you can anticipate.

The purpose of making these detailed projections of expected cash inflows and outflows is to point out any future cash shortages or deficits, so you can take steps in advance to prevent such occurrences. For example, if your projections indicated you were going to experience a severe cash crunch in about three months, you might take any of a number of steps to avert it, such as:

- Seeking to raise new capital;
- Borrowing money;
- Liquidating some of your inventory by cutting prices; or
- Cutting back on planned expenditures.

If you have a computer, microcomputer models are available to assist you in preparing projections of cash flows. If you don't own a computer, your accountant may have such models available to assist you.

If you are able to increase available cash by speeding up collections, delaying payments, or by other means, you can use the extra cash to reduce your borrowings — thus saving interest expenses — or you can invest the surplus cash to earn interest. Either way, improving your cash flow should increase your net earnings and should also help you avert cash shortages.

Controlling and Maximizing Cash Flow

Here are some basic ways to improve your business' cash flow.

- Bill your customers promptly. The later they receive the bill, the later you will usually collect for a particular sale.
- If you know that certain large customers must receive bills by certain days of the month so you can get paid in that month, try to bill them before those deadlines.
- Deposit your cash receipts daily, if possible.
- Keep close tabs on credit customers. Send them past due notices as soon as payments become overdue.

- If you can do so without hurting business, add late charges to overdue accounts.
- Never pay bills until just before they become due, unless there is a worthwhile discount for quick payment.
- Try to keep inventories as lean as possible. Even if you occasionally lose a small sale because you are temporarily out of an item, you should be far ahead of the game by substantially reducing the amount of cash you have tied up in inventory.
- Look for items in your inventory that are moving slowly or not at all. Consider slashing the price on those articles to convert them to cash and also to reduce the cost of storing them or having them take up valuable shelf space.
- Consider leasing equipment items instead of buying.
- Do not pay more on your estimated income taxes than you have to. You may qualify — without incurring interest charges or late payment penalties — under one or more exceptions that will allow you to delay paying much of your tax for the year until the tax return is due. If you realize that you have already overpaid your corporate estimated tax for the year, there is a procedure for obtaining a refund prior to the time when you can file a return.[3]
- If your business has a net operating loss for tax purposes that can be carried back to prior years, a procedure exists for filing a claim for a quick refund of the prior years' taxes. File it as early as you can because the IRS no longer pays interest on these refunds.
- Instead of keeping all your business cash in a local bank account, consider putting a significant portion of your cash in an out-of-town money market-type fund that pays interest and allows you to write checks against the account. Since you continue to earn interest on funds on deposit until the checks clear, consider using a fund in a distant part of the country, since it will take longer for your checks to clear when you make payments to local firms.

9.4 Protecting Your Assets

Starting a new business is almost always a risky proposition, and if the business fails, you may be forced into bankruptcy and could lose everything except what the bankruptcy laws allow you to keep. This is one reason why many small businesses incorporate at the outset, since a corporation will generally limit your liability to business creditors to the amount you invest in the corporation, plus any loans to the corporation you guarantee.

Accordingly, if you incorporate, be cautious about committing too much of your personal assets to the business. For example, instead of putting a building or piece of land you own into the corporation, it may be better —

and may save income and property taxes — for you to keep the property and lease it to the corporation. Even if you incorporate, the leases or bank loans you find it necessary to guarantee on behalf of the corporation could still wipe out your personal assets if the business folds. Thus, it often makes sense to have your corporation set up a tax-qualified pension or profit-sharing plan and to have it contribute as much as possible to the plan on your behalf. Not only does this provide substantial tax savings and deferral, but the law in most states will in many cases protect your account under such a plan from your creditors or the corporation's creditors.

So, if you can build up a significant retirement fund in your corporation's pension plan, you have at least some degree of assurance that the failure of the business or a disastrous lawsuit will not touch that nest egg. In a divorce, however, your spouse may be able to claim his or her share of the pension plan account.

9.5 Protecting Trade Names and Trademarks

If you intend to use some type of distinctive trade name for your business or trademark for your product or in advertising your services, consider taking steps to protect the use of the name or mark by registering it under state or federal law, or both. When considering your trade name or trademark, it may be necessary to perform a search, which can be expensive, to determine whether someone else has already registered the same or a very similar name or symbol. You do not want to open yourself up to a lawsuit for infringement. Since not every trade name can be registered, you will need to consult a trademark attorney if you are interested in protecting a particular name used by your business.

Advantages to Trade Name or Trademark Registration

Federal registration of a name confers a number of significant benefits to registering your trade name or trademark, including:

- Nationwide notice to others of your exclusive right to use the name or mark.
- Prima facie evidence of the validity of the registration and your exclusive right to use the mark throughout the country.
- With certain exceptions, registration gives you an unquestionable right to use the name or mark.
- If you prove in court that someone violated your rights under the Trademark Act of 1946,[4] you will be entitled to recover their profits and damages from its use.
- The right to sue in federal court for trademark infringement regardless of the amount at stake and whether or not there is diversity of citizenship — that is, regardless of whether you and the defendant operate in the same or different states.

- The right to have customs officials halt importation of counterfeit goods using your trademark.

Federal registration is permitted only if you will use the trade name or trademark in more than one state.

9.6 Section 1244 Stock

If you invest directly in a small corporation by transferring money or property (other than securities) to the corporation in exchange for its common stock — or preferred stock, if issued after July 18, 1984 — the stock will usually qualify as Section 1244 stock.[5] If it does, and the stock later becomes worthless or you sell it at a loss, Section 1244 of the Internal Revenue Code permits you to deduct up to $50,000 of your loss — $100,000 for a couple filing a joint return — as an ordinary deduction instead of as a capital loss for that year. This can be very important, since you can fully deduct an ordinary loss from your taxable income, while capital losses can only be used to offset capital gains, if you have any, or $3,000 of ordinary income per year until your capital losses are used up.[6] The $50,000/$100,000 limit on the amount of loss that can qualify for ordinary loss treatment is an annual limitation.

Any stock issued by a small business corporation will generally qualify as Section 1244 stock unless the corporation obtained half or more of its gross receipts from passive kinds of income, such as interest, dividends, and the like, in the five years before your loss is incurred.[7] A corporation qualifies as a small business corporation if the total invested in its stock is one million dollars or less.[8]

If the stock issued by your corporation meets the requirements of Section 1244, it will automatically qualify for ordinary loss treatment, up to the first one million dollars of stock issued. You should be aware, however, that capital contributions you make, where no stock is received by you for such money, will not qualify for ordinary loss treatment.[9]

See Section 11.9 as to whether state law also provides favorable tax treatment for losses on stock in a small business corporation.

9.7 U.S. Small Business Administration and Other Government Loans

If you need to borrow money for your business and cannot obtain regular bank financing, don't overlook the possibility of obtaining a loan through the U.S. Small Business Administration (SBA). Many small business owners are under the impression that it is virtually impossible to obtain an SBA loan unless a member of a minority group; this is not the case. Although the SBA does make special efforts to provide financing for minority-owned businesses, only a relatively small percentage of SBA loans are made to minority firms. Furthermore, a very high percentage of applications for SBA loans are approved when applications are properly submitted, often within three to six weeks.

SBA Loan Programs

The SBA, an agency of the U.S. government, guarantees intermediate and long-term loans to small firms, and to a limited extent, also makes direct loans to some small businesses. The SBA is not allowed to grant such financial assistance unless the borrower is unable to obtain private-sector financing on reasonable terms. The SBA does not compete with banks or other lenders; instead, it works with private lenders to assure availability of capital to potentially profitable small firms. Contrary to what you may have heard on late-night television infomercials, the SBA does *not* have a grant program for starting a small business.

For your business to qualify for SBA financial assistance, it must come within the current definition of a small business. In general, these are the types of small businesses eligible for SBA financing:

- Manufacturers with a maximum of 500 to 1,500 employees, depending upon the industry in which the applicant is engaged;
- Retailers with less than $3.5 million in annual sales — up to $13.5 million for some types of retailers;
- Wholesaling firms with 100 or fewer employees;
- General construction firms, whose annual sales have averaged less than $9.5 million for the last three fiscal years; lower limits apply to various special trade construction firms;
- Service firms with annual receipts not in excess of $3.5 to $14.5 million, depending on the industry; and
- Other definitions apply for businesses engaged in activities, such as agriculture and transportation.

Private lenders that are eligible to make SBA-guaranteed loans or participate in SBA financing packages include banks, savings and loans, and certain other lenders. The SBA has several types of loan programs for small businesses, the largest of which is the 7(a) Loan Program.

Guaranteed Loans

Most SBA financing actually consists of loans by banks or other lenders that are guaranteed by the SBA. This enables the small business to obtain such loans at reasonable interest rates because the bank's risk is largely eliminated. SBA-guaranteed loans are tied to the bank prime rate, as published in *The Wall Street Journal*, at a rate of 2.25% above prime rate for loans of less than seven years, or 2.75% above prime for loans of seven or more years. The SBA charges lenders a 2.0% guarantee fee on the portion of a loan that is guaranteed. Lenders are allowed to charge this fee to the borrower.

The SBA has recently adopted an alternate standard for the 7(a) Loan Program, under which a prospective borrower that does not qualify as a small business under the various standards listed above, may now qualify as such if its net worth is no more than six million dollars and if it had annual after-tax net income of two million dollars or less in each of the two preceding years.

As the borrower, you put up a reasonable amount of equity or collateral. These loans are usually secured by fixed assets, real estate, and inventory and are limited in term to 7 years for working capital loans or 10 years for purchasing fixed assets. Construction loans can be for as long as 25 years.

Under this program, the bank or other private lender deals with the SBA, and you deal with the bank, not the SBA. You will, however, need to do the following in applying for such a loan or any other SBA financing:

- Define the amount you need to borrow and the purposes for which the funds will be used.
- Describe the collateral you will offer as security.
- Determine from a bank that a conventional loan is not available.
- Prepare current financial statements, preferably with your accountant's assistance. These would include, at a minimum, a relatively current balance sheet and an income statement for the previous full year and for the current year up to the date of the balance sheet.
- Prepare personal financial statements of the owners, partners, or stockholders owning more than 20% of the stock of the company.

Direct Loans

If you are unable to obtain sufficient conventional financing or SBA-guaranteed loan funds, it may be possible, in rare instances, to obtain a direct loan from the SBA. When made, these direct loans are usually offered on a participation basis with a bank or other lender, where the bank oversees the loan payments and loan servicing on behalf of itself and the SBA. In recent years, the SBA has largely ceased making direct loans because it has had only minimal funds available, from time to time. Even when it does occasionally have funds to lend, there are always far more qualified applicants than funds to lend to them. Consequently, you will have very little chance of obtaining such a direct loan.

In 1992, however, the SBA began, as part of its direct loan program, to make "microloans" at slightly below-market interest rates to veterans, business owners with disabilities, and persons desiring to start companies in economically depressed areas. These loans, ranging from as little as $100 to a maximum of only $25,000, are intended to help very small businesses, particularly those run by minorities, women, and low-income people, who generally have a difficult time raising capital. As such, microloans are designed to empower people, such as single mothers, disabled individuals, and public housing tenants, to become self-employed and self-supporting. The SBA's microloans are modeled after microloan programs that have been operated for a number of years by nonprofit agencies in the United States and in a number of Third World countries, generally with great success. For the smallest microloans — often only a few hundred dollars — no collateral is generally required, only a good character reference or a good reputation in the community.

The SBA microloan program is generally run in cooperation with local nonprofit organizations. To find an SBA microlender, contact an SBA district office or:

SBA Answer Desk
(800) 827-5722

Other SBA Programs

New legislation frequently adds to and modifies the number and scope of SBA loan programs. Other such programs include:

- Seasonal lines of credit;
- Economic opportunity loans for entrepreneurs who are physically handicapped or members of a minority group;
- Short-term contract loan guarantees;
- Energy loans to small firms to install, sell, service, develop, or manufacture solar energy or energy-saving devices; and
- Disaster recovery loans to firms harmed by natural disasters.

Since the nature, scope, and availability of funds under these numerous programs are constantly changing, consult your bank or local SBA offices if you think your firm may qualify under one of these special financial assistance programs.

U.S. Department of Housing and Urban Development

The U.S. Department of Housing and Urban Development (HUD) makes Urban Development Action Grants (UDAG) to cities in economically distressed areas. The cities are then able to use these UDAG funds to make second-mortgage loans to private developers who are able to leverage these loans by borrowing at least five times such amounts — three times in small towns — from private sources. The purpose of such loans is to encourage new investment and development in depressed areas.

U.S. Department of Commerce

The Economic Development Administration (EDA) of the U.S. Department of Commerce makes direct loans and offers loan guarantees to businesses in areas with low family incomes or areas suffering from high unemployment. The purpose of these loans is to promote creation or retention of jobs for the residents living in these areas.

To qualify for this financing, your business must be located in an EDA redevelopment area and you need to demonstrate that the venture will directly benefit local residents and will not create local over-capacity for the industry in question. Application for EDA loan assistance is a long and complex process, taking much longer for processing than typical SBA loans.

Farmers Home Administration

The Farmers Home Administration (FmHA) can perhaps be thought of as an SBA for rural areas. It offers insured and guaranteed loans to develop business and industry in nonurban areas with populations of under 50,000. Like the SBA program, FmHA loan guarantees are for up to 90% of the total amount of the loan and are made for up to 30 years for financing real estate acquisition, 15 years for machinery and equipment, and 7 years for working capital. FmHA loan guarantees are not available for agricultural production.

Unlike SBA loan guarantees, there is no dollar limit on FmHA loan guarantees, nor does the FmHA make direct loans. Applicants for FmHA loan guarantees must not only have adequate collateral and good business histories, they must also demonstrate that the project will have a favorable economic impact and will create new jobs in the area — not merely shifting business activity and jobs from one area to another. Preference is given:

- To businesses who are expanding rather than transferring into an area;
- To projects in open country areas or towns with populations of under 25,000; and
- To business owners who are military veterans.

Other Federal Loan Programs

Other major federal loan programs are provided through the Federal Land Bank Association, Production Credit Association, and the Federal Intermediate Credit Bank. These organizations offer loans to businesses that provide services to farmers. These loans can be for purchasing land and equipment and for obtaining start-up working capital.

SBICs and MESBICs

In addition to direct loans and guarantees from government agencies, don't overlook possible loans or equity financing from Small Business Investment Companies (SBICs) and Minority Enterprise Small Business Investment Companies (MESBICs). Both are licensed and regulated by the SBA to provide equity capital, long-term loans, and management assistance to small businesses.

SBIC and MESBIC loans are usually subordinated to loans from other creditors and are typically made for five- to seven-year terms. Both types of investment companies are privately owned and thus tend to favor loans to established companies with significant net worth rather than new business start ups.

You may have to give up a large part of the equity in your business if you obtain SBIC financing. An SBIC is not permitted to control a company (50% or greater ownership) it lends to, but typically an SBIC lender will insist on debt that is convertible into common stock, warrants, and options, which may give it up to 49% ownership in your company. An SBIC will also want seats on your board of directors, will impose controls and restrictions on the way your business operates, and may insist upon salary limits for the principal owners. SBIC financing does not come without a price.

MESBICs serve only those small firms that are owned by members of economically or socially disadvantaged minority groups.

Business Development Corporations are Local Development Companies (LDCs) and Certified Development Companies (CDCs) organized by local residents to promote economic development in their particular communities. These entities do not make working capital loans or loans to purchase free-standing equipment.

Business Development Corporations

Instead, LDCs or CDCs will arrange for SBA-guaranteed bank loans and sale of SBA-guaranteed debentures for up to 90% financing for 25 years for land acquisition, building construction, or renovation and purchase of fixed assets, such as machinery and equipment. For information on what state business loan programs may be available in this state, refer to Section 11.9.

9.8 Mail Order Sales

If your business involves selling goods by mail order, become familiar with Rule 435.1, a regulation issued by the Federal Trade Commission (FTC).[10] This federal regulation requires any business soliciting mail order sales to be prepared to ship the merchandise within 30 days after an order is received, unless it has clearly stated in its solicitation that orders will not be shipped for a longer period. Otherwise, the solicitation will be considered as an unfair and deceptive trade practice. In addition, if you receive an order and for some reason you cannot ship it within 30 days, or the period stated in your solicitation, you must:

- Immediately notify the customer and offer to either cancel the order and receive a refund or consent to the delay in shipment.
- Indicate when you will be able to ship or that you do not know when you will be able to ship the order.
- Provide other required information to the customer, which will vary in content depending upon when you expect to be able to ship.

Since March 1, 1994, the coverage of Rule 435.1 has been extended to all orders you receive, including those received by modem, fax, or telephone, in addition to those received by mail.

If you are going into the mail order business and want a single source of information on state and federal mail order laws, obtain the *Mail Order Legal Guide*, by Erwin J. Keup, from your book source or:

The Oasis Press
(800) 228-2275

Rule 435.1 is fairly complex and difficult to understand, but you need to understand and be familiar with it if you sell goods by mail order. For a free guide on this FTC rule, contact the FTC at the number listed below and request *A Business Guide to the Federal Trade Commission's Mail Order Rule.*

Federal Trade Commission
(202) 326-2222

State Sales and Use Taxes

If you sell across state lines to customers in states where you have no offices, employees, or other presence, the sale is usually not subject to sales tax in either state, since it is an interstate sale; however, technically, such sales are subject to use tax in the customer's state. A use tax is sort of a shadow of the sales tax and, in most states, applies where the sales tax doesn't.

The U.S. Supreme Court and other courts generally have not supported attempts of the various states to force out-of-state retailers to collect use tax on mail order or other sales made to residents of the taxing state, so that most mail order firms tend to treat such interstate sales as being tax-free, or tell the customers that it is up to them to report the purchase and pay the use tax, which they rarely do.

Unfortunately, in the last few years, many states have enacted new and broader sales and use tax laws. Many of these laws require out-of-state retailers, who advertise in the local media or send substantial amounts of direct mail/catalog solicitations into the state, to register as retailers subject to sales or use tax in the state and to treat such direct sales as taxable. The U.S. Supreme Court has finally ruled that these aggressive new sales tax laws are unconstitutional in the 1992 case of *Quill Corporation v. North Dakota.* Thus, it appears most of the broad new mail order sales and use tax laws — which have been adopted in some 34 states and are targeted to hit out-of-state mail order firms — may be invalid. While this is good news for mail order retailers, the bad news is the court also indicated in its decision that Congress could, if it chose to do so, constitutionally enact legislation that would permit the states to require use tax collection on mail order and similar sales by out-of-state retailers.

In fact, just such a bill has already been introduced in the U.S. Senate by Senator Dale Bumpers (D) of Arkansas, inaptly named the "Tax Fairness for Main Street Business Act of 1994." This bill, if enacted, would grant states the right to enact laws requiring out-of-state sellers of tangible personal property to collect and remit state and local sales-use taxes if the following requirements were met:

- The seller is subject to the personal jurisdiction of the taxing state;
- The tangible personal property has a final destination in the state in question;
- The seller's gross receipts from sales of such property in the twelve months ending September 30 of the calendar year before the year of the sale exceeded $100,000 in the taxing state or $3 million in the United States as a whole; and

- The taxing state collects and administers all of the local sales-use taxes imposed on behalf of its local jurisdictions, such as cities and counties.

Where a state has nonuniform local sales tax rates, the proposed legislation would give the seller the choice of either collecting tax at the appropriate rate in each local jurisdiction, or collecting tax at a flat statewide rate, based on an average rate determined by the state, rounded to the nearest 0.25%. Each state passing such a law would have to maintain a toll-free help line, which small mail order sellers could call at any time to determine the appropriate sales tax rate for sales to residents of that state.

Thus, if this or another federal law authorizing such use tax collections is enacted, it seems likely it will provide some exemption for smaller retailers and a simplified, statewide tax rate and payment method for sellers who have only minimal sales in each of a number of states. Otherwise, most small mail order sellers would instantly be forced out of business without such an exemption, due to the impossible complexity and enormous cost of filing sales or use tax returns for every state and local taxing district where a sale is made.

9.9 Environmental Laws Affecting Your Business

As the world becomes more crowded and as the damaging effects of two centuries of unrestrained industrial development becomes more apparent on the environment, political attempts to remedy these problems, particularly the problems of pollution and toxic emissions, have resulted in a flood of legislation, regulations, and litigation involving environmental matters. While this is probably all to the good in the larger sense, some of the immediate effects of these new environmental restrictions have been to create another whole layer of complex and often conflicting government regulations on business, plus a virtual minefield of legal exposure for companies of all sizes.

For small businesses — most of which do not have in-house legal staffs and can hardly afford the large legal fees needed for professional guidance through this maze of regulations — the effect of the growing body of environmental laws is especially harsh. Small businesses are also disproportionately affected by the heavy costs of complying with various mandated emissions requirements, which often require large capital expenditures for sophisticated new pollution control equipment.

While this section cannot do much more than scratch the surface of the environmental law exposure and increased operational complexities most businesses are going to face, the discussion below explains some of the main problem areas you need to be at least passingly familiar with. This section also provides a capsule description of the major areas of federal environmental law that may currently apply to your business or which may apply at some time in the future.

Environmental Clean-up Laws

Perhaps the most pervasive of the environmental laws, with the most devastating potential consequences for the unwary, are the environmental clean-up laws, and the legal liability these laws attach to real estate that has been contaminated by hazardous substances. The main laws that apply in this area are the Comprehensive Environmental Response, Compensation and Liability Act[11] (CERCLA or the Superfund law) and the Resource Conservation and Recovery Act (RCRA).[12]

CERCLA and RCRA apply to virtually every real estate transaction. While RCRA applies primarily to currently generated hazardous waste, including limits on creation of waste and requirements for disposing of it, CERCLA is more focused on cleaning up hazardous substances that have been spilled or dumped in the past.

CERCLA Liability

CERCLA deals with all kinds of pollution: air, surface water, groundwater, and soil. It covers virtually every type of hazardous substances as defined under CERCLA, the Clean Water Act, the Clean Air Act, or the Toxic Substances Control Act. There are, however, major exceptions for petroleum and certain petroleum derivatives. The main thrust of CERCLA is to impose liability on private owners of property to clean up hazardous wastes they have created. CERCLA would also apply to owners of the inherited property, if the property in question was already contaminated when it was acquired.

In short, even if you were not responsible for creating a contamination problem, if you acquire real estate that is already contaminated — and it later becomes apparent there has been a spill or dumping that requires an environmental cleanup, possibly at astronomical cost — you are liable for the costs of the cleanup, if you are the current owner. You can't simply walk away from the property and let the government take it in lieu of paying the clean-up costs.

Once the owner, you are the responsible party and may be held liable for costs that exceed the value of the property many times over. You may even become liable somewhere down the road if you sell a business — an existing corporation, for instance — that has formerly owned contaminated property. The government could eventually institute environmental proceedings against the current property owner, who then sues all the prior legal owners of the property, including you, for indemnity or reimbursement.

Of course, you may be able to sue the prior owner or anyone in the chain of prior owners for indemnification, if they are still in existence and can be found. However, since that is a pretty slim thread upon which to hang your financial survival, you need to take precautions up front, before acquiring any real property, to protect yourself from possible environmental liability for cleanup under CERCLA.

The following are some things you can and should do to reduce your risk in any real estate or existing business acquisition:

- Exercise considerable diligence concerning the current condition and past uses of any real estate involved in a transaction. Also, if buying an existing corporation, you need to find out what properties it owned in the past and be concerned whether any such properties may have been contaminated by hazardous substances.

- Be particularly wary of any sites that have been used as gas stations, landfill areas, locations of dry cleaners, chemical or other industrial production processes, battery production, recycling, or metal plating. Be extremely cautious if the site contains underground storage tanks.

- Consider retaining an environmental audit firm to do detailed site inspections and evaluations to determine if there may be a contamination problem.

- In a business or real estate purchase agreement, require written representations and warranties about the site from the seller and include provisions under which he or she will indemnify you if there is a problem. Be mindful of the seller's financial viability, in case you should be forced to seek indemnity from him or her. A promise isn't worth the paper it is written on, if the seller doesn't have the wherewithal to make good on it.

Even though under the Superfund law there is an innocent purchaser defense, you must be able to demonstrate that you made appropriate inquiry before acquiring the property to determine any pre-existing contamination problem. There is little guidance in the law at this point as to what constitutes an appropriate inquiry, so perhaps you should not expect to escape liability under that rule. The best defense is to avoid purchasing property that is contaminated by taking the steps outlined above. Even if such steps fail to discover a lurking environmental problem, at least you will have a much stronger argument to make under the innocent purchaser defense if you have done a due-diligence survey and had an environmental audit performed by a reputable firm.

RCRA Requirements

RCRA contains a comprehensive set of rules for managing hazardous wastes, including petroleum-based substances, and regulating those who generate hazardous wastes, transport them, and store, treat, or dispose of them. Penalties for violations include fines of up to $25,000 a day, plus imprisonment.

One important focus of RCRA is on underground storage tanks (USTs), many of which are known to be leaking gasoline or other contaminants into the surrounding soil and groundwater. Under RCRA, much of the regulation of USTs is left to state governments. Thus, under federal regulations, the owner of a UST must notify the state of the tank's existence, including tanks that were taken out of service after January 1, 1974.[13]

New USTs must satisfy federal performance standards, which generally require that they be constructed of fiberglass-reinforced plastic or steel that is cathodically protected from corrosion.[14] Furthermore, all existing USTs must be upgraded to federal standards by December 22, 1998,[15] which will result in some major expenditures for many small businesses, such as service stations.

Clean Water Act

Under the Clean Water Act, the federal Environmental Protection Agency (EPA) and individual states are the watchdogs of water pollution standards.[16] It also allows private citizens to sue to enforce the act. Penalties for violations can be as high as $50,000 a day, and even negligent, but unintentional violations can result in imprisonment. For certain existing facilities, this law provides for a system of EPA permits for discharging certain amounts of water pollutants.

Wetlands Development

Portions of the Clean Water Act require that all proposed development activities, which involve the dredging or filling of wetlands, obtain permits from the U.S. Army Corps of Engineers.[17] Thus, before you acquire real property that you plan to develop in any way, you need to do a careful survey to determine if the property lies within an area that is considered to be a wetland. Otherwise, you may end up with a piece of property which is undevelopable and which can hardly be sold at all, even for a huge loss.

This has been a trap for more than one unwitting buyer of land in wetlands districts, since wetlands include much more than swamps and marshes. Many dry-looking parcels may also fall within the regulatory definition. Furthermore, be aware that many states have adopted wetlands restrictions, which may require you to also obtain state development permits.

Clean Air Act

The Clean Air Act of 1970, which was substantially amended and strengthened by the Clean Air Act of 1991, among other things, restricts the ability of stationary sources of air pollutants to emit various pollutants into the atmosphere at new or modified facilities.[18] States are allowed to implement their own rules for controlling air pollution levels. The Clean Air Act of 1991 has greatly expanded the impact on small businesses. As this act's amendments go into effect, they will require a diverse number of air pollution controls. Some will include:

- Gasoline stations will need vapor-recovery devices on gasoline pumps.
- Furniture makers may need incinerators to burn off hydrocarbons released from spray-paint booths.
- Restaurants in smoggy areas will have to install containment units that collect hydrocarbon emissions from charcoal grills.
- Many bakeries will have to install oxidation devices or catalytic converters to neutralize the gases produced by fermenting yeast when dough is baked.
- Auto-body paint and repair shops will have to install extremely expensive equipment to catch hydrocarbon emissions from spray painting.
- Print shops will have to neutralize or eliminate use of chemicals that contribute to ozone formation.

As the above examples indicate, the requirements under the Clean Air Act of 1991 are very pervasive and will affect many nonindustrial types of businesses who would never have considered themselves to be polluters in the past. Companies that are sources of air pollutant emissions will have to obtain state-issued construction and operating permits under EPA rules. Small businesses will have to apply for permits at least every five years and file reports of their compliance with the law every six months, if they produce more than 100 tons per year of any ozone-forming pollutant. Ozone-forming pollutants are the main targets of the act.

According to some experts, once these rules go into effect, a small business' main cost of complying with the clean air regulations is likely to be all the required paperwork. Penalties for violations are also very severe, with civil penalties as high as $25,000 a day for each violation, plus felony imprisonment and huge fines for willful or negligent releases of hazardous air pollutants. In addition, the EPA has set emissions fees of $25 a ton for every ton of regulated pollutants that a firm emits, up to $4,000 per year.

Toxic Substances Control Act

If your business is one that engages in the manufacturing, processing, or distribution of chemical substances, you may be required under the federal Toxic Substances Control Act (TSCA) to report certain information to the EPA regarding the chemical substances and mixtures you use.[19] The TSCA requires manufacturers to give a 90-day notification before producing a new chemical substance and, in some cases, for older chemicals. The EPA may require safety testing before approval of such a chemical. The TSCA also has extensive recordkeeping rules regarding use and disposal of toxic chemicals.

There are severe penalties for failing to make the required reports to the EPA, including civil and criminal penalties of $25,000 and up, plus up to a year's imprisonment for each violation. Each day the violation continues is considered a separate violation for purposes of the fines levied under the TSCA.

Pesticide Regulations

The Federal Insecticide, Fungicide and Rodenticide Act (FIFRA), which amends the Federal Environmental Pesticides Control Act of 1972 (FEPCA), regulates both the manufacture and distribution of pesticides.[20]

Environmental Impact Statements

The National Environmental Policy Act of 1969 (NEPA) requires an environmental impact statement (EIS) to be prepared with respect to major federal actions that significantly affect the quality of the human environment.[21] While this would not, at first impression, seem to directly affect you, as a small business owner, the EIS requirement also applies in any situation where a federal agency approves some action by other persons, such as a private company.

In addition, many states have adopted similar EIS requirements; for instance, when a local planning board approves a real estate development, an EIS may be required under state law, if not federal.

Asbestos Regulation

As lung disease, cancer, and other health risks attributed to the exposure to asbestos have come to light, a number of state and federal laws have been enacted to deal with this problem. In addition, huge numbers of individual damage suits for alleged harm to individuals, who were exposed to asbestos in the workplace and elsewhere, have resulted in enormous judgments against many companies, even forcing a giant building materials firm, Johns-Manville Corporation, into Chapter 11 bankruptcy to protect itself from a host of asbestos-related lawsuits.

Federal amendments to the TSCA and the Asbestos Hazard Emergency Response Act of 1986 (AHERA) have given the EPA power to issue regulations regarding asbestos in school buildings. In addition, Occupational Safety and Health Administration (OSHA) regulations have been issued to limit asbestos exposure in the workplace and to set construction standards regarding use of asbestos.[22]

Noise Control

Both OSHA and the EPA have issued regulations on noise emission standards, ranging from aircraft noise to protections of workers from hearing impairment in the workplace.

9.10 Consumer Credit Laws and Regulations

Many of the largest and most successful companies in America have gotten where they are, in part, by providing consumer credit to persons who buy their products. Classic examples would include such giant companies as Sears and General Motors, although countless smaller companies have also found that financing their customers' purchases can be a major boon to sales and that the interest earned on such credit can also become an important profit center in its own right.

The definition of consumer credit does not refer to the practice of allowing a client or customer to charge it and pay you at the end of the month, which is largely unregulated by the government. Instead, the following discussion deals with the situation where your business extends credit and charges interest during the period over which the loan amount (or amount financed) is being paid off by the customer.

The three main areas of the law regulating the extension of consumer credit, which affects nearly all businesses that grant such credit, are the federal Equal Credit Opportunity Act, the federal Truth-in-Lending Act, and state laws that prohibit usury.

If your business is engaged in providing consumer credit, you will most likely be subject to the provisions of the federal Equal Credit Opportunity Act (ECOA).[23] In general, the ECOA prohibits discrimination in credit transactions on the basis of race, color, religion, national origin, sex, age, or marital status.

The basic principle of this law is that each person applying for credit must be considered as an individual. This means, primarily, that there are very strict limits regarding what you may ask about marital status and about the spouse of the applicant. You may ask about marital status, but only to determine what rights and remedies you might have as a creditor — such as in a community property state — to refuse an applicant's credit.

The ECOA also forbids discrimination in providing credit because some or all of the applicant's income derives from public assistance programs, or because a person exercised a right, in good faith, under the Consumer Credit Protection Act.

Equal Credit Opportunity Act

If your business activities involve lending money, or if you sell to consumers on credit terms, you may have to comply with the federal Truth-in-Lending Act and state laws such as those that prohibit the charging of usurious interest rates on loans or other credit transactions.[24]

Regulations under the Truth-in-Lending Simplification and Reform Act provide that a business is not subject to the truth-in-lending rules unless it extended consumer credit at least 25 times in either the previous year or the current calendar year.[25] For loan transactions, required disclosures include:

- The annual percentage rate of interest;
- When the finance charge begins to accrue;
- The total amount of the finance charge;
- The number of payments to be made and the dollar amount of each payment;
- When payments are to be made;
- The total dollar amount of all payments;
- How any prepayment penalty and any late charges are to be computed;
- The amount of any prepaid finance charges and any deposit, plus the sum of the two;
- The amount financed;
- The existence of any balloon payment and its dollar amount;
- Annual statements of billing rights;
- Other information regarding security interests and rights to rescind; and
- Periodic billings to credit customers must include a number of disclosures regarding outstanding balances, how finance charges have been computed, and other items.

The rules regarding the Truth-in-Lending Act are far too complex to cover satisfactorily in a book of this nature; it can only alert you to the

Truth-in-Lending Act

possibility that you may be required to comply with those rules and give you some sense of what will be required if the rules do apply to you. If you plan to extend credit to consumers — other than sending out bills requesting payment in full, without interest charge, after you have provided goods or services — you need to consult an attorney experienced in this area.

Fortunately, legislation has considerably simplified the truth-in-lending rules, and the Federal Reserve Board has published model disclosure statements and billing rights statements that can be used to satisfy the requirements of the truth-in-lending regulations.

Cash Discount Act

The Cash Discount Act permits sellers to offer a discount of any amount to customers who pay in cash or by check without running afoul of the truth-in-lending rules. The discount, in this case, has to be clearly disclosed and made available to all customers.[26] In the past, if you offered more than a 5% cash discount, you were considered to be imposing a finance charge on credit customers and had to give them all the required truth-in-lending disclosures.

Usury Laws

See Section 11.9 for a brief description of how this state's usury laws may apply to your business.

9.11 Employee or Independent Contractor?

As was pointed out in Section 5.2, there are some major advantages in hiring independent contractors rather than employees to work in your business. Not only do you gain considerable payroll tax savings by retaining independent contractors, but there are far fewer administrative headaches.

Unfortunately, just because you hire someone and you agree that he or she will be an independent contractor, it does not necessarily make it so for tax and legal purposes. So before you hire anyone to work for you as an independent contractor, you need to take a hard look at whether the IRS or a court of law would consider that person to be your employee rather than an independent contractor. While the IRS uses a 20-factor test to evaluate whether a person is or is not an employee, a few major warning flags will indicate to you whether or not the person is your employee. These include:

- The person works mostly or only for your firm. That is, the person is not like a lawyer, for example, who has a number of clients besides you that he or she works for.
- The worker is subject to your control, and you have the right to direct how the work is done, not just to demand a particular result.

- The person works in your office or establishment and does not have his or her own place of business, business cards, business name, etc.
- The kind of work the person does for you is normally done by employees, such as secretarial work.
- The person is not a licensed professional of any type.

Unless you are quite clear that the work relationship will not be considered that of employer/employee, be very careful about hiring someone as a so-called independent contractor. The consequences of being wrong can be severe. Here are just a few of the things that can happen if your independent contractor is determined to be an employee:

- You are liable for not only the employer payroll taxes you failed to pay, but also for a portion of the employee taxes you failed to withhold, for example, income taxes and FICA tax.
- If you treat someone as an independent contractor, report payments of $600 or more a year to that person on IRS *Form 1099-MISC*. If you do, and the IRS later determines the person was really an employee, the back taxes you are liable for are limited to the employer payroll taxes, 20% of the employee's FICA tax you failed to withhold, and income tax withholding equal to only 1.5% of the wages you paid the person.

  If you do not file *Form 1099-MISC* and the person is reclassified as an employee, you are liable for 40% of the employee's FICA tax and income tax withholding equal to 3% of the wages — twice as much as if you would have filed *Form 1099-MISC*. Furthermore, there is a $100 penalty for failure to file *Form 1099-MISC* and you will owe interest on the taxes due. It is no longer a bargain to "borrow" from the IRS.

  You may also be assessed other penalties if you did not have a reasonable basis for treating the person as a nonemployee and may be liable for up to 100% of the employee's FICA and income tax which you failed to withhold.

- If the person is hurt on the job and you have not provided workers' compensation insurance coverage, you will be liable for extensive legal damages.
- If your business has a qualified retirement plan and you have not contributed to the plan on behalf of the person because he or she was not thought to be an employee at the time, the retirement plan could be disqualified for tax purposes for failing to cover the employee in question.

Thus, do not get stampeded into the independent contractor game by your friends and business associates who tell you how simple it is to avoid all those payroll taxes.

The above discussion of independent contractors summarizes federal rules only. Many states take an even more restrictive view than the IRS on the employee versus independent contractor issue.

Independent Contractor Treatment Tips

There are a number of steps you may be able to take to make a stronger case for someone who works for you to be treated as an independent contractor. Obviously, not all of the following will necessarily be feasible in every case, and a number of these steps, if implemented, may require some significant changes in the way you do business.

But if you can follow most of the suggestions below with regard to a given worker, you will improve your odds against having that worker reclassified as an employee by the IRS.

- Have a written agreement, signed by both parties, that makes it clear the company doesn't have the right to control the methods or procedures for the worker to accomplish the work contracted for. Include language in the agreement that states it is the worker's obligation to pay income and self-employment taxes on amounts earned, and that he or she will receive a *Form 1099* reflecting amounts earned, if the amount earned is $600 or more.

- Try to avoid setting working hours by hour or week. It would be all right to specify starting and completion dates for the work.

- Make it clear that if additional workers are needed to help, the contractor will hire and pay them.

- The arrangement should make it clear that the contractor is not limited to working exclusively for you, but is free to take on other work from other customers.

- Compensation should be based on what work is performed rather than the time spent to do it. This may require careful estimates so that the worker is fairly paid, not overpaid, for the work done.

- Avoid providing office space to the contractor on a regular basis.

- Let the workers be responsible for their own training, if that is possible.

- Each worker should be advised, in writing, to provide for their own liability, workers' compensation, health, and disability insurance coverage.

- Costs such as meals, transportation, and clothing should be built into the contract price of the job, rather than being billed directly to your account.

- It should be clear in your agreement with the worker that he or she can't be fired and can't quit. The worker's job is to fulfill a given work contract.

- Don't give the worker other work to fill in during downtime. This may mean, of course, that you will have to pay the worker somewhat more for the work done than you otherwise would, if you wish to keep him or her happy.

- Don't pay bonuses to a person you treat as an independent contractor.

Other Alternatives

Hiring individuals as your own employees or treating them as independent contractors may sometimes pose a difficult choice. Fortunately, you have other available options. You could:

- Hire temporary employees from a temporary help agency; or

▪ Lease employees from an employee leasing company.

An increasing number of companies are utilizing these two worthwhile alternatives.

Hiring "temps" is usually quite straightforward, at least for many kinds of positions, but it may cost you a bit more than straight hiring. A temporary help agency has to charge you enough to make a profit, as well as pay for any benefits it provides to the temps, who are the agency's employees — not yours. One benefit to you, other than the simplicity of having someone else handle payroll, benefits, workers' compensation, and other costs of retaining such workers, is that you can send such workers home the moment you no longer need them, with no adverse consequences.

Of even greater importance to many companies is the opportunity to try out temps and offer permanent jobs to those whose performance they like. In effect, you get to "test out" such individuals for as long as you wish, before deciding if you want to offer them employment as your own employee, not the agency's, which is exactly what many temps are seeking.

Employee leasing is a bit more complicated, because in many cases, you do the hiring. In some cases, you may even transfer your existing staff over to the payroll of the leasing company, which then leases them back to you for a fee equal to the salaries, taxes, and benefits paid by the leasing company, plus its mark-up percentage.

Leasing tends to be more of a long-term solution than hiring temps. Do your homework in checking out the reputation and background of any leasing company you will be dealing with. A number of leasing companies have gone broke or absconded with the payroll taxes withheld from employees' salaries, frequently leaving the firms that leased from them holding the bag. While there are many reputable leasing firms, they tend not to be as large and well known as the major temp firms, such as Kelly Services, Manpower, and other well-established firms in the industry.

Similar to hiring temps, leasing can be a major time- and energy-saving convenience. For example, if you lease all of your employees, you may be freed up to do what you do best, such as selling, rather than spending much of your time bogged down with payroll, benefits, and other employee-related paperwork.

You may also actually save money on your costs for workers, particularly if the leasing company is large and has been able to negotiate much less expensive, pooled rates for health insurance or workers' compensation than you could as a small employer.

Thus, leasing can offer substantial advantages to small companies, and usually avoids the problems and risks involved in seeking to treat workers as independent contractors, where such status is somewhat questionable. Be sure you deal with a reputable, established, financially responsible employee leasing company.

9.12 Whether You Should Incorporate Outside Your State

For most small businesses, there is little reason to consider incorporating your business under the laws of some state other than where you live. In fact, there are a few good reasons why you should not incorporate in a different state.

- Your corporation may have to pay a qualification fee to transact business in your home state as a foreign corporation. See Section 11.2 on this point.

- If your attorney is a local lawyer, he or she is likely to be much less familiar with the corporate laws of some other state than those of your state. Thus, your attorney is likely to either charge you more for corporate law advice if he or she has to research the law of an unfamiliar jurisdiction or give you less accurate advice than he or she could about your state's corporate laws.

- In many states, your corporation will have to pay some sort of minimum annual franchise tax or capital tax to the state of incorporation, even if you do no business there.

Don't believe the newspaper ads that tell you to incorporate in wonderful, tax-free Nevada or some other state and avoid your state's corporation income or franchise taxes. It doesn't work. If your corporation does business in your state, it pays the same taxes on its taxable income regardless of whether it is incorporated in your state, Nevada, or in the Grand Duchy of Luxembourg.

Perhaps the only valid reason why you might want to incorporate elsewhere would be to take advantage of some particular provision or flexibility available under the corporate laws of a particular state. If you own all the stock of your company, it is unlikely you would ever need to take advantage of any such provisions, which are usually more important where different groups are struggling for control of a corporation's board of directors or the like.

9.13 Foreign Investment in U.S. Businesses

Under the Foreign Direct Investment and International Financial Data Improvements Act of 1990, foreign individuals owning or acquiring 10% or more voting interest in U.S. businesses, including interests in U.S. real estate, must report certain information, including annual financial and operating data, to the U.S. Department of Commerce. Failure to file can result in civil penalties of $2,500 to $25,000.[27] For more information on this law, write to:

Bureau of Economic Analysis
U.S. Department of Commerce
BE-50 (IN)
Washington, DC 20230
(202) 606-5577

9.14 Emerging Trends and Issues

Today, businesses of every size and type are being buffeted by the ever-accelerating rate of change in the business, economic, social, and political environment in which they must operate. Part of the reason is that Congress, along with 50 state legislatures and countless government agencies, spew out reams of new laws and regulations all year long, in ever greater volume. As Benjamin Franklin once put it, "No man is safe in his bed when the Congress is in session."

To blame all of the disorienting changes that are occurring on lawmakers, however, is unfair since it seems that life in general is becoming more complex and unpredictable by the day. Accordingly, this section attempts to provide you, as a business owner, with a brief overview of developing and current trends in the business environment.

Labor Rates

Low labor rates abroad are causing the permanent shutdown of many large and small U.S. manufacturers, who can no longer keep up with foreign competition or U.S. manufacturers who move their operations overseas where wages are lower. This trend seems likely to continue and will have a rippling effect throughout the U.S. economy, adversely affecting many of the small firms that are either suppliers to large U.S. manufacturers or whose service operations will be drastically affected as larger companies close plants and make massive and permanent layoffs of thousands of employees.

Automation

Increasing automation, both here and abroad, is also likely to have a dramatic effect on employment and competitiveness in this country and throughout the world. Automation has been a factor in replacing blue-collar labor for decades. With the continual explosion in computing power and sophistication, vast numbers of middle managers and other white-collar workers are beginning to be displaced. With the advent of expert systems and "artificial intelligence," which are still in their infancy, but rapidly coming into their own, it is difficult to say whose job, if anyone's, will be safe in a few years.

While the ability to replace workers with computers or computer-driven machinery may be very attractive from a cost-savings standpoint to an employer, its societal effects are hard to predict and may prove to be very adverse to the overall business environment. The field of information processing is moving rapidly, and it is difficult to visualize how the world and the U.S. economy may look in as little as five or six years.

Downsizing

According to an American Management Association (AMA) survey for the year ending in June 1991, 55.5% of the organizations polled engaged in downsizing and 60% of those firms had also made significant staff cutbacks in the previous year, suggesting that firms are now cutting even deeper and deeper. The survey revealed that the cuts were heaviest on the Pacific Coast, averaging 12.6% of the workforce among firms reporting downsizing. Middle management jobs, which are estimated to make up something like 5% to 8% of the total workforce, accounted for more than 16% of the jobs cut in the 1991 survey period.

This trend has continued into 1994, as many of the nation's largest, most successful corporations, including IBM, General Motors, and Boeing, have announced one round of massive layoffs after another. Challenger, Gray & Christmas, a placement firm, says the pace of layoffs among large companies in 1993 ran well ahead of 1991, which was supposedly the bottom of the recent recession.[28]

While much of this change seems frightening to businesspeople, as well as to their employees, it may also give rise to fantastic new opportunities. Many of these people are likely to start their own smaller businesses due to the permanent disappearance of so many middle management or automatable jobs. Many may even keep working for their former firms as independent contractors or consultants.

In addition to enriching the overall business environment by creating a major upsurge in the formation of new, small, and flexible business entities, firms that cater to the needs of other small businesses may find the coming decade to be one of explosive growth and unparalleled opportunity.

Telecommuting

One of the most predictable trends, which is already well under way, is the growth of telecommuting, where more and more people work out of their homes, communicating with their clients or employers by use of personal computers, modems, faxes, or multiple phone lines. Already, some employers, like certain government agencies in Washington, D.C., are taking an intermediate step by setting up satellite telecommuting offices in suburban areas. By going to these nearby satellite offices, equipped with computer workstations, many workers can, on most days, avoid long and arduous commutes to downtown offices by piping their work product electronically to the main office instead.

A 1992 survey by Link Resources Corporation, a research and consulting firm, showed telecommuting has become a major factor in the economy almost overnight. The survey estimated that company employees who work at home part- or full-time increased in 1992 by 39%, over 1991, to

39 million individuals, most of whom are believed to be telecommuting. The survey apparently did not even take into account home-based businesses, which are also believed to be proliferating at startling rates.

Not all the consequences of increased telecommuting are positive. Some unforeseen side effects are already beginning to surface, such as rising workers' compensation costs for employers who have substantial numbers of employees working at home.

Apparently, employees who injure themselves at home tend to claim in many cases that such injuries are work-related, and therefore compensable under the workers' compensation system. In addition, injuries sustained while commuting are also more likely to be compensable, where such workers are constantly taking work back and forth between the office and home.

As a result, workers' compensation insurers have already begun to raise their rates for telecommuting employees. Don't overlook this potential expense when analyzing the costs and benefits of having more of your workforce telecommute.

Pending Law Changes

Now that one political party controls both the White House and Congress, look for significant law changes in 1994 and during the remainder of the Clinton administration. Many of these future law changes are sure to affect your business, for better or worse. Major new legislation to look for in the near future may include:

- Mandatory health care coverage — This is currently the Clinton administration's number one priority. The exact shape of change in this area is anyone's guess at this time. However, it is possible that the initial proposal to pay for universal health care with a payroll tax will not be part of the final plan, due to the enormous opposition to such a tax. Instead, look for some sort of mandated insurance coverage, probably with insurance rates and medical coverage terms set by the government.

  Part of the final package may also include a limit on deductions for medical insurance. Under such a limit, excess premiums paid for health care plans providing more than a defined "standard" level of benefits would not be deductible by employers and the excess payments would also be taxable income to the covered employee. Some portion of the additional costs of universal health care will be borne by the government. It seems likely the government will seek to fund the costs by imposing increased "sin" taxes on alcohol and cigarettes, and a national sales tax or value-added tax (VAT) of some kind cannot be ruled out as a possibility.

- Full deductibility of health insurance for the self-employed — The Clinton health care reform plan and several competing proposals have all endorsed an increase in the percentage of self-employed persons' health insurance deduction from the current 25% to 100%.

Such plans call for this deduction — which has expired and been renewed after the fact several times in recent years — to be made permanent. Such provisions, if enacted, would finally put self-employed business owners on a par with those who are incorporated, with regard to deductibility of their medical insurance costs.

- Taxation of S corporation taxable income as self-employment income — Another proposal that has surfaced in connection with the Clinton health care reform proposals is to tax the income of S corporation shareholders as self-employment income, as has long been the case with partners in partnerships. This would close what has long been perceived as a loophole in the taxation of S corporations, by subjecting owners to self-employment tax on their share of the net taxable income of the S corporation — presumably with exceptions being made for rental income and interest income, which have never been considered self-employment income for owners of unincorporated businesses.

- States may be allowed to tax out-of-state mail order vendors — Legislation is pending in Congress that would authorize states, for the first time, to enact legislation requiring out-of-state sellers to collect sales or use tax on interstate sales for goods shipped to residents of the state in question. For details, see the discussion of this proposed legislation in Section 9.8.

- Federal legislation regarding limited liability companies (LLCs) — Now that some four-fifths of the states have adopted LLC laws and the tax benefits of LLCs threaten to reduce federal income tax revenues, one congressional committee is already looking into the possibility of requiring LLCs to be taxed as corporations. LLCs are generally taxed as partnerships under current federal tax law.

- Striker replacement law — The Clinton Administration supported a striker replacement law in Congress in 1994, which was defeated in July by seven votes in the U.S. Senate. The intent of this proposed law is to overturn a 1938 Supreme Court decision that allows employers to fire workers who go on strike over economic issues, such as wages. If enacted, the proposed legislation will both prohibit employers from hiring permanent replacement workers during a strike and require them to rehire strikers after the strike ends. The proposed bill contains other provisions that tend to shift the balance of economic power to labor unions and impose major burdens on small, nonunion employers by making it easier for labor unions to organize the workforce of smaller firms. Although the bill was defeated in 1994, a Congressional election year, look for it to be reintroduced in the 1995–96 Congressional session.

- Information returns (1099s) for payments to corporations — Under current law, businesses do not have to file 1099 information return forms for most payments they make to corporations; however, Congress may soon eliminate this important exemption. Doing so would greatly increase the paperwork burden on nearly all businesses.

- Increase estimated tax "safe harbor" to 115% — The ink is hardly dry on the 1993 Deficit Reduction Act, which allows high-income individual taxpayers to base-their estimated tax payments on 110% of the prior year tax, and the House Ways and Means Committee is already considering raising the "safe harbor" percentage to 115% of the prior year tax liability.

Listed and discussed below are some other legal trends and new or pending legislation you should know about for future reference. This information provides possible tips for issues or rules which may affect your business.

Other Legal Trends and New or Pending Legislation

From all indications, the Clinton administration will support an early increase in the federal minimum wage, which is currently $4.25 an hour. Look for an increase in the $5.00-an-hour range before the end of 1995.

Minimum Wage

While changes in the minimum wage in the past have usually occurred only at intervals of several years, depending upon the mood and makeup of Congress, current proposals call for indexing the minimum wage so it would automatically increase each year with the cost-of-living or other index.

In 1988 and 1989, the National Conference of Commissioners on Uniform State Laws and the American Law Institute, respectively, both recommended that states should abolish or repeal their bulk sale or bulk transfer laws, which previously were in effect in all states. Both of these prestigious organizations concluded that bulk sale laws — originally adopted in most states in the late nineteenth century for the purpose of protecting creditors from fraud — no longer serve any useful purpose, but are instead a significant burden upon persons buying existing businesses.

Repeal of Bulk Sales Law

Since these recommendations were made, about half the states have repealed their bulk sales laws, and several have amended and simplified theirs. This trend is likely to continue in the next few years. For information on whether your state still has a bulk sale law in effect, contact your state's secretary of state's office.

Until recently, white-collar workplaces or offices generally created very little liability exposure for employers, with regard to hazardous working conditions. This, too, is beginning to change.

Video Display Terminals

In recent years, there have been an increasing number of lawsuits filed by employees in connection with hazards of working long hours on computers; and the city of San Francisco has adopted an ordinance that provides regulatory safeguards for workers using video display terminals (VDTs) for four or more hours per shift. A number of other city and state governments around the nation are also considering similar laws or ordinances because the use of computers in the workplace is such a universal phenomenon and because a number of threats to employees' health have arisen in connection with the heavy use of computers.

These threats range from excessive exposure to radiation emitted by VDTs to carpal tunnel syndrome, a common and debilitating nerve entrapment disorder that can cause severe pain and weakness in the wrist. Carpal tunnel syndrome can result from too many hours spent typing on a computer keyboard — as well as from many other tasks requiring repetitive flexing and extensions of the wrist.

Laws regulating VDTs are likely to begin appearing all over the country in the near future, and offices that don't pay attention to ergonomics — the study of equipment design to reduce workplace injury — may well become sitting ducks for lawsuits or fines. While most legal claims by employees regarding VDT usage have been imposed on workers' compensation insurers thus far, employers may become directly liable:

- If they participate actively in the design of computer systems or workstations that allegedly caused the injury to an employee; or
- If new state legislation removes such claims from the workers' compensation system and places financial responsibility directly upon employers.

Helpful Organizations

Communicate your thoughts on government policy and pending legislation to groups like the National Federation of Independent Business (NFIB), the U.S. Chamber of Commerce, your local chamber of commerce, or a trade association for your industry. It also can be helpful to call or write your senator, U.S. representative, or state legislator to voice your opinion in favor of or opposition to pending legislation or regulations that will affect your business.

Small business has been hit very hard by the government at all levels in recent years, and the more small business owners join and work together through helpful organizations, the better the chances of shaping the future.

Endnotes

1. I.R.C. §168.
2. I.R.C. §179(b)(1).
3. I.R.C. §6425.
4. 15 U.S.C. §§1051–1128.
5. I.R.C. §1244(c). The Tax Reform Act of 1984 §481(a).
6. I.R.C. §1211(b).
7. I.R.C. §1244(c)(1)(C).
8. I.R.C. §1244(c)(3).
9. I.R.C. §1244(d)(1)(B).
10. 16 C.F.R. §435.1.
11. 42 U.S.C.A. §§9601 *et seq.*
12. 42 U.S.C.A. §§6901 *et seq.*
13. 40 C.F.R. §280.22(a) and (b).
14. 40 C.F.R. §280.20.
15. 40 C.F.R. §280.21.
16. 33 U.S.C.A. §§1251–1376.
17. 33 U.S.C.A. §1344(a).
18. 42 U.S.C.A. §§7401–7626.
19. 15 U.S.C.A. §§2601–2629.
20. 7 U.S.C.A. §§135 *et seq.*
21. 42 U.S.C.A. §§4321–4347.
22. 29 C.F.R. §§1910 and 1926.58.
23. 15 U.S.C. §1691.
24. 15 U.S.C. §§1601 *et seq.*
25. 12 C.F.R. §226.2(a)(17).
26. 12 C.F.R. §226.4(c)(8).
27. 15 C.F.R. §806.
28. *Barron's National Financial Weekly.* August 30, 1993.

Internal Accounting Controls Checklist

- ☐ The same person who handles your cash receipts should not be the same person who makes the bank deposits. Cash is too easily misappropriated. Don't tempt an employee by letting him or her handle both of these duties.

- ☐ The person who writes checks should not also sign them or have the authority to sign checks. A different person should sign checks.

- ☐ Whoever signs checks should only sign them when the bill that is being paid is presented at the same time. The check number should be written on the bill to avoid double payments or payments to a nonexistent vendor. When you sign the check, be sure you know what the bill is for.

- ☐ Consider using some type of mechanical check imprinting equipment for all checks that are written, as a further means of preventing unauthorized payments. Such machines keep a record of the amount of any checks written.

- ☐ Use only prenumbered checks and keep all of the cancelled or voided checks in your records. This will help make it readily apparent if any additional checks are written without your knowledge.

- ☐ Complete a monthly bank reconciliation yourself or have your outside accountant do it. Never let the person who writes checks do the reconciliation.

- ☐ Deposit your daily cash receipts in the bank each day. Do not let cash collections for one day get mingled with the next day's collections.

- ☐ Use prenumbered sets of sales checks, invoices, and receipts to keep control of payments made and received. Duplicates will be kept track of by the individuals making sales, etc., and the master copy will enable you to make sure they account for all of their transactions.

- ☐ Use a petty cash fund and voucher system for stamps, small bills, and other small cash outlays. Do not use cash from the day's receipts to pay bills! Put a voucher or bill in the petty cash box each time money is taken out. When the fund is depleted, write a check to bring it back up to the maximum amount (say $50), and record all the vouchers at the time the check is cashed to replenish the fund.

- ☐ Maintain a master or control account for all of your accounts receivable, and reconcile it each month to the subsidiary accounts receivable. If someone is stealing money from customer payments, it will be easier to spot if the master and subsidiary accounts are reconciled regularly.

Chapter 10

Sources of Help and Information

If you're going to sin, sin against God, not the bureaucracy.
God will forgive you, but the bureaucracy won't.

— Admiral Hyman G. Rickover

10.1 General Considerations

Many government and private organizations provide free or low-cost services and publications to small business. Unfortunately, most small business owners only find out about a few of these sources and then only on a haphazard basis. This chapter summarizes many of the services and publications you may need to draw on as an owner or operator of a small business.

10.2 Professional Services

Select your accountant carefully. This is the one person outside your business who is most likely to be closely in touch with almost everything going on in your operation. Besides helping to set up your books and to establish systems for handling cash receipts and disbursements, a good accountant can provide a wealth of practical advice on a wide range of subjects that are important to your business, including planning for taxes, managing your money, obtaining financing, and evaluating business opportunities. Attorneys and bankers are often in a good position to recommend accountants.

Accountants

Attorneys

Unless you are starting out as a sole proprietor, you will usually need an attorney to prepare a partnership agreement or to set up a corporation. You will probably do well to consult an attorney anyway to make sure you are obtaining necessary licenses and permits or to help you obtain them in some cases. In most parts of the country, local bar associations have lawyer referral services that can put you in touch with attorneys in your area. In most cases, you will do better to ask an accountant or banker to recommend a good business lawyer. If you need highly specialized legal advice or representation, ask an attorney you know to recommend a specialist.

Bankers

Establish a good relationship with officers of the bank branch where you open an account for your business. While you may find it tough to borrow from your banker when you first go into business, he or she will be interested in keeping an eye on your business to see how it develops. It pays to cultivate the relationship to create a good impression before you want to apply for a business loan from the bank. Ask around before opening an account; find out if there is a bank in your area that is well known for lending to small businesses. Many of the large banks tend to be more interested in larger accounts, although different branch managers of the same bank may have very different ideas about working with small businesses. Your banker can be a useful source of free financial advice and a good connection when wanting to meet other business owners in your community.

Benefit Consultants

If you intend to establish a corporate pension or profit-sharing plan — or Keogh plan, if you have a number of employees — you may want to seek out a benefit consulting firm and obtain its proposals as to the type of benefit plan you need and how it should be structured. Since many such firms are primarily engaged in selling insurance products, such as life insurance, annuities, and investment contracts, designed for pension plans, the plan these firms design for you will almost invariably involve building in their products. Since an insured retirement plan may not necessarily make sense in your particular situation, ask your attorney or accountant to recommend a benefit consulting firm that does not have products to sell other than its consulting and plan administration services.

10.3 U.S. Small Business Administration and Other Helpful Agencies

The federal Small Business Administration (SBA) is one government agency that is genuinely helpful to small businesses. The SBA not only guarantees financing for many small businesses (see Section 9.7), but it also provides a number of valuable services.

One service you might find helpful is the Service Corps of Retired Executives (SCORE). SCORE is a program in which retired executives with many years of business experience volunteer their services as consultants to small businesses and charge only for their out-of-pocket expenses. Other SBA programs designed to provide assistance to small businesses include:

- Small Business Development Centers (SBDCs) — SBDCs are local centers operated by the state or community, with SBA assistance, to provide a wide range of business counseling and training. To see if your state has an SBDC network, refer to Section 11.10.
- Small Business Institutes (SBIs) — SBIs provide in-depth business counseling at hundreds of universities across the country.

In addition, SBA offices perform a variety of seminars and workshops on topics of interest to people who are starting or operating small businesses. Here are some of the seminars offered by the SBA.

- *Building a Business Plan*
- *Starting a New Business*
- *Preparing the Loan Proposal*

Contact your local SBA office for more information.

Business Information Centers

The SBA has also opened new Business Information Centers — each of which has a full set of all 51 of the books in this *Starting and Operating a Business* series — in Seattle, Houston, and Atlanta, with more coming soon in St. Louis, Los Angeles, and elsewhere. Each of these centers is designed to assist in disseminating helpful information to small business.

Telephone Hotlines

The SBA and several other government agencies maintain toll-free telephone hotline information services to assist businesses and taxpayers. Some of the more important ones to know about are listed below.

SBA Answer Desk

The SBA Answer Desk has a toll-free number of a small business information and referral service offered by the SBA, which you can call from anywhere in the continental United States, except Washington, D.C. For the number in D.C., check the local directory. The telephone Answer Desk offers a wide range of prerecorded, informational messages, any of which you may access if you have a touch-tone phone.

SBA Answer Desk
(800) U-ASK-SBA or 827-5722

SBA Online

The SBA has set up an electronic bulletin board system (BBS), called *SBA Online*, to help distribute information about its services and publications to anyone with a personal computer and modem. Since the service is sponsored by several major corporations, including Sprint, a huge variety of information is available toll-free nationwide via an 800-number. Typical SBA information available at no cost includes:

- Business development
- Financing services
- Government contracting opportunities
- Small business facts and programs
- Local Small Business Development Center and Business Information Center access
- Legislation and regulations
- SBA acquired assets for resale

In addition, the *SBA Online* established two new access numbers for 1994 that offer full usage of electronic mail services, as well as providing gateways to other government agencies and on-line services, including the Internet. The Internet is a world-wide computer database established by the government and research agencies to allow mail and information sharing. It has grown to become a popular backbone of the recently promoted "information superhighway."

Other outside services of *SBA Online* include access to Census Bureau data, the Internal Revenue Service, and the U.S. Patent and Trademark Office, as well as news from NASA, the Environmental Protection Agency, and other regulatory agencies. Internet services include the ability to write and receive Internet e-mail, and access to newsgroups.

Although full usage does require either 900 number charges per minute or a regular Washington D.C. toll call, the BBS provides a helpful *Offline Mail Reader* and estimates of file download time at various modem speeds. In addition, the BBS is well-designed for efficient usage, is accessible from virtually any computer set up, and provides numerous quick access utilities.

To log on to *SBA Online* for the first time:

- Set the following parameters for your modem's communication program:
  - No parity
  - Eight data bits
  - One stop bit
  - VT 102 terminal emulation

- Dial 1-800-697-4636 at any modem speed (2400 to 19.2K)
- Press Control key + "C" after you see a "Connect" message. You will see the SBA logo and be prompted to type in your name and business address.

The BBS then provides easy-to-use menu choices for navigation around the service. Be sure to read the "Help" menu for an excellent explanation of general BBS and computer terminology, as well *SBA Online* access tips.

After you are comfortable with the 800 number service, try the other access numbers:

SBA Online
Direct Dial
(202) 401-9600

900 Service
(900) 463-4636

Technical Support (for questions or problems)
(202) 205-6400

Small Business Hotline

The Small Business Hotline is a specialized free service offered by the Export-Import Bank to small exporters needing general information or problem-solving assistance relating to doing business abroad. It provides information on export credit and on assistance available from other government agencies and the private sector.

Small Business Hotline – Automated Info System
(800) 424-5201

Internal Revenue Service

The IRS has an assistance program called Tele-Tax. The program allows you to call a toll-free number in your state to listen to pre-recorded tax information that will answer many federal tax questions.

About 140 topics are available, including information on the Small Business Tax Education Program (STEP), business income, sole proprietorships, and the self-employment tax.

For more information on Tele-Tax, call the IRS's toll-free number to request *Publication 910, Guide to Free Tax Services*. This publication not only lists the many tax publications you can order, but it also lists the Tele-Tax phone numbers and topic numbers in your state.

Internal Revenue Service
(800) 829-3676

Trade Information Center

The Trade Information Center has a hotline where you can receive general information on exporting that is provided by various U.S. government agencies.

Trade Information Center
U.S. Department of Commerce
(800) USA-TRADE or 872-8723

Environmental Protection Agency Ombudsman

Like certain Scandinavian countries, the Environmental Protection Agency (EPA) has a small business ombudsman who gives easier access to the EPA, helps you comply with EPA regulations, and makes sure you are treated fairly in any EPA disputes.

EPA Small Business Ombudsman
(703) 305-5938
(800) 368-5888

Social Security Administration

If you want to find out what records the Social Security Administration (SSA) has on your earnings and your projected benefits at retirement age, you can file a simple form requesting a detailed printout of this information. This is something everyone should do once every few years because if the SSA has made a serious mistake in your earnings record, you have only a limited number of years in which you can contact them and have your record corrected.

To obtain the request form, call the SSA's toll-free number or write the SSA for this form at the Consumer Information Center address below.

Social Security Administration
(800) 772-1213

Consumer Information Center
Department 72
Pueblo, CO 81009

Corporate Agents, Inc.

There are also companies who can assist in the incorporation process, providing a variety of incorporation kits and services. One such company, Corporate Agents, Inc., can help you form your corporation in any state for as little as $39 (plus state fees), depending on the state. Some examples of complete costs for other states are $115 for Delaware, $169 for Florida, $331 for New York, and $1,014 for California.

The fees cover all costs, including all state filing fees and recording costs, preparing and filing articles of incorporation, and a registered agent's service fee for the first six months. Also available for a nominal additional cost are the corporate kits, which include the corporate seal, minute book, stock certificates, and sample forms and bylaws.

For more information on this company, you can send the preaddressed post card located at the back of this book or call Corporate Agents at the toll-free number below:

Corporate Agents, Inc.
1013 Centre Road
P.O. Box 1281
Wilmington, DE 19899
(800) 877-4224
FAX (302) 998-7078

10.4 Publications Regarding Small Business Operations

U.S. Small Business Administration

The U.S. Small Business Administration (SBA) has more than 50 helpful booklets and other publications on subjects of importance to new and existing small businesses. The publications, which sell for a nominal fee — usually about $0.50 (50 cents) to $1.00 each, and never more than $2.00 — can be obtained through your nearest SBA office or by calling the SBA Answer Desk and asking for a list of publications.

SBA Answer Desk
(800) U-ASK-SBA or 827-5722

You can also use the preaddressed post card in the back of this book to request lists of SBA publications.

Small Business Institutes

Small Business Institutes (SBIs) are located on university campuses throughout the United States. Part of a cooperative program with the SBA, SBIs offer you business assistance while furthering the education of college students. Students, supervised by faculty members, provide your business with:

- Free confidential consulting;
- In-depth analysis of your firm's business situation;
- Alternatives and recommendations to business problems; and
- Written and oral reports.

Headquartered at the University of Central Arkansas, the Small Business Institute Directors' Association (SBIDA) National Center and the Small Business Advancement Network perform research and gather information on small business. The SBIDA National Center is the link between all SBI universities and the government. The SBIDA also:

- Is the center of correspondence for SBI schools;
- Keeps records on all SBI schools;
- Publishes the *SBIDA News*;
- Processes SBIDA membership; and
- Is a center for advocacy.

The Small Business Advancement Network is an electronic bulletin board which provides information on grant opportunities, cooperative ventures between the SBA and SBI, and small business research. The network is available during regular business hours and is updated daily. For information on the SBI nearest you, contact:

SBIDA National Center
University of Central Arkansas
College of Business
UCA P.O. Box 4983
Conway, AR 72035-5002
(501) 450-5300

For more on the Small Business Advancement Network, contact:

Small Business Advancement National Center
University of Central Arkansas
College of Business
UCA P.O. Box 5018
Conway, AR 72035-0001
(501) 450-5377

The Oasis Press

The publisher of this book, The Oasis Press, has a number of how-to business guides and software programs targeted toward small businesses. Some of the most recent titles published by The Oasis Press include:

- *Bottom Line Basics: Understand and Control Business Finances.* This guide goes beyond accounting to help you plan, manage, and control your company's finances. (Paper, $19.95)
- *The Business Environmental Handbook.* Your company can be both environment-friendly and -profitable. This comprehensive guide tells you how. (Paper, $19.95)
- *Buyer's Guide to Business Insurance.* A step-by-step guide that gives you advice and tips for improving your business insurance costs, coverage, and service. (Paper, $19.95) A companion software, The Insurance Assistant, is also available from the publisher.
- *People Investment.* An up-to-date guide for staffing a business and avoiding today's legal hurdles. (Paper, $19.95)
- *Power Marketing.* A comprehensive guide that details successful marketing strategies for your business. (Paper, $19.95)
- *The Secrets to Buying and Selling a Business.* A guide designed to help both buyers and sellers in their quest to make the best deal possible. (Paper, $19.95)
- *Start Your Business: A Beginner's Guide.* This guide is the perfect companion to this *Starting and Operating a Business* book, helping you answer the essential questions regarding money matters, marketing, staffing, business plans, and other important start-up issues. (Paper, $8.95)

Information on these and other related resources from The Oasis Press is provided at the back of this book or it can be obtained by calling:

The Oasis Press
(800) 228-2275

Magazines

Here are some magazines that provide continuing information for businesses in general and small businesses in particular. There are also a number of specialized publications you may find helpful. Most of these publications can be located through your local library or news stand.

The Wall Street Journal
200 Liberty Street
New York, NY 10281
(212) 416-2898

D&B Reports
299 Park Avenue
New York, NY 10171-0002
(212) 593-6723

In Business
419 State Avenue
Emmaus, PA 18049-3717
(215) 967-4135

Success Magazine
P.O. Box 3038
Harlin, IA 51537
(212) 551-9500
(800) 234-7324

**Entrepreneur Magazine
Business Start-ups**
Subscriber Service
P.O. Box 58808
Boulder, CO 80322
(800) 421-2300

Business Review
P.O. Box 777
Cypress, TX 77429-0777
(713) 373-3535

Business Week
Subscriber Service
P.O. Box 506
Hightstown, NJ 08520
(800) 635-1200

Nation's Business
U.S. Chamber of Commerce
1615 H. Street, NW
Washington, DC 20062
(202) 463-5650

Inc.
Subscriber Service
P.O. Box 54129
Boulder, CO 80322-4129
(800) 234-0999

Small Business Opportunities
1115 Broadway, 8th Floor
New York, NY 10010-2803
(212) 807-7100

Small Business Reports
Subscriber Services
P.O. Box 53140
Boulder, CO 80322-3140
(800) 234-1094

Independent Business
National Federation of Independent Business
Membership Development Office
600 Maryland Avenue, SW, Suite 700
Washington, DC 20024
(202) 554-9000

Home Business Opportunities
P.O. Box 1606
Ozark, AL 36360
(205) 774-0990

Statistical Information

Some of the more important sources of statistical information that you will need if you do your own marketing research are:

Title	**Publisher**
Survey of Buying Power **Sales and Marketing Management Magazine** Comprehensive data on population, retail sales, and consumer buying income for states, counties, and cities.	**Bill Communications, Inc.** 355 Park Avenue South New York, NY 10010 (212) 592-6200
Publication Price List Titles on corporate relations, human resources, management, economic and business environments, and consumer research.	**Conference Board** 845 Third Avenue New York, NY 10022 (800) 872-6273
Survey of Current Business U.S. Department of Commerce's monthly survey of business trends and conditions.	**Superintendent of Documents** **U.S. Government Printing Office** Washington, DC 20402 (202) 783-3238
The Complete Information Bank for Entrepreneurs & Small Business Managers, Second Edition An excellent sourcebook which lists and describes hundreds of leading business books and other sources of help and information for small businesses.	**Center for Entrepreneurship** Wichita State University 1845 Fairmont Wichita, KS 67260-0147 (316) 689-3000
Encyclopedia of Business Information Sources, Ninth Edition Arranged by industry, this guide lists trade associations and major sources of statistical information.	**Gale Research, Inc.** 835 Penobscott Building Detroit, MI 48226 (313) 961-2242

U.S. Occupational Safety and Health Administration

The U.S. Occupational Safety and Health Administration (OSHA) provides a number of useful, free publications on OSHA requirements for small businesses. Two of the more important ones are listed below. Each is available from one of OSHA's ten regional offices or from one or more local OSHA offices in every state.

OSHA Handbook for Small Business (OSHA 2209)	Helpful handbook designed to assist small business employers to meet their legal requirements under the OSHA laws and regulations.
Recordkeeping Guidelines for Occupational Injuries and Illness (O.M.B. No. 1220-0029)	Provides useful summary of what records must be kept, who must keep them, and for how long.

OSHA offices can also provide you with a package or folder entitled, *Information from the Occupational Safety and Health Administration,* which includes the above publications, plus required posters and about a dozen other OSHA informational booklets and pamphlets. See the pre-addressed postcard at the back of the book for ordering booklets and required posters.

Securities and Exchange Commission

The SEC's Office of Small Business Policy publishes *Q & A: Small Business and the SEC*, which is a guide to special services, rules, regulations, and suggestions regarding a company's first public offering of stock. It is available from:

Office of Small Business Policy
Securities and Exchange Commission
450 Fifth Street NW
Washington, DC 20549
(202) 942-4040 (publications)

Equal Employment Opportunity Commission

The Equal Employment Opportunity Commission (EEOC) publishes a useful and comprehensive publication on all the discrimination laws that it enforces, such as civil rights, age discrimination, and equal pay. To obtain the publication that is entitled, *Laws Enforced by EEOC*, contact:

Office of Communications and Legislative Affairs
Equal Employment Opportunity Commission
1800 L Street NW
Washington, DC 20507
(202) 663-4900
(800) 669-3362

10.5 Do-It-Yourself Incorporation

If you want to form your own corporation and save several hundred dollars in legal fees, there are books that tell you how to do it and provide the forms you need; however, think carefully before you attempt to do this on your own. In some cases, setting up a corporation is not that complicated, and if you follow the instructions in a self-incorporation book precisely — if one is available for your state — you should be able to do it properly. But you will have to spend many hours carefully figuring out and then doing all that is required. Your time might be worth much more than the money you would save in legal fees because you could concentrate more on getting the business off to a good start. Check Section 11.10 to see if there is an incorporation book for your state.

10.6 Information Regarding Payroll Taxes and Withholding

Major offices of the IRS frequently put on seminars for new employers regarding payroll tax requirements. Call your local IRS office for information as to when such seminars will be held in your area. In addition, you may want to obtain *Circular E, Employer's Tax Guide,* and *Notice 109, Information About Depositing Employment and Excise Taxes.* Both can be obtained from the IRS office nearest you. In addition, the Matthew Bender Company publishes an excellent book called the *Payroll Tax Guide,* which covers almost every aspect of federal payroll tax returns.

Matthew Bender Company
(800) 223-1940

10.7 Other Useful Tax Publications

The publications below can also be obtained from your local IRS office:

Publication	Subject
Publication 334	*Tax Guide For Small Business Income and other Federal Taxes*
Publication 349	*Federal Highway Use Taxes on Heavy Vehicles*
Publication 378	*Fuel Tax Credits and Refunds*
Publication 463	*Travel, Entertainment, and Gift Expenses*
Publication 510	*Federal Excise Taxes*
Publication 541	*Tax Information on Partnerships*
Publication 542	*Tax Information on Corporations*

Publication	Subject
Publication 544	Sales and Other Dispositions of Assets
Publication 552	Recordkeeping Requirements
Publication 583	Taxpayers Starting a Business
Publication 587	Business Use of Your Home
Publication 589	Tax Information on S Corporations
Publication 910	Guide to Free Tax Services
Publication 937	Business Reporting

To order these free tax publications or other tax forms, call:

Internal Revenue Service
(800) 829-3676

10.8 ERISA Compliance

If your business has a pension or profit-sharing plan and you wish to handle your own Employee Retirement Income Security Act (ERISA) filings for the plan, obtain a copy of Charles D. Spencer & Associates' publication, *5500 Annual Reports for Employee Benefit Plans*. This publication will help you prepare the necessary *Form 5500* series through its easy-to-understand, step-by-step instructions. For ordering information, contact:

Charles D. Spencer & Associates, Inc.
250 South Wacker Drive, Suite 600
Chicago, IL 60606
(312) 993-7900

10.9 Information on Franchising

Title and Author	Publisher
Franchise Bible Erwin J. Keup	**The Oasis Press** 300 North Valley Drive Grants Pass, OR 97526 (800) 228-2275
Miscellaneous titles on franchise topics. Write for a catalog.	**International Franchise Association** 1350 New York Avenue, NW, Suite 900 Washington, DC 20005
Business Franchise Guide	**Commerce Clearing House, Inc.** 4025 West Peterson Avenue Chicago, IL 60646
Miscellaneous titles on franchise topics. Write for a catalog.	**Pilot Books** 103 Cooper Street Babylon, NY 11702

Title and Author	**Publisher**
Franchise Opportunities Handbook U.S. Department of Commerce	**Superintendent of Documents** **U.S. Government Printing Office** Washington, DC 20402
Franchising in the U.S. Michael M. Coltman	**Self-Counsel Press Inc.** 1704 North State Street Bellingham, WA 98225 (800) 663-3007
Franchisee Rights — A Self-Defense Manual ***for The Franchisee*** Alex Hammond	**Hammond & Morton** 1185 Avenue of the Americas New York, NY 10036
Franchising: Regulation of Buying and Selling ***A Franchise*** Philip F. Zeidman, Perry C. Ausbrook, and H. Bret Lowell	**Bureau of National Affairs, Inc.** 9435 Key West Avenue Rockville, MD 20850 (800) 372-1033
The Info Franchise Newsletter ***The Franchise Annual***	**Info Press** 728 Center Street Lewiston, NY 14092-0550 (716) 754-4669
Survey of Foreign Laws and Regulations ***Affecting International Franchising*** Compiled by the Franchising Committee of the Section of Antitrust Law of the American Bar Association	**Publications Planning and Marketing** **American Bar Association** 705 North Lake Shore Drive Chicago, IL 60611

Notes

State Laws & Related Resources

Notes to Pennsylvania Chapter

What's New

This update of the Pennsylvania chapter features new information and additions in several areas. The list below will help you locate the most significant changes by chapter–section number.

- Tax rate changes regarding Pennsylvania's unemployment tax – 11.5
- New sources of financial assistance programs – 11.9
- Sample of updated *Form REV 289 AS, Application for Tax License* – back of book
- Updated addresses and phone numbers – throughout chapter

If changes have occurred since publication of this update or if you have any questions, contact this office for assistance or referral to the appropriate agency.

Bureau of Small Business and Appalachian Development
Pennsylvania Department of Commerce
461 Forum Building
Harrisburg, PA 17120
(717) 783-5700

About the Author

The state author of *Starting and Operating a Business in Pennsylvania* is Adam S. Monks, who has updated this chapter through October 1993.

Mr. Monks is a partner in the international accounting firm of Ernst & Young. He is director of the Entrepreneurial Services Group, which includes the High Technology Group of Ernst & Young's Pittsburgh office. He is a certified public accountant with a bachelor's degree in accounting and a master's degree in business administration. He is a director of the Pittsburgh High Technology Council and is a member of several professional organizations, including the American Institute of Certified Public Accountants. Mr. Monks' professional experience spans more than 20 years assisting start-up companies in a variety of ways.

Acknowledgments

Mr. Monks would like to thank the following individuals in the Pittsburgh office of the Ernst & Young Entrepreneurial Services Group for their contributions to this chapter: Richard L. Vareha (CPA), senior manager; Gary A. LeDonne (CPA), senior manager; Karl Schwartz (CPA); David L. Mikan (CPA), manager; and Pamela Masters (CPA).

Chapter 11

State Laws and Taxes

11.1 Introduction

Starting and operating a business in Pennsylvania is made much more attractive because of the commonwealth's highly-diversified economy, well-educated workforce, strong transportation system, and pro-business government. These factors and more have inspired approximately 30 Fortune 500 companies to headquarter within the commonwealth.[1] Possibly your new or existing business will be a future Fortune 500 company to prosper in Pennsylvania!

Pennsylvania has a highly diversified economy, with manufacturing as the commonwealth's most important activity. In fact, employment in manufacturing is exceeded only by California, Ohio, and New York.[2] You will find both Philadelphia and Pittsburgh are the leading manufacturing centers for Pennsylvania. In addition, agriculture, tourism, and a growing service-related industry also contribute to the commonwealth's economic well being.

Diversified Economy

Boasting a workforce of approximately five million people, your business should have no trouble recruiting experienced and well-trained employees. Many of these employees have either taken advantage, or can take advantage, of Pennsylvania's four top-notch state universities or its numerous other public and private colleges. In addition, customized job training programs are available to train employees to match specific job requirements. Pennsylvania provides funds for these programs to help reduce the business costs of start ups and expansions and to provide

Strong Workforce

needed employees. For more information on customized job training programs, refer to Section 11.9.

Comprehensive Transportation Network

Pennsylvania is a Middle Atlantic state that is within one-day access to more than 60% of the retail and industrial consumers in the United States and Canada.[3] Enhancing this state's comprehensive transportation network are roadways, water ports, railroads, and airports. For example, Interstate 80, also known as the Keystone Shortway, is a superhighway that has opened central Pennsylvania to industrial development by providing a link to the Midwest and the Atlantic Coast.

Pennsylvania's waterways offer unique port coverage with a deepwater port at Philadelphia, a Great Lakes port at Erie, and an inland-water port at Pittsburgh.[4] Your business definitely has a good head start due to Pennsylvania's strategic location and effective transportation network.

Pro Business Attitude

In addition to its highly diversified economy, strong industrious workforce, and extensive transportation network, Pennsylvania's government has created specific agencies and programs designed to encourage and help small business. In particular, the Bureau of Small Business and Appalachian Development of the Pennsylvania Department of Commerce is a vital resource for anyone wanting to start or who is already in business within Pennsylvania. This bureau can refer you to appropriate agencies and provide general business information.

To further assist business owners, Pennsylvania offers several financing programs that stimulate the productive use of the significant available resources. The more popular programs are the Pennsylvania Industrial Development Authority (PIDA), the Ben Franklin/IRC Partnership, the Customized Job Training (CJT) Program, and the Enterprise Zone Program.

Several of these programs provide low-interest loans to new and expanding businesses for land, buildings, machinery, and equipment. Other programs offer grants and funds for advanced technology projects, and others provide tax incentives for employment of certain individuals.

You can also find many sources of capital through financial institutions, such as banks and savings and loans, and a significant number of venture capitalists. Pennsylvania has several major banks and many local banks that are interested in having entrepreneurial companies as their clients.

There has been a significant growth in venture capital for technology companies and, more recently, for any type of company requiring funding in industries when growth with profits is anticipated.

As highlighted above, Pennsylvania has much to offer if you are wishing to start, relocate, or operate a business in the commonwealth. The following sections will deal with the state-related aspects of general areas covered in the first ten chapters of this book.

11.2 Choosing the Legal Form of the Business

One of the first decisions you must make when starting your new business is to choose which legal form of business organization you will adopt. There are three basic forms: the sole proprietorship, the partnership, and the corporation. General considerations for choosing a legal form of business are located in sections 2.1–2.4. More state-specific considerations for Pennsylvania are discussed below. Other requirements, such as business name registration, taxes, wage-hour, and labor laws, are discussed in sections 11.4–11.7.

Sole Proprietorships

A sole proprietorship is a business that is owned by one person. Because there are no formal legal requirements for setting up a sole proprietorship, you will find it relatively simple to form and operate. A sole proprietorship offers you greater personal control of your business, fewer tax requirements and filings than other forms of business, and all the profits or losses. You will be personally liable, however, for all your business' debts and obligations, as discussed in Section 2.2.

Similar to federal tax law, as an owner of a sole proprietorship in Pennsylvania, your business earnings or losses will be subject to income taxes and you report them with your personal individual income tax returns.[5] To report your Pennsylvania net income, use *Form PA-40, Pennsylvania Individual Tax Return*. The top individual income tax rate in Pennsylvania is 2.8%.

For additional information on sole proprietorship taxes and requirements, refer to sections 11.4 and 11.5.

Partnerships

Any two or more individuals or entities who agree to contribute money, labor, property, or skill to a business and who agree to share in its profits, losses, and management are considered to have a partnership.

General Partnerships

As a partner in a general partnership, you have the right to share in management and have unlimited personal liability for the partnership's debts, taxes, and other obligations. Partnership agreements are not required by law, but it is sound business practice for you and your partner(s) to draw up a partnership agreement that, at a minimum, outlines basic business issues. Consider consulting an attorney when writing your partnership agreement.

Because the partnership itself is not taxed,[6] you report your earnings from the partnership on your personal income tax return, *Form PA-40*. Be advised your partnership is required to withhold personal income tax for any nonresident partners.

In addition to reporting your personal income tax, the partnership must report its earnings on *Form PA-65*. This form must be filed with the

Pennsylvania Department of Revenue, along with a copy of *Form 1065*, the federal partnership information return.

Limited Partnerships

A limited partnership can be formed between two or more individuals, partnerships, corporations, or other entities. In this type of partnership, limited partners have limited liability and are only liable for the amount of their investment in the partnership. In exchange for this limited liability, limited partners cannot participate in the day-to-day management of the business. That responsibility is left to the general partners who have unlimited liability. A limited partnership must always have at least one general partner and at least one limited partner. There must be a written limited partnership agreement.

To form a limited partnership in Pennsylvania, you are required to file a *Certificate of Limited Partnership* with the department of state's office.

Certain limited partnerships and partnership associations may be treated as either partnerships or corporations for tax purposes by Pennsylvania law.[7] For example, certain real estate investment companies are required to file corporation returns and are taxed as individual entities. To determine your correct tax status, check the specific legal requirements that apply to your particular business.

Corporations

A corporation is a more complicated form of business because it is considered a distinct legal entity and has a legal status or existence separate from you, the incorporator or owner. One of the main advantages to incorporating your business is that you are not personally liable for the corporation's debts, as long as you comply with all the necessary corporate formalities and recordkeeping requirements. To learn more about corporate formalities, obtain a copy of *The Essential Corporation Handbook* by Carl Sniffen from your local bookstore or through The Oasis Press.

If you are considering incorporating your business, consult an attorney to be sure you know what your responsibilities are and to better understand your options. To form a corporation, you will need to know how to file articles of incorporation, what types of taxes to expect, and how to comply with state securities laws.

A brief overview of some of these issues is presented below. Other requirements are discussed in sections 11.4 and 11.5. Keep in mind you will need to research more details once you make your decision to incorporate. One office that can help you with state requirements is:

Corporation Bureau
Pennsylvania Department of State
P.O. Box 8722
Harrisburg, PA 17105-8722
(717) 787-1057

The Corporation Bureau can send you all corporate forms on diskette for a small fee. Call the above office to request an order form.

If yours is a domestic corporation — incorporated in Pennsylvania — you need to: **Domestic Corporations**

- File articles of incorporation with the Pennsylvania Department of State;
- Advertise the intention to incorporate;
- Register with the commonwealth;
- Maintain a registered office within Pennsylvania; and
- Pay the required $100 filing fee.[8]

As a corporate owner, your ownership interest is determined by the amount of stock you purchased and what percentage you own of the total share of the corporation. As an owner, you can receive income in two ways. First, by working in the business, you will be considered an employee and receive a paycheck with appropriate payroll taxes deducted. Second, you can receive distributions of profits in the form of dividends, which are taxable to you as income. This income is reported on your personal income tax return, while the corporation itself must file its own income tax return. See the discussion on corporate taxation which follows for more details.

If your business is incorporated in another state and you seek to do business in Pennsylvania, your corporation will be considered a "foreign corporation." In order to do business in Pennsylvania, your corporation is required to file an application for certificate of authority with the Pennsylvania Department of State along with a $180 filing fee. Your foreign corporation will be subject to taxation and fees.[9] Contact the Pennsylvania Department of Revenue for tax information specific to foreign corporations. **Foreign Corporations**

Pennsylvania recognizes S corporations, and as a general rule, affords them the same tax treatment as is afforded to S corporations under federal law. Under both state and federal law, an S corporation acts as a conduit of income from a corporation to its shareholders. The result is that the corporation itself incurs no corporate income tax liability; rather, individuals who own stock pay tax based on their distributive share of earnings. Each shareholder pays tax on the percentage of earnings which represents the pro rata share of his or her stock ownership.[10] **S Corporations**

S corporations are specifically exempted from Pennsylvania corporate net income tax; however, a Pennsylvania S corporation is subject to both the capital stock tax and corporate loans tax. In addition, S corporations are required to withhold personal income tax for each nonresident shareholder.

When electing S corporation status, your corporation must elect under federal law to be eligible to be an S corporation for Pennsylvania. Election must be by unanimous consent of the shareholders and is limited to corporations with no more than 35 shareholders, one class of stock, a valid election under the Internal Revenue Code, and no investment income in excess of 25% of gross receipts in any year. The election must be made on or before the 15th day of the third month of the current taxable year to be effective for the current year. The election remains in effect until it is either revoked or terminated.

An S corporation in Pennsylvania must file an informational tax return, *Form PA-20S*. This return must reflect all items of gross income and deductions, list the names and addresses of shareholders, and the state amounts distributed to each shareholder. This return, with a copy of your federal return attached, is due 30 days after the deadline for the federal S corporation return.[11] For federal information on S corporations, see Section 2.5.

Professional Corporations

Pennsylvania recognizes professional corporations as corporate entities. In professional corporations, only members of the particular profession involved — such as medical, legal, or accounting — may be shareholders. A professional corporation is taxed as a corporation but does not share limited liability protection against professional malpractice claims.[12]

Annual Reports

Once your corporation has completed its initial filings and registrations, you will have to remember to file its annual report. The annual report must be filed with the Corporation Bureau after the close of the corporation's fiscal year. Failure to file this report could result in your corporation's charter being revoked or suspended.

Corporate Taxation

In addition to federal taxes affecting corporations, as discussed in Section 2.4, Pennsylvania corporations are subject to:

- A corporate income tax
- A capital stock or franchise tax
- A corporate loans tax

Corporate Income Tax

Pennsylvania levies a corporate net income tax on both domestic and foreign corporations. A corporation will be subject to the tax for owning property or capital within Pennsylvania or for conducting business activities within the commonwealth.

Pennsylvania Corporate Tax Report, Form RCT-101, is used to file corporate income tax with the Pennsylvania Department of Revenue. The return is due on the 15th day of the fourth month after the end of the tax year. Pennsylvania uses the corporation's federal taxable income as a base and modifies that figure by statutorily prescribed inclusions and deductions to determine state taxable corporate income.[13]

Multistate corporations are required to apportion income using a three-factor formula to determine Pennsylvania taxable income. The Pennsylvania corporate tax rate is 12.25% of taxable income.[14]

Capital Stock Tax

A capital stock tax is levied on Pennsylvania corporations as a form of property tax and is calculated based on the value of capital stock.[15] The value of capital stock is determined by a fixed formula of average earnings and corporate equity. A fraction of the value of the corporation's capital stock is taxed, based on a taxable asset formula. Certain assets are exempt, including property outside Pennsylvania and those assets employed in manufacturing, processing, research, and development operations.[16]

The capital stock tax is reported with your corporate net income tax return. The current rate for this tax is 1.275% per dollar value of capital stock, with a minimum tax of $300.[17] Corporations are required to make estimated capital stock tax payments on a quarterly basis, just like with income tax. The first $50,000 of capital stock net worth is exempt from this tax.

Franchise Tax

Pennsylvania imposes a franchise tax on foreign corporations. The franchise tax is considered to be a levy on the privilege of doing business in the commonwealth rather than a property tax. This franchise tax is based on the value of capital stock of the corporation and the relationship of that value to the right of the corporation to conduct business in Pennsylvania.[18]

The franchise tax rate is the same rate as the capital stock tax rate.[19] The mechanics and administration of the capital stock and franchise taxes are the same; thus, future references to capital stock tax are equally applicable to the franchise tax.

Corporate Loans Tax

In addition to the corporation net income tax and capital stock tax, a corporation may be required to pay a corporate loans tax. This intangible personal property tax is imposed on loans and other forms of debt issued by corporations to individual residents of Pennsylvania. The tax rate is four mills on the nominal value of indebtedness on which interest is paid.[20] This nominal value is calculated by dividing the interest paid during the year by the interest rate applicable to the debt.

The capital stock tax, franchise tax, and corporate loans tax are administered by the Bureau of Corporation Taxes within the Pennsylvania Department of Revenue.

Securities Laws

When your newly formed corporation issues shares of its stock to you or to any other shareholders, you must be very careful to comply with both federal and Pennsylvania securities laws. Otherwise, you could be a target for lawsuits from disgruntled investors in your corporation or even criminal prosecution.

Stock issued by corporations may be subject to registration requirements of the Securities and Exchange Commission (SEC) or the Pennsylvania Securities Commission. Pennsylvania exempts some classes of stock and types of securities from registering with the commonwealth. Among these are stock in S corporations; securities of credit unions, industrial loan associations, and trade or professional associations; and shares of professional corporations.[21]

In the case of the typical small corporation start up, you will probably be able to qualify for exemption from registering with the Securities and Exchange Commission (SEC), under federal laws, as described in Section 4.14. For more information about the registration of stock, exemptions, and state securities (or blue sky) laws in general, consult your attorney or contact the department of state's office.

11.3 Buying an Existing Business — State Legal Requirements

Buying a business is always a significant undertaking, and as a prospective purchaser, you must investigate the business being acquired as thoroughly as possible to avoid hidden liabilities and pitfalls. Be sure your investigation includes:

- A review of business books and records, including tax returns, payroll records, current receivables and payables, and minute books;
- A physical inventory of all furniture, fixtures, equipment, inventory, and tangible personal or real property being acquired;
- A review of the status of any leases, contracts, or pending litigation;
- A search to determine if the seller has any overdue taxes, such as unemployment tax, owed to the Pennsylvania or federal governments;
- A review of all intangible property rights, such as patent, trade or service marks, and copyrights; and
- Discussions with customers and suppliers of the business.

In many instances, you or the seller may want to keep the potential sale confidential, so your discussions with customers and suppliers may be limited. Any purchasing agreement should contain a detailed set of representations and warranties concerning the business being acquired. You may also wish to consider using an escrow or set-off provisions to provide recourse in the event a hidden liability is discovered after closing.

Purchasing an existing business is one endeavor you should not attempt without the assistance of an attorney. For more information on buying a business, refer to Chapter 3. Important new environmental laws you need to be aware of when purchasing an existing business are discussed in Section 9.9.

Bulk Sales Law

When a business sells all or substantially all of its assets or enters into a major transaction that is not part of its ordinary business activities, the bulk sales law applies. Like most other states, Pennsylvania's bulk sales law follows the general requirements outlined in the Uniform Commercial Code (UCC). The purpose of this law is to protect the rights of creditors, such as suppliers and others, who have advanced goods or money to a business and have not yet been paid.

The bulk sales law is of particular importance to you, because as purchaser of an existing business, you are required to perform certain duties under this law to ensure that the rights of the seller's creditors are protected. To comply with this law, both you and the seller have certain responsibilities.

- The seller must furnish you with a list of the names and correct addresses of all his or her creditors and those claiming to be creditors.
- You and the seller must prepare a list of all items of property to be transferred.
- You must notify each creditor in advance, by certified mail or in person, that a transfer is about to occur.
- You must keep the property list on file and make it available to the public for at least six months.
- You must notify the Pennsylvania Department of Revenue at least ten days before the sale.

Pennsylvania issues a bulk sales clearance certificate to the seller after all corporate tax reports and payment of any tax liability have been made. You must obtain this clearance certificate from the seller. Failure to do so will result in your becoming jointly liable with the seller for any outstanding taxes owed to the state by the seller.[22]

Once you have complied with the Pennsylvania requirements above, the burden shifts to the seller's creditors to take some action to protect their rights. Compliance will also protect you from later claims against the assets you have purchased. If you fail to comply with these provisions, it could cause you major financial hardship. To be sure you meet the requirements of the bulk sales law, consult with your attorney.

Recorded Security Interests

Before closing a deal, it is important for you to know if there are any security interests or liens against any of the assets of the business that would interfere with your receiving clear title to any part of it. To protect yourself, have your attorney thoroughly research county, state, and federal records before you finalize your agreement to acquire the property.

Of course, if the transaction involves a purchase of real property, you should also have a title search performed to find out if the seller has good title and if there are any recorded deeds of trust or other claims against the property that the seller has not disclosed to you. You also want to make sure that the title grants you adequate means of access to the property.

For more information, contact:

Uniform Commercial Code Section
Pennsylvania Department of State
P.O. Box 8721
Harrisburg, PA 17105
(717) 787-8712

Unemployment Tax Experience Rating

A company's unemployment tax experience rate determines the amount that must be contributed to Pennsylvania's unemployment fund. If the seller has earned a better unemployment tax experience rating than you would receive as a new employer, you may wish to explore the option of taking over the seller's rate when you acquire the business.

In Pennsylvania, the new employer's rate is 3.8255%, so if the seller's rate is less than this, contact the Pennsylvania Department of Labor and Industry to see about applying for the lower rate.[23]

Bureau of Unemployment Compensation
Pennsylvania Department of Labor and Industry
(717) 787-4677 (Employer charges)

Unemployment Tax Release

When you purchase an existing business, look into its history of activity with unemployment taxes. You will want to be sure that the seller has made all the required unemployment reports and payments; otherwise, you may be held liable for any unpaid taxes. To avoid becoming liable for any unpaid unemployment taxes owed to the state by the seller, you should require the seller to obtain a tax clearance certificate from the Pennsylvania Department of Revenue. This certificate will show whether or not the seller has filed reports and paid unemployment contributions on schedule, as well as indicate any balance due regarding Pennsylvania withholding taxes.

To protect yourself from having to pay unanticipated back taxes, consider using an escrow or provisions in your purchasing agreement to limit your liability as successor/employer for any prior unpaid contributions.

Sales Tax Release

Pennsylvania requires each business collecting sales tax to register with the Pennsylvania Department of Revenue and to obtain its own identification number. The liability for sales tax collected applies only to the business using a particular identification number. Therefore, when purchasing an existing business, apply for a new identification number and notify the Pennsylvania Department of Revenue of the cancellation of the previous owner's number. As long as you do not use the previous owner's identification number, you will have no liability for his or her sales tax. Forms are provided for these procedures.[24] When you purchase an entire business, the sale is exempt from sales tax. However, real estate and motor vehicle transfer taxes may apply.

Environmental Warranties

Today, many purchasers of businesses are being held liable for the environmental problems created by their predecessors. There are many federal and state laws and regulations regarding the environment which you must consider. Environmental laws pertain to air, water, storage of hazardous materials — including some very common household-type products — waste disposal, underground storage tanks, and other matters. Clean-up costs can sometimes exceed the cost of the property acquired.

As a result, you may want to consider an environmental audit of the property before you buy it. The audit would test the soil and water of any real estate being acquired to determine the environmental condition of the property. The purchase agreement should contain detailed representations and warranties of the seller stating that:

- The seller has not violated any environmental law or regulation; and
- The seller will reimburse you against any cost or liability imposed for environmental matters occurring before the acquisition.

For additional information about environmental issues, refer to Section 9.9.

11.4 State Requirements that Apply to Nearly All New Businesses

Regardless of the legal form of business organization you choose, your business will be required to comply with a number of requirements in Pennsylvania, such as obtaining business licenses, paying various taxes, and registering your fictitious business name.

There are also local requirements, taxes, and restrictions that may apply to your business. Like state requirements and taxes, local requirements can change every year. Before starting your business, contact the appropriate state or local government agencies to make sure your business complies with state and local laws. This section introduces you to several basic state requirements and offers further information on what you need to do.

Business Licenses and Permits

If you start a business in Pennsylvania, you will probably need at least one license from the state and others from the city or county in which you conduct business. To find out what type of local license you may need, contact your city hall or county clerk's office. As stated in sections 4.3 and 9.9, make sure your business also conforms to local zoning laws, building codes, health and environmental requirements, and fire and police regulations by obtaining the necessary permits.

Your business may also require state licenses based on your occupation, as discussed in Section 4.4. For a more detailed listing of occupations and businesses that require state licenses, refer to Section 11.6.

Estimated Income Taxes

One of the most surprising concepts to new entrepreneurs is that, as a business owner, you will have to estimate how much money you will make before you make it. Then, several times each year you must pay taxes on the amount you have estimated.

No matter which business form you choose, filing and paying Pennsylvania estimated taxes must now become part of your regular agenda. If you don't have the money to pay estimated income taxes, get your accountant's advice on whether you should get a loan to cover the tax when due or pay underpayment penalties to the government after the end of the year. Note that any state tax penalties you pay — unlike the state tax itself — will not be allowed as a deduction on your federal tax return.

Individual

If your business is a sole proprietorship or partnership, you must report the business income — whether it is actually distributed to you or not — on your personal tax return. If you expect your Pennsylvania taxable income to exceed $2,500 during the calendar year, you will need to pay estimated income taxes. To do this, contact the Pennsylvania Department of Revenue and obtain *Form PA-40ES, Declaration of Estimated Personal Income Tax.*[25] Your initial filing, however, will be on *Form PA-40ESR.* You and your spouse may file a joint declaration of estimated personal income tax.

The estimated tax payments are due in four equal installments on the 15th of April, June, September, and January. The commonwealth will not impose a penalty for underpayment of tax, provided one of these conditions is true:[26]

- The amount of tax prepaid is at least equal to the tax on the previous year's income at the current year's tax rate.
- The amount of tax prepaid is at least 90% of the tax due in the current year.

If your income falls under any one of the following eight classes of income, you will have to pay individual estimated income taxes:

- Compensation and wages;
- Net profits from a business, profession, or farm;
- Interest income;
- Dividend income;
- Net gain from sale of property;
- Net gain from rents, royalties, patents and copyrights;
- Net gain from estates or trusts; and
- Gambling and lottery winnings.[27]

After your first year of paying estimated taxes, you will probably automatically receive forms to use in future years, but even if the forms don't come, you are still responsible for filing and paying on time.

Corporate

If your business is a corporation subject to capital stock and corporate net income taxes, you are required to pay estimated taxes using *Form REV-857.*

For both taxes, you may use a safe harbor equal to the second prior year's tax liability, provided it meets certain requirements. Pre-payment obligations will be satisfied for both taxes if 90% of the tax due is paid in quarterly installments due on the 15th day of the third, sixth, ninth, and twelfth months of your corporation's tax year. Payments for the capital stock tax should be made in each quarter at the rate of 25% of the amount due.

For both taxes, any amount of the total tax not paid through quarterly installments must be paid by the 15th day of the fourth month following the end of a corporation's tax year. A corporation is required to file *Form RCT 101-PA, Corporate Tax Report*, or *Form REV-853, Annual Extension Request*, with the Pennsylvania Department of Revenue on or before the 15th day of the fourth month following the end of the previous tax year.[28] These forms will be mailed to the corporation by the Pennsylvania Department of Revenue near the end of the tax year.

Failure to make timely payments will result in interest charges. If 100% of the previous year's tax liability was paid in a timely manner during the current year, there is generally no penalty for underpayment of estimated tax.

Sales and Use Taxes

If your business is involved in making retail sales or in providing certain services, you must collect sales tax on each separate sale at retail of tangible personal property or services.[29] The law requires every person maintaining a business in Pennsylvania and involved in the sale or lease of tangible personal property or services to collect and remit sales tax to the Pennsylvania Department of Revenue.[30] "Person," as defined in the statute, includes a natural person, partnerships, corporations, and other entities.[31]

The Pennsylvania sales tax rate is 6%.[32] Sales originating in Philadelphia are subject to an additional 1% local sales tax. Another responsibility you have regarding the sales and use tax is that you must maintain records of sales made and tax collected. The Pennsylvania Department of Revenue may review such records during a period of up to three years.[33]

Sales tax returns are filed on *Form PA-3R, Sales, Use, and Hotel Occupancy Return*. New businesses file returns on a quarterly basis for the first year of operation. Returns are subsequently filed quarterly, unless total tax liability for the third calendar quarter exceeds $600. If that occurs, monthly filings are then required.[34]

Underpayment or failure to pay sales tax may result in penalties and interest in addition to liability for the tax itself.[35]

Sales Tax License

You will need to apply for sales tax licenses from the Pennsylvania Department of Revenue, which will authorize your business to collect sales tax and to resell merchandise.[36]

To obtain a sales tax license, contact the Pennsylvania Department of Revenue and request *Form REV-289, Application for License*. There is no charge for the license. The lack of a license does not excuse you from collecting and paying the tax. Your business is liable for the full amount of the tax whether you collect it or not.[37] A sample of an *Application for*

License is provided at the end of this book. Questions regarding the application should be directed to:

Registration Division
Bureau of Business Trust Fund Taxes
Pennsylvania Department of Revenue
(717) 787-7129

Occasional Sales

Sales tax is not imposed on isolated sales of property or services of exempt organizations, such as charities. Isolated sales are infrequent and nonrecurring in nature. Typically, these would include sales by persons not in the business of providing services, retail sales, or sales by vendors that do not regularly sell such property or services in the ordinary course of business.[38]

Sales Tax Exemption Certificate

When you purchase merchandise your business will resell, lease, or rent to others, you are exempt from paying sales tax on it if you have given the seller a sales tax exemption certificate, *Form REV-1220*, to keep on file.[39] This certificate shows the seller that the state has authorized your business to resell that merchandise, so sales tax does not have to be collected on it until you resell it later and collect the tax.

Use Tax

Use tax is intended to tax the use of all property purchased outside the state — where Pennsylvania sales tax has not been collected — but actually used within Pennsylvania. Use tax also applies to items that were exempt from sales tax when purchased — such as items bought for resale — that you end up using instead of reselling.

Property Taxes

The state does not impose a tax on real property; however, taxes are imposed on real estate by counties, cities, boroughs, townships, and local school districts. Real estate typically includes buildings, houses, land, mills, and factories. Exemptions are provided for churches, burial grounds, public property, and property owned by a public charity.

A personal property tax is levied by counties, the cities of Pittsburgh and Philadelphia, and the school district of Pittsburgh. The tax is only levied on certain classes of intangible personal property owned by a resident of Pennsylvania. There is no tax on tangible personal property. Taxable intangible personal property includes:

- Shares of stock, bonds, notes, judgments, and mortgages you hold against another person;
- Accounts bearing interest; and
- Income from a trust located in another state.

Exemptions include:
- Property held for religious, charitable, or educational organizations;
- Shares of stock in banks and certain financial institutions;

- Shares of stock in corporations doing business within the state; and
- Interest-bearing accounts in financial institutions.

The personal property tax rate is $4 per $1,000 (4 mills) of value. Residents of Pittsburgh are subject to a cumulative tax rate of $12 per $1,000 of value because Allegheny County, the city, and the school district each impose a tax. The personal property tax returns are due the 15th day of February for Allegheny County and Philadelphia.

Business Privilege Taxes

Philadelphia and Pittsburgh impose business privilege taxes on both incorporated and unincorporated entities engaging in business within the cities. Returns and licenses are required to be filed annually. The business privilege tax is based primarily on the taxable receipts of the business, as defined by the local authority. Credits are provided for certain other taxes paid to the city.

Fictitious or Assumed Business Name

A fictitious name is any name used in the course of business that does not include the full legal name of all the owners of the business. If your business goes by any name other than your own real name, your business is operating under a fictitious name. A fictitious name might also suggest the existence of additional owners by using such words as "company," "associates," or "group." If you operate a sole proprietorship and use your own true name in the business name, you probably do not have to register the name.

The use of fictitious names is governed by the Fictitious Names Act of 1982.[40] The scope of this act includes individuals, corporations, partnerships, and any other entities which regularly conduct business activities in Pennsylvania. Expressly exempt from the registration requirements are nonprofit or professional activities, limited partnerships — if registered with the Pennsylvania Department of State — and unincorporated associations. The Pennsylvania Department of State imposes several requirements concerning the application, amendment, cancellation, and withdrawal of fictitious or assumed names.

Although being the first to register a certain name probably keeps any other business in your industry from using that name in your state, it is not a universal guarantee. If name protection is critical to your business — especially if you will be marketing in more than one state — it is best to discuss your situation with an attorney who specializes in this area of law.

To register your business name in Pennsylvania, contact the Corporation Bureau of the Pennsylvania Department of State office for forms and specifics on how to complete the procedure. You can also mail the preaddressed post card provided at the back of this book for more information.

Corporation Bureau – Fictitious Name Search
Pennsylvania Department of State
(717) 787-1057

Electronic Funds Transfer Requirements

You may be required to remit tax payments by Electronic Fund Transfer (EFT) if your tax payments are above a specified dollar amount. This new requirement is applicable to the several taxes listed:

Sales and use	Public utility realty
Employer withholding	Gross receipts
Corporate net income	Motor carrier
Capital stock/franchise	Fuel use
Mutual thrift institutions	Oil company franchise
Bank shares	Liquid fuels
Title insurance and trust shares	Malt beverages
Insurance premiums	

If you remit a total tax payment of $20,000 or more for the above taxes, remit your payments by EFT. If you are unable to comply, remit your payments by certified or cashier's check in person or by courier to the Pennsylvania Department of Revenue.[41]

Checklist of State Requirements

To summarize, you will have many decisions to make when starting a new business. One decision is the type of business to undertake. The specific business you choose may be subject to registration, licensing, taxes, or other requirements that apply only to your particular product, service, or activity.

Another important decision your new business faces concerns location. Counties and cities have different property tax rates, and this may provide an incentive to locate in a certain area. A third decision that confronts your new business is which legal form you will choose. Are the advantages of incorporation greater than the disadvantages caused by corporate taxes and additional recordkeeping and paperwork?

Most businesses, regardless of type, location, or form, will be subject to the taxes and requirements discussed in this chapter. It will be your responsibility as a new business owner to understand and comply with all the regulations and reporting requirements that apply to your business. This checklist summarizes the main requirements that you will need to satisfy to start a business in Pennsylvania whether or not you have employees.

Requirements	Proprietorships	Partnerships	Corporations
Articles of incorporation			X
Estimated income tax	X	X	X
Fictitious name registration	X	X	X
Property taxes	X	X	X
Sales and use tax license	X	X	X
State and local licenses	X	X	X

If you have employees, the following sections will describe additional requirements for your business.

11.5 Additional Requirements for Businesses with Employees

Once you hire an employee to work in your business, you take on several additional responsibilities. In Pennsylvania, you will need to withhold certain payroll taxes, obtain workers' compensation insurance, comply with safety and health regulations, and know your rights and those of your employees under various labor laws.

This section discusses these requirements in further detail and recommends publications and assistance programs offered by various agencies. General considerations and federal requirements are covered in Chapter 5.

For more information regarding Pennsylvania employer taxes, contact the Bureau of Business Trust Fund Taxes. To request necessary forms, you can use the preaddressed post card located at the back of this book.

Registration Division
Bureau of Business Trust Fund Taxes
Pennsylvania Department of Revenue
Department 280901
Harrisburg, PA 17128-0901
(717) 783-8839

Withholding Taxes

As an employer, you are responsible for paying a state withholding tax. You may also be responsible for withholding an occupational tax for various cities.

State Withholding Taxes

If you employ one or more individuals and pay them a wage or salary, you are responsible for withholding a portion of their gross compensation to cover their Pennsylvania income tax liability.[42] Withholding occurs at the time wages are paid.

The amount of tax to be withheld is determined by multiplying the amount of compensation for the period by the personal income tax rate of 2.8%. In addition to the tax required to be withheld, you and an employee may agree on an additional amount to be withheld, if the employee has other income subject to personal income tax.[43]

You must file *Form PA-501, Employer Deposit Statement of Income Tax Withheld*, and remit Pennsylvania personal income tax withheld from compensation.[44] The state will automatically forward return envelopes and preprinted deposit statements to you. You must use these preprinted deposit statements.

If the preprinted deposit statements are destroyed or lost, request duplicate forms listing your name and identification number from the Pennsylvania Department of Revenue, Bureau of Business Trust Fund Taxes.

If you are required to file a deposit statement for the first time, file *Form PA-501R, Employer First Time Deposit Statement*, which can also be requested from the Pennsylvania Department of Revenue. The deposit statements are filed, along with the tax sent, to a regional depositing agent located in Pittsburgh or Philadelphia, depending on the county where your business is registered. *Form REV-415, Instruction for Employer Withholding of Personal Income Tax*, provides a list of counties and the appropriate depositing agent's address.

The frequency of filing deposit statements depends on what amount you expect to withhold for a quarterly period.[45]

- If the expected aggregate withholding is $1,000 or more, the deposits must be made semimonthly within three banking days after the 15th and the last day of the month.
- If the expected aggregate withholding is at least $300, but less than $1,000, the deposits must be made monthly on or before the 15th day of the succeeding month for all months except December. Payment for December is due on or before January 31 of the following year.
- If the expected aggregate withholding is less than $300, the deposits must be made quarterly on or before April 30, July 31, October 31, and January 31 for the four quarters ending on March 31, June 30, September 30, and December 31.

Another form you need to file is *Form PA W-3, Employer's Annual Reconciliation of Pennsylvania Income Tax Withheld*. This form reconciles income tax withheld with related employee withholding statements. A preprinted *Form PA W-3* will be mailed to you automatically and must be filed by January 31 of the following year.

An extension of time for filing *Form PA 501* or *Form PA W-3* may be granted if you can show good cause in a written application to the Pennsylvania Department of Revenue.[46]

You must also provide each employee with a federal/state withholding statement, *Form W-2*, on or before January 31 of the following year or 30 days after termination of employment. This form will reflect the total amount of Pennsylvania income tax withheld from the employee's compensation.

Listed below are the withholding tax records you should retain for a three-year period. The Pennsylvania Department of Revenue may examine these records at any time during this period.[47]

- Names, addresses, Social Security numbers, and occupations of all employees receiving compensation;
- The amount, description, and date of any compensation paid;
- Periods of employment of employees;
- Periods for which employees are paid while absent because of sickness or personal injuries, and the amount and weekly rate of such payments;
- Duplicate copies of the returns filed and the date and amounts of remittances made; and
- Adequate current records to support the apportionment of compensation for services provided within and outside Pennsylvania.

Additional information regarding the Pennsylvania personal income tax withholding requirements is available on *Form REV-415, Personal Income Tax Withholding Instructions for Employers*, which can be obtained from the Pennsylvania Department of Revenue's Registration Division.

City Withholding Taxes

The city of Pittsburgh imposes a $10 occupational tax, which you must withhold from the wages of each of your employees. *Form OT-1, Occupational Tax*, is used to remit the tax withheld to the city treasurer. To register, contact the treasurer's office in Pittsburgh.

This occupational tax is due and payable by April 30 of each year. When you hire a new employee, the tax is due one month after the end of the quarter when the new employee is hired — unless the new employee has evidence that an occupational tax was withheld by a prior employer for the previous year. The occupational tax could have been paid to another municipality other than the city of Pittsburgh.

In addition to the Pittsburgh occupational withholding tax, the city imposes a 1% wage tax on all compensation of residents and nonresidents working within the city, unless the income is taxed by the jurisdiction in which the taxpayer is a resident. For Pittsburgh residents, there is an additional tax of 1.875% imposed by the Pittsburgh School District. Therefore, the combined rate is 2.875%. You must withhold the wage income tax from your employees' wages and remit the tax to the city treasurer.

The city of Philadelphia imposes an earned income tax on all compensation earned by residents and nonresidents who work within the city. This earned income tax rate is 4.96% on wages of residents and 4.3125% on wages of nonresidents.[48] You are required to withhold the tax from the employees' wages and remit the tax to the Philadelphia Department of Revenue.

If your business is located in either Pittsburgh or Philadelphia, contact their respective revenue departments to get further information on filing and payment requirements.

State Unemployment Tax

If your business has one or more employees, you will be responsible for paying unemployment tax. These payments or contributions provide unemployment compensation for workers who become involuntarily unemployed.

The tax rates range from 2.1395% to a maximum of 9.5545% of the first $8,000 of wages paid to each employee during the calendar year.[49] The contribution rate if you are a new employer — except in construction — is 3.8255%. This rate will apply until you establish your own experience tax rating, which usually occurs after the first two or three years of being in business.

This experience tax or contribution rate is based on the amount of unemployment benefits paid to your former employees as it relates to the total wages your company has paid over a period of years. For example, the more former employees who claim benefits, the higher your experience rating. Conversely, the fewer former employees claiming benefits, the lower your rate.

It is illegal to deduct the unemployment tax from your employees' wages, except for 0.15%, which is the employee's portion of the contribution. You, as the employer, are responsible for paying the state unemployment tax. Note that as owner of a sole proprietorship, partnership, or limited partnership, you are not considered an employee of the business; therefore, you do not have to pay unemployment tax for yourself.

As a new employer, you are required to file *Form UC-1, Employer's Initial Statement*, on the date wages are first paid in Pennsylvania. This informational form registers you with the commonwealth. *Form UC-2, Employer's Report for Unemployment Compensation*, is used to report wages after your initial statement; it will automatically be forwarded to you with your assigned contribution rate. *Form UC-2* is required to be filed with the Pennsylvania Department of Labor and Industry one month after the end of each calendar quarter. A remittance for the unemployment compensation tax must accompany *Form UC-2*. To find out how you can save on unemployment taxes, see Section 11.8.

The Pennsylvania unemployment compensation law is administered by the Bureau of Unemployment Compensation. A copy of the unemployment compensation law may be obtained by calling or writing to:

Bureau of Unemployment Compensation
Pennsylvania Department of Labor and Industry
Labor and Industry Building
Seventh and Forester Streets, Room 415
Harrisburg, PA 17121
(717) 783-3140

Magnetic Media Filing Requirements

The Pennsylvania Department of Labor and Industry requires employers with 250 or more employees to file an annual report of employee information — Social Security number, employee name, gross wages, and weeks worked — by magnetic media. Employers reporting on less than 250 employers are encouraged, but not required, to report by magnetic media.

This informational report is due by April 30 of the current year and applies to the information normally provided on *Form UC-1*. It does not apply to the tax information provided on *Form UC-2*. If you have any questions or would like to elect to report by magnetic media, call:

Bureau of Employer Tax Operations
Pennsylvania Department of Labor and Industry
(717) 783-5802

Workers' Compensation Insurance

Workers' compensation insurance is a state-mandated insurance requirement for all Pennsylvania employers. While, as the owner of a sole proprietorship, partnership, or limited partnership, you do not have to obtain workers' compensation for yourself, you are required to provide it for your employees. It provides wage loss and medical benefits to employees injured on the job and it protects you from legal action for damages for injuries suffered by your employees. Be aware that neither general liability nor health and accident insurance can properly substitute for workers' compensation insurance.

You have three choices for obtaining workers' compensation insurance in Pennsylvania.

- Private companies — Obtain insurance from a private casualty company.
- State-operated insurance carriers — Insure with the state-operated insurance carrier, the State Workers' Insurance Fund (SWIF).
- Self-insurance — Self-insurance is permitted only if the insurer has first been approved by the Pennsylvania Department of Labor and Industry, Bureau of Workers' Compensation. Information regarding self-insurance is available from the Self-Insurance Section of the Bureau of Workers' Compensation.

You, as an employer, must provide workers' compensation coverage for all employees from the date of employment. Although it is no longer a statutory or regulatory requirement to post a notice of workers' compensation coverage, it is still considered a good practice to do so.

For more information on workers' compensation insurance, contact the office below or use the preaddressed post card at the back of this book.

Bureau of Workers' Compensation
Pennsylvania Department of Labor and Industry
1171 South Cameron, Room 103
Harrisburg, PA 17104-2501
(717) 783-4467
(800) 482-2383

Safety and Health Regulations

As an employer in Pennsylvania, you will have to comply with state and federal job safety laws designed to prevent injuries resulting from unsafe or unhealthy working conditions.

The Pennsylvania Department of Labor and Industry is responsible for all state employee safety and health regulations. Pennsylvania requires that you report any injuries resulting in a disability lasting more than one workshift. The report must include factual information about the employee, the time and place of the accident, and the probable duration of the disability. For most injuries, there is a ten-day reporting compliance period.

The Pennsylvania Department of Labor and Industry has the authority to inspect locations where labor is performed; examine building plans for structures more than two stories high; receive accident reports; investigate and prescribe means to prevent future occurrences; inspect emergency lighting, sprinkler, and fire alarm systems; and administer and enforce workers' compensation laws.

Pennsylvania businesses must also comply with regulations of the federal Occupational Safety and Health Act (OSHA). To comply with proper standards, check state and federal acts to determine what special rules apply to your particular industry. Refer to Section 5.6 for information on federal OSHA requirements.

Bureau of Occupational and Industrial Safety
Pennsylvania Department of Labor and Industry
(717) 787-3323

Wage-Hour Laws

Before hiring your employees, you need to know about the wage-hour laws that will affect your business. Employee wage-hour laws, as discussed in Section 5.7, cover minimum wage, overtime pay, and child labor laws. The basic requirements your business will have to follow in Pennsylvania are discussed in this subsection. Remember also to maintain an accurate record of each employee's earnings and hours worked. The Bureau of Labor Standards can provide you with a packet that provides more specific information as well as a list of exemptions and posters for each area.

Bureau of Labor Standards
Pennsylvania Department of Labor and Industry
Labor and Industry Building
Seventh and Forster Streets, Room 1302A
Harrisburg, PA 17121
(717) 787-4671

Minimum Wage

The state's minimum wage law requires that you pay all your covered employees at least $4.25 per hour. This is the same as the federal minimum wage, as set by the federal Fair Labor Standards Act (FLSA).

Exemptions to the Minimum Wage Act exist for qualifying students and learners. "Students" are those in either high school or college who work no more than 20 hours per week during the school year, no more than 8 hours per day, and no more than 40 hours per week during vacation periods. "Learners" are employees in a training program which lasts a maximum of eight weeks. In both cases, a special certificate must be obtained, and the rate allowed to be paid is 85% of the current minimum wage.

To determine the hourly wage of a tipped employee — one who makes $30 a month — you may take a tip credit not to exceed 45%.

Equal Pay

Federal and state equal opportunity statutes require equal pay for men and women performing similar services.[50] Failure to do so can result in a claim based on wage or sex discrimination.

Overtime Pay

Pennsylvania's overtime pay law requires that all employees be paid at a rate of one and one-half times their regular rate for all hours worked in excess of 40 per week.[51] Since there are exceptions, check with the Bureau of Labor Standards.

You may pay your employees on a periodic basis, such as weekly, biweekly, semimonthly, or monthly. You must, however, notify your employees of the schedule on which they will be paid at the time they are hired.[52]

Like most states, Pennsylvania regulates the employment of children.[53] If you intend to hire children in your business, check with the Pennsylvania Bureau of Labor Standards to find out what specific restrictions and exemptions there are relating to acceptable occupations and conditions and to allowable hours of employment. An information sheet is available from the office.

In general, the minimum age for working in Pennsylvania is 14 years of age. Minors under that age may not be employed or permitted to work in any occupation. There are exceptions, however, and you should check with an office of the Bureau of Labor Standards.

Pennsylvania also requires an employment certificate for any employee under the age of 18.

In Pennsylvania, students are categorized in two groups: those who are 16 and 17 years old, and those who are 14 and 15 years old. After classification, two standards are applied for vacation periods and for regular school periods.

A 16- or 17-year-old student attending a regular school day program can not work more than 28 hours during a school week nor more than 8 hours on a given school day. On weekends, however, a student may work an additional 8 hours on Saturday or Sunday, or both, with a limitation of six work days in one week. A restriction also applies to such a student by prohibiting work after midnight and before the hour of 6:00 A.M. on a school day. There is, however, an extension until 1:00 A.M. for weekends.

During vacation periods, a 16- or 17-year-old student may work up to 44 hours in a week, limited to 8 hours on any one day and no more than six days in that week. During summer vacations, there is no limitation as to when a student must end work.

Different rules apply for 14- and 15-year-old students. These youths may not work more than 4 hours in one day and are restricted to a maximum of 18 hours in a week. On a Saturday or Sunday, this student may work 8 hours; however, the weekly 18-hour maximum still applies, as does the total of six different work days in one week. These students are not allowed to begin work before 7:00 A.M. and must end their workday by 7:00 P.M. The 7:00 P.M. limit is extended to 10:00 P.M. during summer vacation.

For all employees less than 18 years old, a 30-minute meal break must be provided after 5 hours of continuous work.

Refer also to Section 5.7 for a discussion of federal laws that apply to the employment of minors.

Other State Labor Laws

You will also have to deal with other employee-related state requirements, which may vary depending upon how many employees you have. To correctly determine your policies on issues such as family leave and breaks, review the general guidelines below, then obtain more complete information from the Pennsylvania Department of Labor.

If you have not yet written your company policy manual regarding these and other employee-related issues, consider getting a copy of The Oasis Press' *A Company Policy and Personnel Workbook* to streamline the process.

Breaks, Holidays, and Sick Leave

Most employers allow employees breaks for meals and rest. Generally, employees also receive at least seven paid holidays a year and are granted sick leave, which is paid time off for an employee who is temporarily incapacitated.

Family Leave

More companies today are voluntarily providing family or parental leave or a combination of both for their employees. Family/parental leave generally allows employees several weeks of paid or unpaid leaves of absence for family or medical purposes, such as:

- The birth or adoption of a child; or
- A serious health condition of the employee, spouse, child, or parent.

Maternity Leave

Closely related to family leave is maternity leave, which typically allows pregnant employees up to twelve weeks of paid or unpaid leave during pregnancy or following the birth of the child, or both. The employee is usually returned to her previous job or a comparable one at equal pay, benefits, and seniority.

Right-to-Work

In about half of the states, right-to-work laws have been enacted to guarantee that no person may be denied employment for refusing to join a union. Many also prohibit mandatory payment of union dues by non-union workers in order to retain employment.

Pennsylvania does not have a right-to-work law and allows "union shop" or "agency shop" contracts, or both, between a company and a union. In a union shop, an employee not belonging to a union may be hired but then must join the union, usually within 30 days. In an agency shop, an employee need not join the union but, to remain employed, must pay dues to the union.

Anti-Discrimination

Section 5.8 provides you with a detailed discussion of the federal anti-discrimination laws you need to follow when hiring and employing your staff.

11.6 State Licenses

As noted in Chapter 6, many businesses and professions are required to obtain licenses before engaging in business. State governments have traditionally licensed professionals, such as doctors, lawyers, and accountants. To further protect consumers, Pennsylvania has expanded the list to include other occupations. A partial listing of occupations and businesses that require licensing in Pennsylvania follows. For further information on state licenses, contact:

Professional and Occupational Affairs Bureau (BPOA)
P.O. Box 2649
Harrisburg, PA 17105-2649
(717) 787-8503
FAX (717) 787-7769

Bureau of Small Business and Appalachian Development
Pennsylvania Department of Commerce
461 Forum Building
Harrisburg, PA 17120
(717) 783-5700

Business or Occupation	Agency
Architects	State Architects Licensure Board
Auctioneers, auctioneer apprentices	State Board of Auctioneer Examiners
Barber shops, beauty shops, and barber teachers	State Board of Barber Examiners
Certified public accountants	State Board of Accountancy
Chiropractors	State Board of Chiropractic Examiners
Cosmetologists, manicurists, and cosmetology schools	State Board of Cosmetology
Dentists and dental hygienists	State Board of Dentistry
Professional engineers and surveyors	State Registration Board for Professional Engineers, Land Surveyors & Geologists
Funeral directors	State Board of Funeral Directors
Landscape architects	State Board of Landscape Architects
Motor vehicle dealers and salespersons	State Board of Vehicle Manufacturers, Dealers, and Salespersons
Nursing home administrators	State Board of Examiners, Nursing Home Administrators
Occupational therapists	State Board of Occupational Therapy, Education, and Licensure
Optometrists	State Board of Optometry
Osteopathic physicians	State Board of Osteopathic Medicine
Pharmacists and pharmacies	State Board of Pharmacy
Physical therapists	State Board of Physical Therapy
Physicians and physician's assistants	State Board of Medicine

Podiatrists	State Board of Podiatry
Psychologists	State Board of Psychology
Real estate brokers and salespersons	State Real Estate Commission
Real estate appraisers	State Board Certified Real Estate Appraisers
Registered and practical nurses	State Board of Nursing
River pilots	Navigation Commission for the Delaware River
Social workers	State Board of Social Work Examiners
Speech, language, and hearing specialists	State Board of Speech, Language, and Hearing Examiners
Veterinarians and animal health technicians	State Board of Veterinary Medical Examiners

Apprenticeship Programs

More than 800 apprenticeable occupations are approved by the U.S. Department of Labor. Following is a list of the foremost apprenticeable occupations in Pennsylvania, some of which require that a license be obtained for employment in certain cities.

Selected Apprentice Occupations in Pennsylvania

Air conditioning, refrigeration, and heating mechanic	Glazier
Auto mechanic	Lithographer
Automobile body repairer	Machinist
Boilermaker	Millwright
Bricklayer and stonemason	Painter
Butcher	Patternmaker
Carpenter	Photoengraver
Cook	Plumber and pipefitter
Drafter	Printing press operator
Electrician	Roofer
Electronics	Sheetmetal worker
	Tool-and-die maker

For additional information on state apprenticeship programs, contact:

Pennsylvania Apprenticeship and Training Council
Department of Labor and Industry Building, Room 1303
7th and Forester Streets
Harrisburg, PA 17120
(717) 787-3681

For additional information on federal apprenticeship programs, contact:

Bureau of Apprenticeship and Training
U.S. Department of Labor
Federal Building, 3rd and Walnut Streets
P.O. Box 1046
Harrisburg, PA 17108
(717) 782-3496

11.7 State Excise Taxes

Pennsylvania imposes a number of excise taxes and certain license fees. Some excise taxes are imposed on the production, importation, use, or sale of certain goods. Others are imposed on services and certain types of businesses. Excise taxes that may apply to your business are listed below. Refer to Chapter 7 for information on federal excise taxes. For additional information on commonwealth excise taxes, contact:

Pennsylvania Department of Revenue
(717) 787-8201

Alcoholic Beverages

If you sell, possess, produce, or distribute liquor or other alcoholic beverages in Pennsylvania, you must pay a tax on all sales within the state at the rates listed below. The taxes must be paid on a monthly basis no later than the 15th day of the current month. You pay these taxes to the Pennsylvania Department of Revenue.

Type of Beverage	Tax Rate
Distilled spirits	$1.00 (per gallon)
Wines	$0.005 (per unit)
Rectified spirits	$0.30 (per gallon)
Malt beverages	$2.48 (per barrel)[54]

You may also be required to purchase a license from the Pennsylvania Liquor Control Board. Licenses range in cost from $250 to $700.[55] For more information, contact:

Pennsylvania Liquor Control Board – Licensing Information
(717) 783-8250

Tobacco Products

Pennsylvania taxes the possession or sale of cigarettes.[56] The tax is imposed one time on any cigarette, whether the transfer is of an individual cigarette, in packages, cartons, or cases.[57] The tax is charged at a rate of $0.0155 (1 55/100 of a cent) per cigarette or $0.31 (31 cents) per standard pack of 20 cigarettes.[58]

If you are a wholesaler or retailer of cigarettes, you must be licensed by the state.[59] License fees vary depending on the type of cigarette license you desire. A wholesale cigarette dealer's license is $500. A retail cigarette dealer's license — and a cigarette vending machine license — is $25. A cigarette stamping agency license is $1,000.

As a licensed dealer, you will file reports and pay the tax in accordance with Pennsylvania Department of Revenue requirements.[60] For more information, contact:

Registration Division
(717) 783-9374

Gasoline and Motor Fuel or Special Fuels

If you use or sell gasoline or motor fuels in Pennsylvania, you are responsible for two taxes imposed on these fuels. The liquid fuels tax is charged on all liquid fuels sold or used by distributors of qualifying products. The tax is collected by the distributor but paid for by the consumer.[61] The current rate of this tax is $0.12 (12 cents) per gallon.[62] The fuel use tax is imposed on dealer/users at a rate of $0.12 (12 cents) per gallon of fuel used in Pennsylvania.[63] A fuel that is taxed under the liquid fuels act is not subject to the fuel use tax. Diesel fuel is not considered a liquid fuel for purposes of this tax.[64]

Businesses engaged in the distribution of liquid fuels must apply for appropriate permits or licenses from the Pennsylvania Department of Revenue.[65] A monthly report on *Form REV-1096* detailing the amount of fuel sold and tax due is required by the state.

Motor Vehicle Registration

Pennsylvania requires all motor vehicles to be registered with the Department of Transportation. Certain classifications of vehicles, such as motorcycles and passenger cars, are subject to a flat rate fee. Trucks and motor homes are examples of vehicles that pay a fee based on gross vehicle weight.[66] Vehicles owned or operated by Pennsylvania residents and businesses must register and pay the appropriate fee. Trucks owned by domestic or foreign corporations, which are registered outside of Pennsylvania, have to meet special requirements regarding fees and registration determined by whether or not they are involved in interstate or intrastate transportation.[67] Vehicles qualifying for exemption from registration and fees in Pennsylvania include those owned by residents of other states and vehicles owned by federal, state, or local government units.[68]

Motor vehicle rentals and retail sales are subject to the Pennsylvania 6% sales tax.[69] Leases of motor vehicles are subject to an additional tax of 3% for a total tax of 9%. Rentals of motor vehicles are also subject to a fee of $2 for each day or portion of a day the vehicle is rented. Sales to registered dealers for resale purposes or to nonresidents for use outside Pennsylvania are exempt from the sales tax.[70]

Other Taxes

Beside the major excise taxes discussed above, Pennsylvania also imposes taxes on hotel rooms and real estate transfers.

11.8 Planning for Tax Savings in a Business — State Tax Laws

As discussed in Chapter 8, there are effective legal ways to reduce your taxes. This section continues that discussion and provides you with state specifics on those tax strategies that can help you in your business. Before implementing any of the following tax-saving tips, be sure to consult your tax adviser or accountant.

Your best strategy for reducing the unemployment tax your company pays is to plan and hire carefully, so you have minimal layoffs. Over time, this will lower your unemployment tax rating. An effective way to pre-screen employees and to test your long-term need for a new position is to use a temporary help agency as a source for workers at all skill levels.

If you operate your business as a sole proprietorship, there are some minor tax advantages in hiring certain family members as employees in your business. In Pennsylvania, any wages your sole proprietorship pays to your spouse, or children under 18 years of age, are exempt from state unemployment tax. Keep in mind, however, that because you don't pay unemployment tax for them, they are not eligible to collect benefits if you fire or lay them off. Another way you can reduce your state unemployment tax liability is to have your typical evaluation period of new employees last less than 16 weeks.[71] A person cannot claim unemployment benefits from you unless the claimant worked at least 16 credit weeks.

Pennsylvania provides a wide array of tax credits and exemptions for businesses. Some that might apply to your business are discussed below.

The federal targeted jobs and new jobs tax credits are not allowed for Pennsylvania computation of net income tax; however, Pennsylvania does allow a credit for wages paid under a targeted jobs or new jobs program.

The Pennsylvania Inheritance and Estate Tax Act does not provide for an unlimited marital deduction as does federal law. The Pennsylvania statute, however, does provide for property owned in joint tenancy by husband and wife to pass tax free at death by right of survivorship.[72] Property held in other forms — such as tenancy in common and tenants by entireties — is subject to the state inheritance tax, a rate of 6% for spouses.[73]

If your company does significant export business, you may want to form a separate Domestic International Sales Corporation (DISC) or Foreign Sales Corporation (FSC) to take advantage of the federal export incentives described in Section 8.4. Pennsylvania generally follows the federal tax rules for both DISCs and FSCs so that use of such special entities can reduce or defer income taxes on export sales.[74]

If your corporation owns stock in another corporation, your company can qualify for a dividends received deduction which could reduce the income tax it has to pay on dividends it receives. To find out if your corporation can take advantage of the federal dividends received deduction, consult with your accountant.

A 50% credit against the Pennsylvania corporate net income tax is allowed on approved investments in specific designated areas for neighborhood assistance, job training, or education and community service.

Unemployment Tax Savings

State Tax Credits and Exemptions

State Jobs Tax Credits

Estate Planning and Marital Deduction

Sheltering Profits on Export Sales

Dividends Received Deduction

Investment Tax Credit

This credit may increase to 70% of the amount invested in special program areas, such as enterprise zones, designated by the commonwealth. See Section 11.9 for more information on enterprise zones.

11.9 Miscellaneous Business Pointers

This section provides general business information on such topics as financial assistance, usury laws, and emerging trends in Pennsylvania. Refer to Chapter 9 for information on federal assistance programs and other basic business pointers.

State Business Loan Programs

A wide variety of financial incentive programs are available in Pennsylvania for new or expanding businesses. The Office of Program Management was established under the Pennsylvania Department of Commerce to assist businesses through the programs discussed below.[75]

For more information, please contact:

Office of Program Management
Pennsylvania Department of Commerce
The Forum Building, Room 479
Harrisburg, PA 17120
(717) 787-1909

Pennsylvania Economic Development
 Financing Authority
466 Forum Building
Harrisburg, PA 17120
(717) 783-1109

Pennsylvania Industrial Development Authority

The Pennsylvania Industrial Development Authority (PIDA) was the first state government lending program in the nation to provide long-term, low-interest financing to businesses engaged in manufacturing or industrial enterprises. PIDA lends millions of dollars each year to various targeted industries, including advanced technology companies and small businesses which create new employment opportunities within the state.

Loan terms range up to 15 years at interest rates significantly less than prime rates. Financing up to $2 million is available. The loans are generally used to finance up to 70% of the cost of land, buildings, and expansion of manufacturing facilities and small businesses. In addition to funding, the Pennsylvania Department of Commerce provides plant location specialists, regional representatives, and other consultants deemed appropriate. Loans are also available for job retention projects for quality firms.

Pennsylvania Capital Loan Fund

The Pennsylvania Capital Loan Fund (PCLF) program receives funds from both federal and state appropriations. Commonwealth-funded PCLF loans may finance up to 50% of the project cost or $100,000, whichever is less. Federally funded loans may be used to finance up to 50% of a project's total cost or a $100,000 maximum.

The purpose of these funds reflects Pennsylvania's emphasis on creating long-term job opportunities and on spurring small businesses and advanced technology enterprises. These loans can be used to finance the purchase of land, buildings, machinery, equipment, and, in some instances, to provide working capital. PCLF financing can be used to complement other state financing programs.

Revenue Bond and Mortgage Programs

Revenue bond and mortgage lending programs allow financial institutions and local industrial development authorities to lend money to a business at rates below the going rate since no taxes are paid by the lending institution on the interest earned. The proceeds from these loans may only be used for land, building, machinery, and equipment. The minimum cost for an industrial project is $100,000 and must create a minimum of one job for every $50,000 loaned.

The Ben Franklin Challenge Grant Program

The Ben Franklin Challenge Grant Program for Technological Innovation was established to link private, educational, and government resources for the common goal of advancing the development of new technology in Pennsylvania.

The cornerstone of this program was the establishment of four regional Technology Centers (TCs) within Pennsylvania. These centers facilitate education, training, research, development, and entrepreneurial assistance services to businesses throughout the state. Pennsylvania apportioned millions of dollars which must be matched in funds supplied by private sources. For further information on this program, including the location of the nearest TC, refer to Section 11.10.

Machinery and Equipment Loan Fund

The Machinery and Equipment Loan Fund (MELF) provides low interest financing for the purchase of machinery and equipment. Loans are available to companies engaged in manufacturing, industrial, agriculture processing, and mining businesses. The loans generally have a term of seven years and may be used to finance up to 50% of the individual project cost.

Pennsylvania Minority Business Development Authority

The Pennsylvania Minority Business Development Authority (PMBDA) provides long-term, low interest loans to assist in the startup or expansion of minority-owned firms. Financing can be used for a variety of start-up expenses, including purchase or rental of land or buildings, machinery, equipment, furnishings, fixtures, inventory, leasehold improvements, and working capital. In addition, PMBDA can provide loans up to $750,000 and equity investment guarantees. The loan terms may be up to 20 years at interest rates not to exceed 50% of the prime rate at the time of approval. PMBDA requires at least 25% participation in the project by the owner and/or other lending sources, such as banks, venture capital companies, and other financial institutions.

Recycling Industrial Development Account

The Recycling Industrial Development Account (RIDA) is a part of the statewide strategy to explore new technologies and provide capital to recyclers and end users of recycled materials. RIDA provides low interest loans to assist companies working to develop and expand the markets for recyclable materials recovered from the state waste stream. Loans may be used to finance the cost of machinery and equipment. RIDA can finance up 50% of the project cost. Loan amounts cannot exceed $300,000.

Pennsylvania Economic Development Financing Authority

The Pennsylvania Economic Development Financing Authority (PEDFA) is the statewide issuer of tax-exempt and taxable private activity bonds. PEDFA provides access to cost-effective capital by issuing bonds, selling the bonds to investors, and lending the proceeds to eligible businesses. Proceeds from tax-exempt and taxable bonds may be used to finance land, buildings, renovations, and equipment, while taxable bonds may also be used to finance working capital and refinancing.

The interest rate for tax-exempt loans is typically between 80 and 85% of the prevailing prime rate, while the rate for taxable loans is between 95 and 100% of prime. The minimum loan rate is $400,000 with loan terms up to 30 years. Borrowers must have their loan guaranteed by a bank to assure that PEDFA bonds are highly rated, which in turn results in the lowest possible interest cost for the borrower.

Revenue Bond and Mortgage Division

The Revenue Bond and Mortgage Division regulates all tax-exempt and taxable projects financed through local Industrial Development Authorities (IDAs). An IDA issues bonds and then uses the proceeds to finance land, building, renovations, and equipment for eligible projects. Each project must be guaranteed by a bank or other financial institution.

Small Business Investment Companies

A Small Business Investment Company (SBIC) is a privately owned and operated company that has been licensed by the U.S. Small Business Administration (SBA) to provide equity capital and long-term loans to small firms. Often, an SBIC also provides management assistance to the companies it finances.

SBICs invest in all types of manufacturing and service industries and a wide variety of other businesses, including construction, retail, and wholesale concerns. Many investment companies seek out small businesses that offer new products or services because these small businesses usually have the growth potential that is attractive to SBICs. To find out more about SBICs, contact the SBA office nearest you.

Enterprise Zone Program

Pennsylvania's Enterprise Zone Program assists financially disadvantaged communities to prepare and implement business development strategies within enterprise zones. It is intended to increase job opportunities. The program focuses on industrial, manufacturing, and larger business services firms. Eligible applicants must be recognized by the Pennsylvania Department of Community Affairs (DCA) as financially disadvantaged municipalities. Approved applicants first receive planning assistance grants to prepare business development strategies based on a structured survey of local business people.

When the DCA approves the strategy, a planning zone is eligible for designation. Designated enterprise zones receive seed money from DCA to implement the approved business development strategy. Designated zones also may apply for competitive grants which are loaned at below market rates to specific businesses within the zone. These loans can be used for up to 30% of total construction, machinery, and equipment costs. Other loan terms are negotiated locally and subject to DCA approval. Tax credits are available against the state corporate income tax for business property improvements located within an enterprise zone. In addition, a five-year carry forward is available.

When requesting other state resources, designated enterprise zones are given priority consideration to facilitate identified business investment and job creation opportunities.

A listing of currently designated enterprise zones and information on zone benefits can be obtained through:

Bureau of Community Planning
Pennsylvania Department of Community Affairs
551 Forum Building
Harrisburg, PA 17120
(717) 787-7400

Customized Job Training Program

The Customized Job Training (CJT) Program is a state initiative that provides funds to train employees in specific skills to meet an individual employer's needs. In general, CJT funds can be used for instructor salaries and benefits, consumable materials and supplies, rental of tools and equipment, and some travel and overhead expenses.

Entry-level training costs may be supportable up to 100% of eligible costs. Funding for upgrade training costs cannot exceed 70% of eligible costs. The firm selects the most appropriate site for training and is also responsible for selecting trainees and establishing criteria — such as educational and skill levels — to choose and determine which trainees successfully complete the training program. Trainees are guaranteed to receive a job with the company if they successfully complete the training.

If you are interested in CJT, apply through a local educational agency, including area vocational/technical schools, school districts, intermediate units, community colleges, licensed private and proprietary trade and business schools, and state or private universities. The local educational agency is responsible for preparing the project budget and application for funding. It will develop the training plan with your business, package the program application, oversee the delivery of the training program, and handle all the fiscal arrangements.

All applications are submitted to the appropriate regional vocational education field office for initial review. If your application meets program requirements, it is forwarded to the Pennsylvania Department of Education for a review by an interagency task force composed of representatives of the governor's office and the departments of education, labor and industry, public welfare, and commerce. While the task force recommends approval or disapproval, the final review and decision rests with the secretaries of the departments of education and commerce. The approval process takes ten to twelve weeks. You may contact a local educational agency, a regional vocational education field office, or the Pennsylvania Department of Education for more information on CJT.

Usury Laws

Usury laws define the maximum amount of interest that may be charged on a credit transaction, such as a promissory note or other instrument, that requires the payment of interest. Currently, Pennsylvania law provides for a maximum interest rate of 6% on loans of $50,000 or less in which no express contract has been made.

Section 1244 Stock

As discussed in Section 9.6, if you take a loss on small business corporation stock that qualifies as section 1244 stock you get favorable tax treatment from the IRS. For Pennsylvania tax purposes, however, this preferential treatment does not apply.

Environmental Regulations

If your business will have any impact on the surrounding environment, such as erecting a new building or renovating an existing structure, contact the U.S. Environmental Protection Agency (EPA) to make sure you meet their requirements.

Emerging Trends and Issues

If you would like to keep abreast of emerging trends and issues that will affect your business, consider joining the National Federation of Independent Business (NFIB). The NFIB is the nation's largest organization representing the interests of small business owners. Through NFIB, you will learn more about pending state and federal legislation, regulations, and taxes that will affect you and, more importantly, you will be able to speak out on these issues through NFIB's state and national lobbying efforts. As an NFIB member, you would receive:

- *Independent Business (IB)*, the bimonthly national magazine for small business owners; and
- *State Reports*, that specifically cover issues in Pennsylvania.

For more information on NFIB, contact:

National Federation of Independent Business
Attn: Membership Services
53 Century Boulevard, Suite 205
Nashville, TN 37214
(800) NFIB NOW (634-2669)

If you ever have a question regarding a particular legislative bill, contact:

Pennsylvania Reference Bureau – Status Unit
(717) 787-2342

You can also contact the Pennsylvania Chamber of Business and Industry, which can help you understand Pennsylvania regulations, legislative issues, bills, and laws.[76]

Pennsylvania Chamber of Business and Industry
One Commerce Square
417 Walnut Street
Harrisburg, PA 17101
(717) 255-3252
(800) 225-7224

11.10　State Sources of Help and Information

Throughout the state, you will be able to find many public and private agencies and organizations that can assist you with your business. For your convenience, many of these sources of help and information are listed below.

Do-It-Yourself Incorporation

You can incorporate your business on your own in Pennsylvania, but if you have an existing partnership or sole proprietorship that you want to convert to a corporation, see your accountant first. There may be important tax consequences that will influence the way you transfer assets and structure the corporation.

Your tax accountant, attorney, or Department of State's office may also be able to refer you to a do-it-yourself incorporation book that can assist you through the incorporation process, providing state-specific information, ready-to-use forms, and stock certificates. One such book is *Incorporating In Pennsylvania Without A Lawyer*. Published by Consumer Publishing, Inc., this $24.95 book is updated monthly by the author, W. Dean Brown. To order this book, contact:

The Oasis Press
(800) 228-2275

Commonwealth Agency Assistance

For your specific questions regarding Pennsylvania laws, regulations, taxes, incentives, and other requirements and programs, these agencies and offices can be very helpful.

One-Stop or Business Assistance Center

The Office of Small Business of the Bureau of Small Business and Appalachian Development is Pennsylvania's one-stop business information center. This office can answer questions regarding general business requirements and licenses and permits or refer you to the appropriate agency. You can also request from this office the free publication, *Pennsylvania Small Business Operations & Resources Guide*.

Office of Small Business
Bureau of Small Business and Appalachian Development
461 Forum Building
Harrisburg, PA 17120
(717) 783-5700

Publications Office

The State Bookstore of Pennsylvania carries many books and publications that can help you answer questions concerning starting a business in Pennsylvania. Two useful publications the State Bookstore carries are:

- *The Pennsylvania Manual* — This book describes the functions and types of assistance provided by the various state departments, agencies, and commissions. A valuable directory is included that can help you determine who to contact for additional information concerning various regulatory, licensing, and filing requirements that affect business in Pennsylvania.

- *Questions and Answers on Workers' Compensation in Pennsylvania* and *A Primer on Pennsylvania Workers' Compensation* — These pamphlets were prepared by the Bureau of Workers' Compensation and are a good starting point for learning about employer responsibilities under the workers' compensation law.

For more information on these and other publications, request the State Bookstore's publication directory or call:

State Bookstore
1825 Stanly Drive
Harrisburg, PA 17103
(717) 787-5109

Tax or Revenue Office

If you have questions regarding sales and use taxes, corporate income taxes, or personal income taxes, contact a Pennsylvania Department of Revenue office nearest you or call the main office in Harrisburg below. You can also order any Pennsylvania tax form or schedule by calling a 24-hour answering service, also listed below.

Pennsylvania Department of Revenue
(717) 787-8201 (General information)
(717) 787-6229 (Sales and use taxes)
(717) 783-6035 (Corporate income tax)
(717) 787-8094 (Tax forms and schedules)
(800) 362-2050 (Tax forms – outside Harrisburg)

Economic Development

The Office of Small Business, described earlier, also administers the Enterprise Development Program (EDP), which promotes local business expansion and job creation through business and community support services.

The support services include assistance in finance, federal procurement, and export outreach. Seven Local Development Districts (LDDs) provide these services to Pennsylvania's 52 Appalachian counties.

For the counties of Carbon, Lackawanna, Luzerne, Monroe, Pike, Schuylkill, and Wayne, contact:

Economic Development Council of Northeastern Pennsylvania
1151 Oak Street
Pittston, PA 18640-3795
(717) 655-5581

For Cameron, Clearfield, Elk, Jefferson, McKean, and Potter counties, contact:

North Central Pennsylvania Regional Planning and Development Commission
651 Montmorenci Avenue
Ridgway, PA 15853
(814) 772-6901

For Bradford, Sullivan, Susquehanna, Tioga, and Wyoming counties, contact:

Northern Tier Regional Planning and Development Commission
507 Main Street
Towanda, PA 18848
(717) 265-9103

For Clarion, Crawford, Erie, Forest, Lawrence, Mercer, Venango, and Warren counties, contact:

Northwest Pennsylvania Regional Planning and Development Commission
614 Eleventh Street
Franklin, PA 16323
(814) 437-3024

For Bedford, Blair, Cambria, Fulton, Huntingdon, and Somerset counties, contact:

Southern Alleghenies Planning and Development Commission
541 58th Street
Altoona, PA 16602
(814) 949-6500

For Centre, Clinton, Columbia, Juniata, Lycoming, Mifflin, Montour, Northumberland, Perry, Snyder, and Union counties, contact:

SEDA – Council of Governments
Timberhaven
R.D. #1
Lewisburg, PA 17837
(717) 524-4491

For Allegheny, Armstrong, Beaver, Butler, Fayette, Greene, Indiana, Washington, and Westmoreland counties, contact:

Southwestern Pennsylvania Regional Development Council
The Waterfront
200 First Avenue
Pittsburgh, PA 15222-1573
(412) 391-5590

Department of State

The Pennsylvania Department of State can help you with questions regarding incorporation, limited partnerships, and fictitious names.

Pennsylvania Department of State
(717) 787-1057

Labor/Industrial Relations Office

If you have questions regarding Pennsylvania labor standards, unemployment taxes, and workers' compensation, call:

Pennsylvania Department of Labor and Industry
(717) 787-4671 (in Harrisburg)
(814) 946-7374 (in Altoona)
(215) 560-1858 (in Philadelphia)
(412) 565-5300 (in Pittsburgh)
(717) 963-4577 (in Scranton)
(717) 787-2097 (Unemployment compensation)
(800) 482-2383 (Workers' compensation)

The Ben Franklin/IRC Partnership

The Ben Franklin Partnership (BFP) Fund was created in 1982 through an act of the Pennsylvania General Assembly.[77] It has developed into perhaps the most comprehensive state technology-oriented, economic development program in the nation, in that it promotes both the development and application of advanced technologies. In 1993, the fund was expanded to include Industrial Resource Centers and it was renamed the Ben Franklin/IRC Partnership.

The Ben Franklin/IRC Partnership contains programs unique among the states that promote advanced technology — the use of new techniques and processes both in mature industries and in new fields and enterprises. Furthermore, a comprehensive array of financing assistance and business services is provided locally through four regional privately managed technology centers (TCs).

The partnership links private and educational resources — particularly those educational institutions with research capabilities — to develop and commercialize new technologies; to creatively apply existing technologies for commercial advantage; and to spin off new small businesses on the leading edge of technological innovation.

Seed funding is provided to selected early stage and other small businesses for development of innovative products. It also supports education and training activities, provides entrepreneurial development services, and funds small business incubator facilities. Ben Franklin/IRC Partnership Challenge Grants provide the matching funds for local projects through four regional TCs. This funding is provided in the following areas:

- Joint research and development between private companies and universities;
- Research and development by small companies;
- Technology transfer;
- Centers of excellence;
- Entrepreneurial development;

- Education and training for technology work forces;
- Regional or statewide technology development initiatives; and
- Incubators.

In addition to the Challenge Grant Program for Technological Innovation, other programs funded through the Ben Franklin/IRC Partnership appropriation include:

- Small Business Research Seed Grant Program
- Pennsylvania Technical Assistance Program (PENNTAP)

The board of the Ben Franklin/IRC Partnership Fund administers these programs as well:

- Small Business Incubators Program
- Seed Venture Capital Fund Program
- Engineering School Equipment Grant Program
- Environmental Recycling Technology Research Fund

Information on these programs is also available from the four regional TCs. The four centers and their primary areas of research are listed below.

- Northeast Tier Ben Franklin Technology Center — This center, based at Lehigh University, includes 25 other private and public colleges and universities; 1,100 industrial, labor, and financial organizations; 4 small business development centers; and 21 economic development or local government groups and organizations, as well as foundations. The center supports activities in any technology area that shows commercial promise. The majority of past support has been in the areas of microelectronics, materials, and biotechnology. For more information, contact:

Northeast Tier (NET) Ben Franklin Technology Center
125 Goodman Drive
Bethlehem, PA 18015-3715
(215) 758-5200

- Ben Franklin Technology Center of Southeastern Pennsylvania — This consortium is based at the University City Science Center and includes the University of Pennsylvania, Drexel University, Temple University, Thomas Jefferson University, Pennsylvania Hospital, 60 other public and private colleges and universities, 350 private sector firms, and other groups and organizations. The primary areas of research and development are advanced sensor technologies, computer science and information, medical biotechnologies, and materials engineering and processing. The southeastern office is located in Philadelphia.

Ben Franklin Technology Center of Southeastern Pennsylvania
University City Science Center
3624 Market Street
Philadelphia, PA 19104
(215) 895-3103

- Western Pennsylvania Ben Franklin Technology Center — This center is a consortium consisting of Carnegie-Mellon University, the University of Pittsburgh, 21 other public and private academic institutions, more than 100 private firms, labor groups, and other economic development organizations. The primary areas of research and development are robotics and intelligent systems; computers; advanced materials; processes and devices; and biological/biomedical technologies. The western Pennsylvania office is in Pittsburgh.

Ben Franklin Technology Center of Western Pennsylvania
4516 Henry Street, Suite 103
Pittsburgh, PA 15213
(412) 681-1520

- Ben Franklin Technology Center of Central/Northern Pennsylvania — This center is located at Pennsylvania State University and has two satellite centers at Behrend College in Erie and the Penn State Capital Campus in Middletown. The center works with more than 20 other colleges and universities, 85 private sector firms, and other groups and organizations. The primary areas for research and development are food; forestry and agricultural sciences; advanced materials, coal, and minerals; manufacturing, management, and control systems; and biotechnology. For more information, contact one of these three offices.

Executive Director
Ben Franklin Technology Center of
** Central/Northern Pennsylvania**
105 Barbara Building II
North University Drive
University Park, PA 16802-1013
(814) 863-4558

Director
Erie Satellite
Behrend College
Station Road
Erie, PA 16563-0601
(814) 898-6255

Director
South Central Satellite
Pennsylvania State Capitol College
Middletown, PA 17057
(717) 948-6339

Industrial Resource Centers

In addition to these four TCs, Pennsylvania also has Industrial Resource Centers (IRCs). The IRCs are private nonprofit corporations managed by private industry and supported by the commonwealth of Pennsylvania.

The objective of the IRCs is to assist manufacturers to identify, learn about, and adopt modern production techniques, technologies, and philosophies. The IRCs will assist in assessing your business needs, developing manufacturing strategies, educating and training employees, marketing, and referencing to a network of professionals. There are several IRC locations:

Bioprocessing Resource Center
519 Wartik Laboratory
University Park, PA 16802
(814) 863-3650

Delaware Valley IRC
12265 Townsend Road, Suite 500
Philadelphia, PA 19154
(215) 464-8550

Northeastern Pennsylvania IRC (NEPIRC)
Garden Village Professional Center
16 Luzerne Avenue, Suite 125
West Pittston, PA 18643-2817
(717) 654-8966
FAX (717) 655-8931

**The Industrial Modernization Center
(IMC), Inc.**
P.O. Box 220-62A
Farm Complex, R.D. #5
Montoursville, PA 17754
(717) 368-8361

Northwest Pennsylvania IRC
2107 West 12th Street
Erie, PA 16505
(814) 456-6299

Manufacturers Resource Center (MRC)
125 Goodman Drive
Bethlehem, PA 18015
(215) 758-5599

**Manufacturing Technology Industrial
Resource Center (MANTEC)**
P.O. Box 5046
York, PA 17405
(717) 843-5054

**Southwestern Pennsylvania Industrial
Resource Center (SPIRC)**
Business Innovation Center
One Library Place
Duquesne, PA 15110
(412) 469-3530
(800) 444-2504

The Ben Franklin/IRC Partnership are supported by the Pennsylvania Department of Commerce's Office of Technology Development. This office can be contacted at the following address for further information on the activities and programs it supports:

**Office of Technology Development
Pennsylvania Department of Commerce**
352 Forum Building
Harrisburg, PA 17120
(717) 787-4147

There are many offices in Pennsylvania that assist women and minority-owned businesses. The offices provide information and referral services.

Assistance for Women and Minorities

Bureau of Women's Business Development
(717) 787-3339

Governor's Advisory Commission on African American Affairs
(717) 787-1954

Governor's Advisory Commission on Latino Affairs
(717) 783-3877

Minority Business Development Agency
(215) 597-9236

Office of Minority and Women Business Enterprise
(717) 787-7380

Small business incubators can provide to new or fledgling businesses a sheltered environment in which a business can grow and prosper. If your small business qualifies, your company may be offered:

Small Business Incubators

- Financial, management, and other business services — such as office equipment, clerical services, and telephone answering — you may share with other incubator tenants;

- Rental space in an incubator building at a lower than market rate; and
- Assistance with relocation once your company is mature enough to leave the incubator.

To qualify as a tenant in a small business incubator, your company will go through a selection process in which your business plan will be reviewed. For more information on incubators in Pennsylvania, contact the Pennsylvania Department of Commerce.

Federal Agency Assistance

The federal agencies described in Chapter 10 also have regional and local offices in Pennsylvania that you can contact.

U.S. Small Business Administration

The SBA publishes pamphlets and books covering the myriad aspects of business and provides limited financing for qualified borrowers. There are four U.S. Small Business Administration (SBA) offices in Pennsylvania.

Harrisburg SBA Office
100 Chestnut Street, Suite 309
Harrisburg, PA 17101
(717) 782-3840

Philadelphia Regional SBA Office
475 Allendale Road, Suite 201
King of Prussia, PA 19406
(215) 962-3805

Pittsburgh SBA Office
Convention Tower, 5th Floor
960 Penn Avenue
Pittsburgh, PA 15222
(412) 644-5441

Wilkes-Barre SBA Office
Penn Place, Room 2327
20 North Pennsylvania Avenue
Wilkes-Barre, PA 18701
(717) 826-6497

Service Corps of Retired Executives

Sponsored by the SBA, the Service Corps of Retired Executives (SCORE) is an association of retired businesspeople in your area who provide counseling. To find the nearest chapter, write or call SCORE at the U.S. Small Business Administration office above.

Small Business Institute

The Small Business Institute (SBI) program is a joint effort of the SBA and Pennsylvania universities. As part of their course work, senior-level college students, under the direction of faculty members, provide management consulting, market surveys, and other assistance for small business owners. To learn more about this program, contact the SBA office above.

Internal Revenue Service

To ask questions or request forms from the Internal Revenue Service, you can call the toll-free information number below. You can also hear prerecorded tax information from the IRS Tele-Tax number. The codes and topics which may be of interest to you include:

- 101 – IRS help available
- 103 – Small Business Tax Education Program
- 309 – Business use of home
- 310 – Business use of car

- 311 – Business travel expense
- 312 – Business entertainment expenses
- 352 – Self-employment tax
- 455 – Forms/Publications – How to order

For a complete list of codes, contact the IRS forms and publications number and request *Publication 910, Guide to Free Tax Services.*

Internal Revenue Service
(215) 574-9900 (Philadelphia office)
(412) 281-0112 (Pittsburgh office)
(800) 829-1040 (Questions)
(800) 829-3676 (Forms and publications)
(717) 627-1040 (Pennsylvania Tele-Tax)
(800) 829-4477 (Tele-Tax)

Local Government Sources of Help and Information

Local chambers of commerce and public libraries can be very helpful when it comes to assisting businesses.

Chambers of Commerce

Local chambers of commerce can be an excellent resource to learn more about the area or community in which you plan to locate your business. These offices are usually very helpful sources of information and referrals. The chamber of commerce can provide information about general business conditions, available space and rentals, and local business organizations and associations. These offices are usually listed in the White Pages of the local telephone directory.

Public Libraries

Your local public library offers a wealth of useful information. You can locate the answer to a number of business-related questions in the reference section. Statistics available on your industry and your competition can contribute to your market research and business plan.

In the periodical section, you will find publications that can provide information on emerging trends and issues in the business world. Telephone and specialized directories, available in libraries, can help you locate hard-to-find suppliers, potential buyers, associations, and organizations.

Many of the larger libraries also offer a reference assistance section. If a library in your area has this service, you may even be able to call the reference librarian for the information you need. Specialized, private, or college libraries may be available in your area, as well.

To find a library near you, look under the Yellow Pages or the Government Section of your phone directory.

State Business Publications

Trade and business journals can keep you up-to-date on business-related activities and issues in Pennsylvania. Daily newspapers are also helpful since they cover state and local news and information that could affect your business.

Allegheny Business News
471 Lincoln Avenue
Pittsburgh, PA 15202-3673
(412) 734-2300

Business Digest of Lehigh Valley
911 North Jerome Street
Allentown, PA 18103-1968
(215) 821-8350

Central Penn Business Journal
409 South Second Street, Suite 3D
Harrisburg, PA 17104
(717) 236-4300

Eastern Pennsylvania Business Journal
5000 Tilghman Street, Suite 215
Allentown, PA 18104
(215) 398-1026

Executive Report
3 Gateway Center #5, South
Pittsburgh, PA 15222-1004
(412) 471- 4585

Northeast Pennsylvania Business Journal
3185 Lackawanna Avenue
Bloomsburg, PA 17815-3329
(717) 784-2121

Pennsylvania CPA Journal
1608 Walnut Street, Third Floor
Philadelphia, PA 19103-5457
(215) 735-2635

Philadelphia Business Journal
400 Market Street, Suite 300
Philadelphia, PA 19106
(215) 238-1450

Pittsburgh Business Times-Journal
2313 East Carson Street, Suite 200
Pittsburgh, PA 15203
(412) 481-6397

Small Business Development Centers

Pennsylvania Small Business Development Centers (SBDCs) are located throughout the state to help you start and grow your business. Located at colleges and universities, SBDCs provide free management consulting and affordable business training workshops. The SBDCs help entrepreneurs with business plans, identify sources of financing, develop new markets, and manage cash flow. Call the SBDC nearest you for more information.

State SBDC Director's Office
University of Pennsylvania
Vance Hall, 4th Floor
3733 Spruce Street
Philadelphia, PA 19104-6374
(215) 898-1219

SBDC: Bucknell University
Dana Engineering Building
Lewisburg, PA 17837
(717) 524-1249

SBDC: Clarion University of Pennsylvania
Still Hall, Room 102
Clarion, PA 16214
(814) 226-2060

SBDC: Duquesne University
Rockwell Hall
Pittsburgh, PA 15282
(412) 396-6233

SBDC: Gannon University
Carlisle Building, 3rd Floor
Erie, PA 16541
(814) 871-7714

SBDC: Indiana University of Pennsylvania
Robert Shaw Center
650 South 13th Street
Indiana, PA 15705
(412) 357-7915

SBDC: LaSalle University
1900 West Onley Avenue
P.O. Box 828
Philadelphia, PA 19141
(215) 951-1416

SBDC: Lehigh University
Rauch Business Center
621 Taylor Street
Bethlehem, PA 18015
(215) 758-3980

SBDC: Kutztown University
University Center at Harrisburg
2986 North 2nd Street
Harrisburg, PA 17110
(717) 233-3120

SBDC: St. Francis College
P.O. Box 600
Loretto, PA 15940
(814) 472-3200

SBDC: St. Vincent College
Alfred Hall, 4th Floor
Latrobe, PA 15650
(412) 537-4572

SBDC: Temple University
Speakman Hall, Room 6
Philadelphia, PA 19122
(215) 204-7282

SBDC: University of Pittsburgh
Bellefield Hall, Room 208
315 South Bellefield Avenue
Pittsburgh, PA 15213
(412) 648-1544

SBDC: University of Scranton
St. Thomas Hall, Room 588
800 Linden Street
Scranton, PA 18510
(717) 941-7588

SBDC: West Chester University
906 Springdale Drive
Exton, PA 19341
(215) 363-5175

SBDC: Wilkes University
192 South Franklin Street
Wilkes-Barre, PA 18766
(717) 824-4651, ext. 4340
(800) 572-4444, ext. 4340 (in Pennsylvania)

Endnotes

1. *The 500 by State*, FORTUNE. 19 April 1993.
2. "Pennsylvania" *Academic American Encyclopedia*. 1993 ed., p. 149.
3. "Pennsylvania Fact Sheet," PENNSYLVANIA DEPARTMENT OF COMMERCE, 1990.
4. "Pennsylvania" *Academic American Encyclopedia*. 1993 ed., p. 150.
5. 1971 Pa. Laws 6, § 303.
6. 1971 Pa. Laws 6, § 306.
7. 1971 Pa. Laws 6, § 401.
8. 1933 Pa. Laws 364, § 201, *et seq.*
9. 1971 Pa. Laws 6, § 402.
10. 1971 Pa. Laws 6, § 330.1.
11. Id.
12. 1970 Pa. Laws 461, § 160.
13. 1971 Pa. Laws 6, § 401.
14. 1971 Pa. Laws 6, § 402.
15. 1971 Pa. Laws 6, § 601.
16. 1971 Pa. Laws 6, § 602.
17. 1971 Pa. Laws 6, § 602.
18. *Commonwealth v. Columbia Gas & Electric Corporation*, 336 Pa. 209, 8 A.2d 404 (1939).
19. 1971 Pa. Laws 6, § 602.
20. 1935 Pa. Laws 414, § 17.
21. 64 Philadelphia Code §§ 202–203.
22. 1971 Pa. Laws 6, § 240.
23. 1971 Pa. Laws 6, §§ 302–303.
24. 1971 Pa. Laws 6, § 240.
25. 1971 Pa. Laws 6, § 325.
26. 1971 Pa. Laws 6, § 352(b).
27. PA. STAT. ANN. tit. 43, § 781.
28. 1971 Pa. Laws 6, § 403.
29. 1971 Pa. Laws 6, § 202.
30. 1971 Pa. Laws 6, § 237.
31. 1971 Pa. Laws 6, § 201.
32. 1971 Pa. Laws 6, § 202.
33. 1971 Pa. Laws 6, § 271.
34. 1971 Pa. Laws 6, § 217.
35. 1971 Pa. Laws 6, §§ 266–267.
36. 1971 Pa. Laws 6, § 208.
37. 1971 Pa. Laws 6, § 237.
38. 1971 Pa. Laws 6, § 204.
39. 1971 Pa. Laws 6, § 201.
40. *Corporate Guide*, PENNSYLVANIA DEPARTMENT OF STATE, Jan. 1984, pp. 27–30.
41. *Pennsylvania Tax Update*, DEPARTMENT OF REVENUE, January/February 1992, Number 36.
42. 1971 Pa. Laws 6, § 316.
43. Pers. Income Tax Reg. § 113.3.
44. Pers. Income Tax Reg. § 113.5.
45. 1971 Pa. Laws 6, § 319.
46. Pers. Income Tax Reg. § 113.10.
47. Pers. Income Tax Reg. § 113.8.
48. 1937 Pa. Laws 2897, § 301.
49. Philadelphia Code § 19-1502(1) (Amended 1983).
50. PA. STAT. ANN. tit. 43, § 336.3.
51. PA. STAT. ANN. tit. 43, § 333.104.
52. PA. STAT. ANN. tit. 43, § 260.7.
53. PA. STAT. ANN. tit. 43, § 46.
54. 47 PA. CONS. STAT. ANN. § 747(a) and (b).
55. 1929 Pa. Laws 177, § 614-A, art. VI-A.
56. 1971 Pa. Laws 6, § 1206.
57. 1971 Pa. Laws 6, § 1208.
58. 1971 Pa. Laws 6, § 1206.
59. 1971 Pa. Laws 6, § 1223 and 971 Pa. Laws 6, § 1224.
60. 1971 Pa. Laws 6, § 1242.
61. 1931 Pa. Laws 149, § 4.
62. 1981 Pa. Laws 98, § 9511.1.
63. 1981 Pa. Laws 98, § 9511.1.
64. 1931 Pa. Laws 149, § 2.
65. 1931 Pa. Laws 149, § 3(a).
66. 75 PA. CONS. STAT. ANN. § 1304.
67. 75 PA. CONS. STAT. ANN. § 6143.
68. 75 PA. CONS. STAT. ANN. § 1901.
69. 1971 Pa. Laws 6, § 238.
70. 61 PA. CODE § 31.46.
71. *Resource Directory for Small Business*, PENNSYLVANIA DEPARTMENT OF COMMERCE.
72. 72 PA. CONS. STAT. ANN. ch. 17, § 1716 (a).
73. PA. STAT. ANN. tit. 43, § 801.
74. 72 PA. CONS. STAT. ANN. ch. 17.
75. *Ben Franklin Partnership Challenge Grant Program for Technological Innovation, Five-Year Report (March 1, 1983–February 29, 1988)* and Pennsylvania Department of Commerce brochures.
76. *Pennsylvania Small Business Operations & Resources Guide*, PENNSYLVANIA DEPARTMENT OF COMMERCE.
77. 72 PA. CONS. STAT. ANN. § 7601.

Index

Appendix

Checklist of Tax and Other Major Requirements for Nearly All Small Businesses

Requirement	None	1–4	5–10	11–14	15–19	20–99	100+	Section Reference
Federal estimated taxes	√	√	√	√	√	√	√	Sec. 4.6
Federal income tax returns	√	√	√	√	√	√	√	Sec. 4.12
Form SS-4, Application for Federal I.D. Number:								
Sole Proprietorships		√	√	√	√	√	√	Sec. 5.2
Partnerships	√	√	√	√	√	√	√	Sec. 5.2
Corporations	√	√	√	√	√	√	√	Sec. 5.2
Form 1099 returns	√	√	√	√	√	√	√	Sec. 4.7
Federal payroll tax returns		√	√	√	√	√	√	Sec. 5.2, 5.3
Provide and file W-2's to employees at year-end		√	√	√	√	√	√	Sec. 5.2
ERISA compliance:								
For unfunded or insured employees' welfare plan:								
Provide a Summary Plan Description to employees		√	√	√	√	√	√	Sec. 5.5
File a Summary Plan Description							√	Sec. 5.5
File *Form 5500, Annual Report*							√	Sec. 5.5
Provide a Summary Annual Report to employees							√	Sec. 5.5
File and provide to employees a Summary of Material Plan Modifications							√	Sec. 5.5
File a Terminal Report, if plan terminated							√	Sec. 5.5
For funded employee welfare plan:								
File and provide all items described in ERISA list		√	√	√	√	√	√	Sec. 5.5
For employees' pension or profit-sharing plan:								
Provide a Summary Plan Description to employees and file with U.S. Department of Labor		√	√	√	√	√	√	Sec. 5.5
File *Form 5500, Annual Report*							√	Sec. 5.5
File *Form 5500-C* or *Form 5500-R*		√	√	√	√	√	√	Sec. 5.5
Provide to employees and file a Summary of Material Modifications		√	√	√	√	√	√	Sec. 5.5
File a Terminal Report, if plan terminated		√	√	√	√	√	√	Sec. 5.5
Provide a Summary Annual Report to employees		√	√	√	√	√	√	Sec. 5.5
Bonding requirement for plan officials		√	√	√	√	√	√	Sec. 5.5
Federal Wage and Hour Laws and Regulations — coverage depends on nature of business and employee types not covered		√	√	√	√	√	√	Sec. 5.7

Checklist of Tax and Other Major Requirements for Nearly All Small Businesses (continued)

Requirement	Number of Employees of Business:							Section Reference
	None	1–4	5–10	11–14	15–19	20–99	100+	
Federal Fair Employment Laws:								
Americans with Disabilities Act anti-discrimination rules					√*	√*	√	Sec. 5.8
Anti-discrimination laws regarding race, color, sex, etc.					√	√	√	Sec. 5.8
Anti-discrimination laws regarding age						√	√	Sec. 5.8
Anti-discrimination laws regarding federal contracts		√	√	√	√	√	√	Sec. 5.8
Equal Pay Act for Women		√	√	√	√	√	√	Sec. 5.8, 11.5
File *Form EEO-1*							√	Sec. 5.8
Post notice regarding discrimination: racial, sexual, etc.					√	√	√	Sec. 5.8
Post notice regarding age anti-discrimination laws						√	√	Sec. 5.8
Post other anti-discrimination notices by certain federal contractors		√	√	√	√	√	√	Sec. 5.8
Federal Family and Medical Leave Act						√**	√	Sec. 5.12
Post notice regarding Federal Family and Medical Leave Act						√**	√	Sec. 5.12
Immigration Laws:								
Complete *INS Form I-9* for each new hire		√	√	√	√	√	√	Sec. 5.9
OSHA Job Safety Regulations:								
Health and safety		√	√	√	√	√	√	Sec. 5.6
Post *Job Safety and Health Notice*		√	√	√	√	√	√	Sec. 5.6
Post *Employee Rights Notice* regarding OSHA		√	√	√	√	√	√	Sec. 5.6
Record industrial injuries and illnesses				√	√	√	√	Sec. 5.6, 11.5
Report job fatalities or multiple injuries to OSHA		√	√	√	√	√	√	Sec. 5.6, 11.5
Federal and State Child Labor Laws		√	√	√	√	√	√	Sec. 5.7, 11.5
Local business licenses	√	√	√	√	√	√	√	Sec. 4.3, 11.4
Sales and use tax permit and returns, if selling tangible personal property	√	√	√	√	√	√	√	Sec. 11.4
Fictitious business name statement, if using fictitious business name	√	√	√	√	√	√	√	Sec. 11.4
Pennsylvania estimated taxes	√	√	√	√	√	√	√	Sec. 11.4
Pennsylvania income taxes	√	√	√	√	√	√	√	Sec. 11.2, 11.4
Pennsylvania Wage and Hour Laws and Regulations — most employees are covered, yet some types are not		√	√	√	√	√	√	Sec. 11.5
Workers' compensation insurance		√	√	√	√	√	√	Sec. 11.5
Pennsylvania Fair Employment Laws: General prohibition of discrimination		√	√	√	√	√	√	Sec. 11.5

* Applies to companies with 25 or more employees until July 26, 1994 when it will apply to companies with 15 or more employees.

** Only applies to companies with 50 or more employees.

Checklist of Official Government Posters and Notices Required to be Displayed by Businesses

Type of Poster or Notice	When required	Where to obtain
Local business license	Required to be obtained by nearly all businesses operating in a particular locality.	Local city hall or county courthouse
Sales tax license	Required to be displayed at each place of business where tangible personal property is sold.	State tax office
OSHA poster regarding job safety and health	Required to be posted by all employers.	U.S. Department of Labor, Occupational Safety and Health Administration
U.S. Fair Labor Standards Act Federal Minimum Wage poster *(WH Publication 1088)*	Required to be posted by employers with employees whose wages and working conditions are subject to the U.S. Fair Labor Standards Act.	U.S. Department of Labor, Employment Standards Administration, Wage and Hour Division
Federal Equal Employment Opportunity poster	Required to be posted by all employers with 15 or more employees 20 weeks of a calendar year or with federal contracts or subcontracts of $10,000 or more.	Federal Equal Employment Opportunity Commission
Federal Age Discrimination poster	Required to be posted by all employers with 20 or more employees, 20 or more weeks in a calendar year.	U.S. Department of Labor, Wage and Hour Division
Federal Rehabilitation Act poster regarding hiring of disabled persons	Required to be posted by employers with federal contracts or subcontracts of $2,500 or more.	Assistant Secretary for Employment Standards, U.S. Department of Labor, Washington, D.C.
Poster regarding hiring of Vietnam-era veterans	Required to be posted by employers with federal contracts or subcontracts of $10,000 or more.	The government contracting officer on the federal contract
Employee Polygraph Protection Act Notice	Required to be posted by most private employers.	Local office of the Wage and Hour Division, U.S. Department of Labor

Instructions for Completing Application for Sales, Use, and Hotel Occupancy Tax License

INSTRUCTIONS FOR COMPLETING
APPLICATION FOR SALES, USE AND HOTEL OCCUPANCY TAX
LICENSE

This is an application for a Sales Tax License Number which will authorize the holder to collect sales tax on taxable sales. Qualified exempt organizations, such as charitable or religious, requesting an exemption number should use form REV-72 UNLESS the exempt organization intends to make taxable sales of property or services.

APPLICATION INSTRUCTIONS

Providing complete and accurate information expedites processing. Incomplete applications will be returned.

Lines 1 - 10 - Revenue use only. Do not write in these spaces.

Lines 11 - 27 - Applicants must answer all questions. Write N/A if not applicable.

SPECIAL APPLICATION TIPS

LINE 11 - THIS INFORMATION MUST BE COMPLETED. LICENSES ARE NOT ISSUED MORE THAN 90 DAYS PRIOR TO THE OPENING OF A BUSINESS.

Lines 12, 12a and 12b - Complete both lines if they apply to your business. Enter legal name of owner on 12. Complete with the Federal Identification Number assigned by the I.R.S.

Example - "Joe Smith" operates as a sole proprietorship under the registered fictitious name of "Joe's Plumbing". "Joe Smith" should be entered on line 12. "Joe's Plumbing" should be entered on line 12b.

Example - "A Company, Inc." operates "X Division" for which it requests a sales tax license number. "A Company, Inc." should be entered on line 12. "X Division" should be entered on line 12b.

Line 14 - Enter physical location of business, Example: "R.D.2, 14 Center Street", etc. DO NOT USE post office boxes or other addresses which do not represent the actual physical location.

Line 15 - Complete this line only if tax returns and correspondence should be sent to an address OTHER THAN the physical location (listed on line 14.)

Line 21 - Records involving Pennsylvania transactions MUST be retained within the Commonwealth unless written authorization is obtained from the Revenue Department under the provisions of Section 271 (c) of the Tax Reform Code of 1971. Authorization may be obtained by writing the PA Department of Revenue, Bureau of Audits. Harrisburg, PA 17128-1001.

Line 27 - Applications must be signed.

*Those who are conducting business for a period of LESS THAN 90 days in any calendar year must contact a local Revenue Department District Office (listed in the blue pages of your telephone directory) to obtain a TEMPORARY LICENSE.

ALL NEW LICENSEES WILL BE PLACED ON A QUARTERLY FILING BASIS

PURCHASING AN EXISTING BUSINESS

Those purchasing an existing business are advised to request from the seller a "Tax Clearance Certificate" to ensure there are no outstanding sales tax liabilities. 72 p.s. 7240 of the Tax Reform Code requires the seller to give the PA Department of Revenue ten days written notice of the sale or transfer.

TRANSIENT VENDORS

Transient Vendors must obtain a Transient Vendor Certificate and a permanent Sales Tax License or a Temporary License from a local Revenue District Office if participating with a licensed promoter. Handcrafters are not Transient Vendors; but, if not permanently licensed, must obtain a Temporary License number from the local Revenue Office and remit the sales tax.

Form REV 289 AS – Application for Tax License: Sample

REV-289 AS + (5-90)

COMMONWEALTH OF PENNSYLVANIA
DEPARTMENT OF REVENUE
BUREAU OF BUSINESS TRUST FUND TAXES
DEPT. 280901
HARRISBURG, PA 17128-0901

APPLICATION FOR TAX LICENSE
☐ Sales
☐ Use
☐ Hotel Occupancy
Please Print in Black Ink or Type

BUREAU USE ONLY

| U | N | CC | I | RE |

FOR BUREAU USE ONLY

1 License Number
2 Form M Q SA F T
3 License Number
4 License Date
5 Start Date
6 OOB Date
7 I P PC FC O
8 PIC
9 No. Cos.
10 Legal Name

11 Date first taxable sales or use made in PA
Month Day Year

11a This application is a request for:
☐ A new license   ☐ Revision of an existing license   ☐ Addition of another business location

11b Applicant is operating as: (check appropriate block)
☐ An Individual   ☐ A Partnership   ☐ An Association   ☐ A Corporation   ☐ Other (Explain) _____

12 Name of owner (individual, partnership, corporation, association, etc.) If corporation, provide legal name.

12a Federal EIN

12b Legal name of business if other than line 12.

13 Business Phone ( )

14 Location of principal place of business (Post Office Box is not acceptable.)

Street and Number/or R.D. Number

| City or Town | County | State | Zip Code |

15 Mailing Address, if different than #14.
OFFICIAL USE ONLY

Street and Number/or R.D. Number and Box

| City or Town | County | State | Zip Code |

16 Name, title, social security number and home address of the owner of the business and/or all elected officers constituting the Partnership, Association, or Corporation. (Attach a separate sheet if more space is required).

Name-Last	First	Middle Initial	Title	Social Security Number
Home Street Address		City	State	Zip Code
Name-Last	First	Middle Initial	Title	Social Security Number
Home Street Address		City	State	Zip Code
Name-Last	First	Middle Initial	Title	Social Security Number
Home Street Address		City	State	Zip Code

16a List the name(s), title(s) and social security number(s) of individual(s) responsible for remitting the PA sales tax.

| Name | Title | Social Security Number |
| Name | Title | Social Security Number |

17 If a Corporation, give date, state of incorporation and corporation tax file (box) number

| Date | State | Corporation Tax File (Box) Number |

If out-of-state corporation, also give date acquired PA Certificate of Authority:
Date:

17a - OFFICIAL USE ONLY -
Effective change or reinstatement date
Month Day Year
☐ Address Change   ☐ County Change

18 Are you operating under the Fictitious Names Act?   ☐ Yes   ☐ No   If yes, give date and location of registration.

| Date: | Location: Street Address | City | State | Zip Code |

18a Are you registered with the Pennsylvania Department of State?   ☐ Yes   ☐ No

Form REV 289 AS – Application for Tax License: Sample (continued)

19 From the chart on the reverse side of the instruction sheet:

A. Choose the principal activity your business will perform in Pennsylvania and insert applicable business standard industrial code.

B. If any portion of the business will involve retail sales/services, or rentals, insert applicable standard industrial code.

20 Describe business activities.

_____

20a Do you presently or in the future intend to make retail sales?

☐ Yes   ☐ No

20b Do you presently or in the future intend to lease motor vehicles or equipment?

☐ Yes   ☐ No

21 Address at which records involving Pennsylvania transactions will be retained.

Street Address   City   State   Zip Code

22 Will owner operate at locations in Pennsylvania other than at the address entered on line 14?   ☐ Yes   ☐ No

If yes, list the name and physical location of each additional address (Post Office Box is not acceptable). Attach a separate sheet if additional space is required.

Name

Street Address   City   State   Zip Code

Name

Street Address   City   State   Zip Code

23 Was business on line 12 or line 12b acquired from another?   ☐ Yes   ☐ No   If yes, complete the following information.

A. Date Acquired   – | Did you acquire: ☐ All of business   ☐ Part of business | Former Federal E.I.N.

B. Name of Former Owner

C. Former Legal Name (if other than B)

D. Sales Tax License/Registration Number of Former Owner | ☐ Keep Active   ☐ Cancel

24 Were you previously registered under the Pennsylvania Sales and Use Tax Act?   ☐ Yes   ☐ No

☐ Keep Active   ☐ Cancel

If yes, list all previous business names and account numbers. Attach a separate sheet if additional space is required.

Business Name	Sales Tax License Number	Federal E.I.N.
Business Name	Sales Tax License Number	Federal E.I.N.

25 Do you maintain an established office, distribution house, sales house, warehouse, service enterprise, residence from which business is conducted or another place of business within the Commonwealth?   ☐ Yes   ☐ No

26 Will you be delivering tangible personal property in Pennsylvania?   ☐ Yes   ☐ No

26a If yes, will you solicit sales of tangible personal property or services pursuant to orders placed by mail or other means; e.g., telephone?   ☐ Yes   ☐ No

Please specify.

27 I certify that the information provided on this application form has been examined by me and is, to the best of my knowledge, true and correct.

Print Name   Telephone Number   Date

(   )

Signature of Above Individual   Title

- The Bureau of Business Trust Fund Taxes, Registration Division, must be notified of any changes to the information included on this form.
- Questions pertaining to this form can be referred to (717)787-7129, Registration Division.
- Separate this sheet from the instruction sheet, and send to the return address on the front page of this application.

Standard Industrial Code Key

STANDARD INDUSTRIAL CODE KEY
(Sales Tax System)

CODE NUMBER	PRINCIPAL ACTIVITY
	AGRICULTURE
0099	Farms, Fisheries, Forestry, Allied Services
2411	Logging
	CONSTRUCTION CONTRACTING
1500	Buildings, Residential and Commercial
1750	Carpeting, Flooring
1752	Carpet Installation and Removal Services
1770	Concrete, Asphalt (other than highway and street)
1730	Electrical Work (electric heat) (burglar and fire alarm)
1600	Heavy Construction (except highway and street)
1610	Highway and Street Construction
0780	Landscaping
1740	Masonry, Stonework, Tile Setting, Plastering
5270	Mobile Homes (Contract Sales)
1720	Painting, Paperhanging, Building Decorating
1710	Plumbing, Heating (except electric), Air Conditioning
1760	Roofing, Sheet Metal, Siding
1790	Special Trade Contractors not listed Elsewhere
1623	Water, Sewer, Pipe Line and the like
1781	Water Well Drilling
	FINANCE, INSURANCE, REAL ESTATE
6000	Banks and Trust Companies
6611	Combination Real Estate, Insurance, Loans, Law Offices
6100	Credit, Savings, and Financial Agencies other than Banks
6700	Holding and Other Investment Offices
6411	Insurance Agents and Brokers
6300	Insurance Companies and Pension, Health and Welfare Funds
6500	Real Estate Agents, Developers, Lessors and the like
6200	Securities Dealers
	HOTELS AND LODGING
7030	Camps and Trailer Parks
7011	Hotels, Motels and Tourist Courts
7041	Organization Hotels and Lodging Houses on Membership Basis
7021	Rooming and Boarding Houses
	MANUFACTURING/PROCESSING
2300	Apparel Manufacturers
3900	Artists' Instruments, Jewelry, Toys, Recreation Equipment
2800	Chemical, Drug and Paint Products
3800	Clocks, Measuring Instruments et al, Photographic, Medical Goods
2000	Food Products
2500	Furniture and Fixtures, Metal, Wood, Plastic
3100	Leather Products
3600	Machinery, Equipment and Supplies - Electrical and Electronic
3500	Machinery, except electrical
3400	Metal Products, Fabricated
3300	Metal Products, Primary
2451	Mobile Homes
3200	Non-metallic Mineral Products - Asbestos, Clay, Glass, Stone
2600	Paper and Paper Board Products, Pulp Mills
2900	Petroleum Products
3000	Plastic and Rubber Products
2700	Publishing, Printing and Allied Services
2421	Sawmills and Planing Mills
2200	Textiles
2100	Tobacco Products
3700	Transportation Equipment
2400	Wood Products other than Furniture
3900	Miscellaneous Manufacturing
	MINING, GAS AND OIL EXPLORATION, QUARRYING
1000	Mining, Gas and Oil Exploration, Quarrying
1781	Water Well Drilling
	PUBLIC ADMINISTRATION
9000	Public Administration
	RETAIL
5599	Air Craft Dealer
5931	Antique Stores and Used Furniture Stores
5531	Auto and Home Supply Stores
7510	Automotive Rental and Leasing Without Drivers
5600	Apparel and Accessory Stores, Men, Women, Children
5181	Beer Distributors
5551	Boat Dealers
5942	Book Stores
5946	Camera and Photographic Supply Stores
2899	Chemicals and Chemical Preparations
2842	Cleaning Supplies
7333	Commercial Art and Photography
5999	Cosmetic Stores
7379	Data Processing Equipment Sales and Rentals
5300	Department and Variety Stores
5963	Direct Selling Establishments (Door-to-Door)
5912	Drug and Proprietary Stores
5812	Eating and Drinking Places (food sales more than 50%)
5813	Eating and Drinking Place (food sales 50% or less)
5811	Eating Places (No alcoholic beverages)
7394	Equipment Rental and Leasing
5499	Food Stores Miscellaneous
5713	Floor Covering Sales
5992	Florists

CODE NUMBER	PRINCIPAL ACTIVITY
	RETAIL (Continued)
5982	Fuel and Ice Dealers, except Fuel Oil Dealers and Bottled Gas Dealers
5983	Fuel Oil Dealers
5700	Furniture, Home Furnishings, Appliance, and Equipment Stores (except floor covering)
5541	Gasoline Service Stations
5399	General Merchandise Stores (Country General Stores)
5947	Gift, Novelty and Souvenir Shops
5411	Grocery Stores, Supermarkets, Delicatessen, etc
7699	Guns, Sales and Returns
5251	Hardware Stores
5945	Hobby, Toy and Game Shops
5944	Jewelry Stores
0279	Kennels
5984	Liquified Petroleum Gas (Bottled Gas) Dealers
5948	Luggage and Leather Good Shops
5211	Lumber and Other Building Materials Dealers
5961	Mail Order Houses
5271	Mobil Home Dealers
5511	Motor Vehicle Dealers, New and Used Cars
5571	Motorcycle Dealers
5733	Musical Instrument and Record Stores
5994	Newsstands - Retail
5261	Nurseries, Lawn and Garden Supply Stores
5943	Office Forms and Supplies
3579	Office Machines and Devices
5231	Paint, Glass and Wallpaper Stores
5999	Pet Foods and Pet Shops
7221	Photographers
3662	Radio and T.V. Transmitting Equipment
5500	Recreational Vehicle Dealers, off highway (go-carts, Snowmobiles, etc)
3576	Scales and Balances, Except Laboratory
5949	Sewing, Needlework and Piece Goods Stores
7319	Sign Painting and Lettering, General Advertising
5941	Sporting Goods Stores and Bicycle Shops
5943	Stationery Stores
3433	Stoves, Household Heating - Except Electric
7999	Swimming Pools
7699	Taxidermy
3661	Telephones and Equipment
7399	Telephone Solicitation or Message Service
5063	Testing and Measuring Equipment, Electrical (Radon Kits, etc.)
5561	Trailer Dealers, Recreational and Utility
7824	Video Sales and Rental
5962	Vending Machine Operators
5999	Retail Stores not elsewhere classified
	SERVICES
7311	Advertising Agencies
7319	Advertising, Miscellaneous
7900	Amusement and Recreation Center, Miscellaneous
7520	Automobile Parking
7530	Automotive Repair Shops
7241	Barber Shops
7231	Beauty Shops
7399	Business Services, Miscellaneous
7379	Data Processing Equipment Repairs
7374	Data Processing Services
7360	Employment Agencies and Personnel Supply Services
7991	Exercise Salon
8000	Health Services (Doctors, Dentists, Clinics, etc.)
7948	Horse Breeding and Racing
7219	Laundries, Dry Cleaning Plants, etc
8111	Legal Services
7330	Mailing, Reproduction and Stenographic Services
8900	Miscellaneous Services (Engineering, Accounting, Research, etc.)
7800	Motion Pictures
8400	Museums, Art Galleries, Botanical and Zoological Gardens
7312	Outdoor Advertising Services
7299	Personal Services, Miscellaneous
7395	Photo Finishers
7699	Repair Shops and Related Services, Miscellaneous
7340	Services to Dwellings and Other Buildings
7299	Tanning Salon
0740	Veterinary Services
	TRANSPORTATION, COMMUNICATIONS, ELECTRIC, GAS AND SANITARY SERVICES
4511	Air Transportation, Common Carriers
4580	Air Transportation, Fixed Facilities and Services Related Thereto
4521	Air Transportation, non-common carriers
4800	Communication Services, Telephone, Telegraph, Radio, Television
4911	Electricity Production and/or Distribution
4920	Gas Production and/or Distribution
4100	Passenger Transportation, Common Carrier (Motor Vehicle)
4140	Passenger Transportation, Non-common Carrier (Motor Vehicle)
4610	Pipelines except Natural Gas
4000	Railroads and Railway Express
4953	Refuse Systems
4952	Sewage Systems
4961	Steam Production and/or Distribution
4231	Terminal Facilities, Motor Freight
4170	Terminal Facilities, Motor Vehicle Passenger
4700	Transportation Services not elsewhere listed
4210	Trucking, Common Carrier
4200	Trucking, Non-common Carrier
4941	Water Supply Systems
4400	Water Transportation and Services incidental Thereto
	NON-CLASSIFIED ESTABLISHMENTS
9999	Non-classified Establishments

Notes

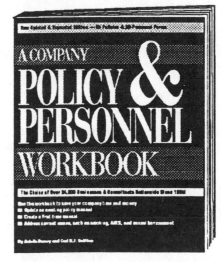

Get business tips from over 157 seasoned experts.

Business Formation and Planning

Start Your Business:
A Beginner's Guide

 Book

This handy, easy-to-read book is full of checklists to help answer your start-up questions. Helps you ask the right questions and find out where you can get the answers. The Plan of Action Worksheets make it easy to compile and coordinate your to-do list. The book is divided into sections covering business, legal, marketing, human resources, sales, taxes, and other decisions.

The Successful Business
Plan: Secrets & Strategies

 Book and software for IBM & compatibles

Start-to-finish guide on creating a successful business plan. Includes tips from venture capitalists, bankers, and successful CEOs. Features worksheets for ease in planning and budgeting with the Abrams Method of Flow-Through Financials. Gives a sample business plan, plus specialized help for retailers, service companies, manufacturers, and in-house corporate plans. Also tells how to find funding sources.

Starting and Operating a
Business in... series
Book available for each state in the
United States, plus District of Columbia

One-stop resource to current federal and state laws and regulations that affect businesses. Clear "human language" explanations of complex issues, plus samples of government forms, and sources for additional help or information. Helps seasoned business owners keep up with changing legislation, and guides new entrepreneurs step-by-step to start and run the business. Includes many checklists and worksheets to organize ideas, create action plans, and project financial scenarios.

The Essential Corporation
Handbook

 Book

This comprehensive reference for small business corporations in all 50 states and Washington, D.C. explains the legal requirements for maintaining a corporation in good standing. Features many sample corporate documents which are annotated by the author to show what to look for and what to look out for. Tells how to avoid personal liability as an officer, director, or shareholder.

Surviving and Prospering
in a Business Partnership

 Book

From evaluation of potential partners, through the drafting of agreements, to day-to-day management of working relationships, this book helps avoid classic partnership catastrophes. Discusses how to set up the partnership to reduce the financial and emotional consequences of unanticipated disputes, dishonesty, divorce, disability, or death of a partner.

California Corporation
Formation Package and
Minute Book

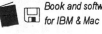 *Book and software for IBM & Mac*

Provides forms required for incorporating and maintaining closely held corporations, including: articles of incorporation; bylaws; stock certificates, stock transfer record sheets, bill of sale agreement; minutes form; plus many others. Addresses questions on fees, timing, notices, regulations, election of directors and other critical factors. Software has minutes, bylaws, and articles of incorporation already for you to edit and customize (using your own word processor).

Franchise Bible:
A Comprehensive Guide

 Book (New edition)

Complete guide to franchising for prospective franchisees or for business owners considering franchising their business. Includes actual sample documents, such as a complete offering circular, plus worksheets for evaluating franchise companies, locations, and organizing information before seeing an attorney. This book is helpful for lawyers as well as their clients.

Home Business Made Easy

Book

Thinking of starting a business at home? This book is the easiest road to starting a home business. Shows you how to select and start a home business that fits your interests, lifestyle and pocketbook. Walks you through 153 different businesses you could operate from home full or part time. Author David Hanania has boiled the process down to simple steps so you can get started now to realize your dreams.

The Small Business Expert
Software for IBM-PC & compatibles

Generates comprehensive custom checklist of the state and federal laws and regulations based on your type and size of business. Allows comparison of doing business in each of the 50 states. Built-in worksheets create outlines for personnel policies, marketing feasibility studies, and a business plan draft. *Requires 256K RAM and hard disk.*

Starting and Operating a
Business: U.S. Edition
Set of eleven binders

The complete encyclopedia of how tc do business in the U.S. Describes laws and regulations for each state, plus Washington, D.C., as well as the federal government. Includes lists of sources of help, plus post cards for requesting materials from government agencies. This set is valuable for businesses with locations or marketing activities in several states, plus franchisors, attorneys, and other consultants.

To order these business tools, use the enclosed order form, FAX 503-476-1479 or call us toll-free at 800-228-2275

Step-by-step techniques for generating more profit.

Financial Management

Top Tax Saving Ideas for Today's Small Business
New Book

An extensive summary of every imaginable tax break that is still available in today's "reformed" tax environment. Deals with the various entities that the owner/manager may choose to operate a business. Identifies a wide assortment of tax deduction, fringe benefits, and tax deferrals. Includes a simplified checklist of recent tax law changes with an emphasis on tax breaks.

Financial Management Techniques for Small Business
Book and software for IBM-PC & compatibles

Clearly reveals the essential ingredients of sound financial management in detail. By monitoring trends in your financial activities, you will be able to uncover potential problems before they become crises. You'll understand why you can be making a profit and still not have the cash to meet expenses, and you'll learn the steps to change your business' cash behavior to get more return for your effort. Software makes your business' financial picture graphically clear, and lets you look at "what if" scenarios.

The Buyer's Guide to Business Insurance
New Book
(Available Spring 1994)

Straightforward advice on shopping for insurance, understanding types of coverage, comparing proposals and premium rates. Worksheets help identify and weigh the risks a particular business is likely to face, then determine if any of those might be safely self-insured or eliminated. Request for proposal form helps businesses avoid over-paying for protection.

Collection Techniques for Small Business
New Book
(Available Spring 1994)

Practical tips on how to turn receivables into cash. Worksheets and checklists help businesses establish credit policies, track accounts, and flag when it is necessary to bring in a collection agency, attorney, or go to court. This book advises how to deal with disputes, negotiate settlements, win in small claims court, and collect on judgments. Gives examples of telephone collection techniques and collection letters.

The Secrets to Buying and Selling a Business
New Book
(Available Spring 1994)

Prepares a business buyer or seller for negotiations that will achieve win-win results. Shows how to determine the real worth of a business, including intangible assets such as "goodwill." Over 36 checklists and worksheets on topics such as tax impact on buyers and sellers, escrow checklist, cash flow projections, evaluating potential buyers, financing options, and many others.

Business Owner's Guide to Accounting & Bookkeeping
Book

Makes understanding the economics of business simple. Explains the basic accounting principles that relate to any business. Step-by-step instructions for generating accounting statements and interpreting them, spotting errors, and recognizing warning signs. Discusses how banks and other creditors view financial statements.

Controlling Your Company's Freight Costs
Book

Shows how to increase company profits by trimming freight costs. Provides tips for comparing alternative methods and shippers, then negotiating contracts to receive the most favorable discounts. Tells how to package shipments for safe transport. Discusses freight insurance and dealing with claims for loss or damage. Appendices include directory of U.S. ports, shipper's guide, and sample bill of lading.

Financial Templates
Software for IBM-PC & compatibles

Calculates and graphs many business "what-if" scenarios and financial reports. Twenty-eight financial templates such as income statements, cash flow, and balance sheet comparisons, break-even analyses, product contribution comparisons, market share, net present value, sales model, pro formas, loan payment projections, etc. *Requires 512K RAM hard disk or two floppy drives, plus Lotus 1-2-3 or compatible spreadsheet program.*

Yes, we accept credit cards — VISA, MasterCard, American Express, Discover, or your personal or business check.

Proven tools and ideas to expand your business.

Marketing & Public Relations

Power Marketing
Book

A wealth of basic, how-to marketing information that easily takes a new or experienced business owner through the essentials of marketing and sales strategies, customer database marketing, advertising, public relations, budgeting, and follow-up marketing systems. Written in a friendly tone by a marketing educator, the book features worksheets with step-by-step instructions, a glossary of marketing terms, and a sample marketing plan. Also available: *Power Marketing Tools for Small Business*—two hours of audio tapes by author Jody Hornor that reveal 81 tools you can use to increase your market power.

How To Develop & Market Creative Business Ideas
Book

Step-by-step manual guides the inventor through all stages of new product development. Discusses patenting your invention, trademarks, copyrights, and how to construct your prototype. Gives information on financing, distribution, test marketing, and finding licensees. Plus, lists many useful sources for prototype resources, trade shows, funding, and more.

Cost-Effective Market Analysis
Book

Workbook explains how a small business can conduct its own market research. Shows how to set objectives, determine which techniques to use, create a schedule, and then monitor expenses. Encompasses primary research (trade shows, telephone interviews, mail surveys), plus secondary research (using available information in print).

Customer Information and Tracking System (CITS)
Software for IBM-PC & compatibles
(Available Spring 1994)

Stores details of past activities plus future reminders on customers, clients, contacts, vendors, and employees, then gives instant access to that information when needed. "Tickler" fields keep reminders of dates for recontacts. "Type" fields categorize names for sorting as the user defines. "Other data" fields store information such as purchase and credit history, telephone call records, or interests.

Has massive storage capabilities. Holds up to 255 lines of comments for each name, plus unlimited time and date stamped notes. Features perpetual calendar, and automatic telephone dialing. Built-in word processing and merge gives the ability to pull in the information already keyed into the fields into individual or form letters. Prints mail labels, rotary file cards, and phone directories. This program is a great contact manager — call 1-800-228-2275 for information. *Requires a hard disk, 640K RAM and 80 column display. (Autodial feature requires modem.)*

International Business

Export Now
Book

Prepares a business to enter the export market. Clearly explains the basics, then articulates specific requirements for export licensing, preparation of documents, payment methods, packaging, and shipping. Includes advice on evaluating foreign representatives, planning international marketing strategies, and discovering official U.S. policy for various countries and regions. Lists sources.

EXECARDS®
International Communication Cards

EXECARDS offer unique cards you can send to businesspeople of many nationalities to help build and maintain lasting relationships. One distinguished EXECARD choice is a richly textured and embossed white card of substantial quality that expresses thank you in thirteen languages; Japanese, Russian, French, Chinese, Arabic, German, Swahili, Italian, Polish, Spanish, Hebrew, and Swedish, as well as English. Another handsome option is an ivory card with thank you embossed in Russian and English. To each, you can add a personal note or order a custom printed message. *Please call for more information.*

Now – Find Out How Your Business Can Profit By Being Environmentally Aware

The Business Environmental Handbook
Book

Save your business while you are saving the planet. Here's your chance to learn about the hundreds of ways any business can help secure its future by starting to conserve resources now. This book reveals little-understood but simple techniques for recycling, precycling, and conservation that can save your business money now, and help preserve resources. Also gives tips on "green marketing" to customers .

Gain the power of increased knowledge — Oasis is your source.

Acquiring Outside Capital

Raising Capital: How to Write a Financing Proposal

New Book

Valuable resource for writing and presenting a winning loan proposal. Includes professional tips on how to write the proposal. Presents detailed examples of the four most common types of proposals to secure venture capital and loans: Private Placement Circular; Prospectus or Public Offering; Financing Proposal; and Limited Partnership Offering.

The Money Connection: Where & How to Apply for Business Loans

New Book

Comprehensive listing of funding sources. Lists hundreds of current nationally recognized business loan and venture capital firms. Describes the latest federal, state, county, and community loan, investment and assistance programs. Gives addresses and phone numbers of federal agency offices in each state.

Financing Your Small Business

Book

Essential techniques to successfully identify, approach, attract, and manage sources of financing. Shows how to gain the full benefits of debt financing while minimizing its risks. Outlines all types of financing and walks you step by step through the process, from evaluating short-term credit options, through negotiating a long-term loan, to deciding whether to go public.

The Loan Package

Book

Preparatory package for a business loan proposal. Worksheets help analyze cash needs and articulate business focus. Includes sample forms for balance sheets, income statements, projections, and budget reports. Screening sheets rank potential lenders to shorten the time involved in getting the loan.

The Successful Business Plan: Secrets & Strategies

Book and software for IBM & compatibles

Now you can find out what venture capitalists and bankers really want to see before they will fund a company. This book gives you their personal tips and insights. The Abrams Method of Flow-Through Financials breaks down the chore into easy to manage steps, so you can end up with a fundable proposal. Software is available for this book—see the back page of this catalog or call 1-800-228-2275 for a free software catalog. *Software requires a hard drive.*

Financial Templates

Software for IBM & compatibles

Software speeds business calculations. Includes 28 financial templates including various projections, statements, ratios, histories, amortizations, and cash flows. This is just one of many useful software packages designed specifically for small businesses. Call 1-800-228-2275 for information. *Requires Lotus 1-2-3, Microsoft Excel 2.0 or higher.*

Human Resource Ideas

A Company Policy and Personnel Workbook

Book and software for IBM & compatibles

Saves costly consultant or staff hours in creating company personnel policies. Provides model policies on topics such as employee safety, leave of absence, flextime, smoking, substance abuse, sexual harassment, performance improvement, grievance procedure. For each subject, practical and legal ramifications are explained, then a choice of alternate policies presented. Software is available for this book. Check our software catalog or call 1-800-228-2275 for more information.

People Investment

Book

Written for the business owner or manager who is not a personnel specialist. Explains what you must know to make your hiring decisions pay off for everyone. Learn more about the Americans With Disabilities Act (ADA), Medical and Family Leave, and more.

Managing People: A Practical Guide

Book

Focuses on developing the art of working with people to maximize the productivity and satisfaction of both manager and employees. Discussions, exercises, and self-tests boost skills in communicating, delegating, motivating, developing teams, goal-setting, adapting to change, and coping with stress.

Safety Law Compliance Manual for California Businesses

Book

Now every California employer must have an Injury and Illness Prevention Program that meets the specific requirements of Senate Bill 198. Already, thousands of citations have been issued to companies who did not comply with all seven components of the complicated new law. Avoid fines by using this guide to set up a program that will meet Cal/OSHA standards. Includes forms.

Plus optional binder for your company's safety program

Also available — Company Injury and Illness Prevention Program Binder — Pre-organized and ready-to-use with forms, tabs, logs and sample documents. Saves your company time, work, and worry.

Why hesitate? If any product you order doesn't meet your needs, just return it for full refund or credit. 800-228-2275.

IH 2 12 3

Unique cards get you noticed. Books & software save you time.

Business Communications

Proposal Development: How to Respond and Win the Bid

📖 *Book*

Orchestrates a successful proposal from preliminary planning to clinching the deal. Shows by explanation and example how to: determine what to include; create text, illustrations, tables, exhibits, and appendices; how to format (using either traditional methods or desktop publishing); meet the special requirements of government proposals; set up and follow a schedule.

Write Your Own Business Contracts

📖 *Book*

Explains the "do's" and "don'ts" of contract writing so any person in business can do the preparatory work in drafting contracts before hiring an attorney for final review. Gives a working knowledge of the various types of business agreements, plus tips on how to prepare for the unexpected.

Complete Book of Business Forms

📖 *Book*

Over 200 reproducible forms for all types of business needs: personnel, employment, finance, production flow, operations, sales, marketing, order entry, and general administration. Time-saving, uniform, coordinated way to record and locate important business information.

EXECARDS®
The Original Business-To-Business Communication Tools

EXECARDS, business-to-business message cards, are an effective vehicle for maintaining personal contacts in this era of rushed, highly-technical communications. A card takes only seconds and a few cents to send, but can memorably tell customers, clients, prospects, or co-workers that their relationship is valued. Many styles and messages to choose from for thanking, acknowledging, inviting, reminding, prospecting, following up, etc. *Please call 800-228-2275 for complete catalog.*

PlanningTools™
Paper pads, 3-hole punched

Handsome PlanningTools help organize thoughts and record notes, actions, plans, and deadlines, so important information and responsibilities do not get lost or forgotten. Specific PlanningTools organize different needs, such as Calendar Notes, Progress/Activity Record, Project Plan/Record, Week's Priority Planner, Make-A-Month Calendar, and Milestone Chart. *Please call 800-228-2275 for information.*

Business Relocation

Company Relocation Handbook: Making the Right Move

📖 *Book*

Comprehensive guide to moving a business. Begins with defining objectives for moving and evaluating whether relocating will actually solve more problems than it creates. Worksheets compare prospective locations, using rating scales for physical plant, equipment, personnel, and geographic considerations. Sets up a schedule for dealing with logistics.

Retirement Planning

Retirement & Estate Planning Handbook

📖 *Book*

Do-it-yourself workbook for setting up a retirement plan that can easily be maintained and followed. Covers establishing net worth, retirement goals, budgets, and a plan for asset acquisition, preservation, and growth. Discusses realistic expectations for Social Security, Medicare, and health care alternatives. Features special sections for business owners.

Mail Order

Mail Order Legal Guide

📖 *New Book*

For companies that use the mail to market their products or services, as well as for mail order businesses, this book clarifies complex regulations so penalties can be avoided. Gives state-by-state legal requirements, plus information on Federal Trade Commission guidelines and rules covering delivery dates, advertising, sales taxes, unfair trade practices, and consumer protection.

Need it tomorrow? In most cases that's possible if you order before noon, PST. Just give us a call at 800-228-2275.

BOOKS FROM THE OASIS PRESS® Please check the edition (binder or paperback) of your choice

TITLE	BINDER	PAPERBACK	QUANTITY	COST
The Business Environmental Handbook		☐ $ 19.95		
Business Owner's Guide to Accounting & Bookkeeping		☐ $ 19.95		
Buyer's Guide to Business Insurance	☐ $ 39.95	☐ $ 19.95		
California Corporation Formation Package and Minute Book	☐ $ 39.95	☐ $ 29.95		
Collection Techniques for Small Business	☐ $ 39.95	☐ $ 19.95		
A Company Policy and Personnel Workbook	☐ $ 49.95	☐ $ 29.95		
Company Relocation Handbook	☐ $ 39.95	☐ $ 19.95		
Complete Book of Business Forms	☐ $ 49.95	☐ $ 19.95		
Controlling Your Company's Freight Costs	☐ $ 39.95			
Cost-Effective Market Analysis	☐ $ 39.95			
The Essential Corporation Handbook		☐ $ 19.95		
Export Now	☐ $ 39.95	☐ $ 19.95		
Financial Management Techniques For Small Business	☐ $ 39.95	☐ $ 19.95		
Financing Your Small Business		☐ $ 19.95		
Franchise Bible	☐ $ 39.95	☐ $ 19.95		
Home Business Made Easy		☐ $ 19.95		
How to Develop & Market Creative Business Ideas		☐ $ 14.95		
The Loan Package	☐ $ 39.95			
Mail Order Legal Guide	☐ $ 45.00	☐ $ 29.95		
Managing People: A Practical Guide	☐ $ 39.95	☐ $ 19.95		
The Money Connection	☐ $ 39.95	☐ $ 24.95		
People Investment	☐ $ 39.95	☐ $ 19.95		
Power Marketing for Small Business	☐ $ 39.95	☐ $ 19.95		
Proposal Development: How to Respond and Win the Bid (hardback book)	☐ $ 39.95	☐ $ 19.95		
Raising Capital	☐ $ 39.95	☐ $ 19.95		
Retirement & Estate Planning Handbook	☐ $ 39.95	☐ $ 19.95		
Safety Law Compliance Manual for California Businesses		☐ $ 24.95		
Company Illness & Injury Prevention Program Binder (OR Get kit WITH BOOK AND binder $49.95)	☐ $ 34.95	☐ $ 49.95 BOOK & BINDER KIT		
Secrets to Buying and Selling a Business	☐ $ 39.95	☐ $ 19.95		
Start Your Business		☐ $ 8.95		
Starting and Operating A Business in... book INCLUDES FEDERAL section PLUS ONE STATE SECTION —	☐ $ 29.95	☐ $ 24.95		
PLEASE SPECIFY WHICH STATE(S) YOU WANT:				
STATE SECTION ONLY (BINDER NOT INCLUDED) – SPECIFY STATES:	☐ $ 8.95			
U.S. EDITION (FEDERAL SECTION – 50 STATES AND WASHINGTON, D.C. IN 11-BINDER SET)	☐ $295.00			
Successful Business Plan: Secrets & Strategies (GET THE BINDER...IT'S A BUSINESS PLAN KIT)	☐ $ 49.95	☐ $ 21.95		
Surviving and Prospering in a Business Partnership	☐ $ 39.95	☐ $ 19.95		
Top Tax Saving Ideas for Today's Small Business		☐ $ 14.95		
Write Your Own Business Contracts (HARDBACK BOOK)	☐ $ 39.95	☐ $ 19.95		

BOOK TOTAL (Please enter on other side also for grand total)

SOFTWARE Please check whether you use Macintosh or 3-1/2" Disk for IBM-PC & Compatibles

TITLE	3-1/2" IBM Disk	Mac	Price	QUANTITY	COST
California Corporation Formation Package Software	☐	☐	$ 39.95		
★ California Corporation Formation Binder book & Software	☐	☐	$ 69.95		
Company Policy & Personnel Software (Standalone)	☐		$ 99.95		
★ Company Policy & Personnel Binder book & Software (Standalone)	☐		$125.95		
Customer Information & Tracking System	☐		$119.95		
Financial Management Techniques	☐		$ 99.95		
★ Financial Management Techniques Binder book & Software	☐		$129.95		
Financial Templates	☐	☐	$ 69.95		
The Small Business Expert	☐		$ 34.95		
Successful Business Plan (Full Standalone)	☐		$ 99.95		
★ Successful Business Plan Binder book & Software (Full Standalone)	☐		$125.95		

SOFTWARE TOTAL (Please enter on other side also for grand total)

Please add above totals on other side to complete your order. Thanks!

PSI Successful Business Library / Tools for Business Success Order Form (please see other side also)
Call, Mail or Fax to: PSI Research, 300 North Valley Drive, Grants Pass, OR 97526 USA
Order Phone USA (800) 228-2275   Inquiries and International Orders (503) 479-9464   FAX (503) 476-1479

Sold to: PLEASE GIVE STREET ADDRESS NOT P.O. BOX FOR SHIPPING

Name _____   Title: _____

Company _____   Daytime Telephone: _____

Street Address _____

City/State/Zip _____

☐   *YES, I want to receive the PSI newsletter, *✱MEMO.*
    Be sure to include: Name, address, and telephone number above.

Ship to: (if different)   PLEASE GIVE STREET ADDRESS NOT P.O. BOX FOR SHIPPING

Name _____

Title _____

Company _____

Street Address _____

City/State/Zip _____

Daytime Telephone _____

Payment Information:

☐ Check enclosed payable to PSI Research (When you enclose a check, UPS ground shipping is free within the Continental U.S.A.)

Charge - ☐ VISA ☐ MASTERCARD ☐ AMEX ☐ DISCOVER   Card Number: _____ Expires _____

Signature: _____   Name on card: _____

EXECARDS — The Proven & Chosen Method of Personal Business Communications

ITEM	PRICE EACH	QUANTITY	COST
EXECARDS Thank You Assortment (12 assorted thank you cards)	$ 12.95		
EXECARDS Recognition Assortment (12 assorted appreciation cards)	$ 12.95		
EXECARDS Marketing Assortment (12 assorted marketing cards)	$ 12.95		
EXECARDS TOTAL (Please enter below also for grand total)			$

Many additional options available, including custom imprinting of your company's name, logo or message. Please request a complete catalog. 800-228-2275

PLANNING TOOLS — Action Tracking Note Pads — 8½" x 11"

ITEM		NUMBER OF PADS
Calendar Note Pad	☐ 1994	
	☐ 94/95	
	☐ 1995	
Total number of pads		
Multiply by unit price: x		
PLANNING TOOLS TOTAL	$	

UNIT PRICE FOR ANY COMBINATION OF PLANNING TOOLS
1-9 pads $3.95 each
10-49 pads $3.49 each

SAFETY PROGRAM FORMS

ITEM	PRICE EACH	QUANTITY
Employee Warning Notification (Package of 20)	$4.95	
Request for Safety Orientation (Package of 20)	$4.95	
Report of Potential Hazard (Package of 20)	$4.95	
SAFETY PROGRAM FORMS TOTAL	$	

YOUR GRAND TOTAL

BOOK TOTAL (from other side)	$
SOFTWARE TOTAL (from other side)	$
EXECARDS TOTAL	$
PLANNING TOOLS TOTAL	$
SAFETY PROGRAM FORMS TOTAL	$
TOTAL ORDER	$

Rush service is available. Please call us for details.

Please send me:

_____ EXECARDS Catalog

_____ Oasis Press Software Information

_____ Oasis Press Book Information

Use this form to register for advance notification of updates, new books and software releases, plus special customer discounts!

Please answer these questions to let us know how our products are working for you, and what we could do to serve you better.

Title of book or software purchased from us:_____

It is a:
- ☐ Binder book
- ☐ Paperback book
- ☐ Book/software combination
- ☐ Software only

Rate this product's overall quality of information:
- ☐ Excellent
- ☐ Good
- ☐ Fair
- ☐ Poor

Rate the quality of printed materials:
- ☐ Excellent
- ☐ Good
- ☐ Fair
- ☐ Poor

Rate the format:
- ☐ Excellent
- ☐ Good
- ☐ Fair
- ☐ Poor

Did the product provide what you needed?
- ☐ Yes ☐ No

If not, what should be added?_____
_____
_____
_____
_____

This product is:
- ☐ Clear and easy to follow
- ☐ Too complicated
- ☐ Too elementary

Were the worksheets (if any) easy to use?
- ☐ Yes ☐ No ☐ N/A

Should we include:
- ☐ More worksheets
- ☐ Fewer worksheets
- ☐ No worksheets

How do you feel about the price?
- ☐ Lower than expected
- ☐ About right
- ☐ Too expensive

How many employees are in your company?
- ☐ Under 10 employees
- ☐ 10 – 50 employees
- ☐ 51 – 99 employees
- ☐ 100 – 250 employees
- ☐ Over 250 employees

How many people in the city your company is in?
- ☐ 50,000 – 100,000
- ☐ 100,000 – 500,000
- ☐ 500,000 – 1,000,000
- ☐ Over 1,000,000
- ☐ Rural (under 50,000)

What is your type of business?
- ☐ Retail
- ☐ Service
- ☐ Government
- ☐ Manufacturing
- ☐ Distributor
- ☐ Education

What types of products or services do you sell?
_____
_____
_____
_____

What is your position in the company?
(please check one)
- ☐ Owner
- ☐ Administration
- ☐ Sales/marketing
- ☐ Finance
- ☐ Human resources
- ☐ Production
- ☐ Operations
- ☐ Computer/MIS

How did you learn about this product?
- ☐ Recommended by a friend
- ☐ Used in a seminar or class
- ☐ Have used other PSI products
- ☐ Received a mailing
- ☐ Saw in bookstore
- ☐ Saw in library
- ☐ Saw review in:
  - ☐ Newspaper
  - ☐ Magazine
  - ☐ TV/Radio

Where did you buy this product?
- ☐ Catalog
- ☐ Bookstore
- ☐ Office supply
- ☐ Consultant
- ☐ Other_____

Would you purchase other business tools from us?
- ☐ Yes ☐ No

If so, which products interest you?
- ☐ EXECARDS® Communication Tools
- ☐ Books for business
- ☐ Software

Would you recommend this product to a friend?
- ☐ Yes ☐ No

If you'd like us to send associates or friends a catalog, just list names and addresses

on back.
Do you use a personal computer for business?
- ☐ Yes ☐ No

If yes, which?
- ☐ IBM/compatible
- ☐ Macintosh

Check all the ways you use computers:
- ☐ Word processing
- ☐ Accounting
- ☐ Spreadsheet
- ☐ Inventory
- ☐ Order processing
- ☐ Design/graphics
- ☐ General data base
- ☐ Customer information
- ☐ Scheduling

May we call you to follow up on your comments?
- ☐ Yes ☐ No

May we add your name to our mailing list?

☐ Yes ☐ No

If there is anything you think we should do to improve this product, please describe: _____
_____
_____
_____

Thank you for your patience in answering the above questions.
Just fill in your name and address here, fold (see back) and mail.

Name _____
Title _____
Company _____
Phone _____
Address _____

PSI Research creates this family of fine products to help you more easily and effectively manage your business activities:
The Oasis Press®   PSI Successful Business Software
PSI Successful Business Library   EXECARDS® Communication Tools

If you have friends or associates who might appreciate receiving our catalogs, please list here. Thanks!

Name_____   Name_____

Title_____   Title_____

Company_____   Company_____

Phone_____   Phone_____

Address_____   Address_____

City/State/Zip_____   City/State/Zip_____

FOLD HERE FIRST

‖‖‖‖

BUSINESS REPLY MAIL

FIRST CLASS MAIL PERMIT NO. 002 MERLIN, OREGON

POSTAGE WILL BE PAID BY ADDRESSEE

PSI Research
PO BOX 1414
Merlin OR 97532-9900

‖‖·‖··‖·‖‖·‖··‖·‖‖·‖·‖‖‖··‖‖···‖‖·‖

Please cut
along this
vertical line,
fold twice,
tape together
and mail.
Thanks!

✂ Cut out these post cards along the dashed lines. Just write in the Information on reverse side, add your return address, then apply the proper postage and drop in the mail.

Name

Title

Company

Address

City

State & Zip

Affix
Stamp
Here

**Bureau of Small Business and
Appalachian Development
Pennsylvania Department of Commerce**

461 Forum Building

Harrisburg, PA 17120

4.15

Name

Title

Company

Address

City

State & Zip

Affix
Stamp
Here

**Registration Division
Bureau of Business Trust Fund Taxes
Pennsylvania Department of Revenue**

Department 280901

Harrisburg, PA 17128-0901

5.1

Name

Title

Company

Address

City

State & Zip

Affix
Stamp
Here

**Corporation Bureau
Pennsylvania Department of State**

P.O. Box 8722

Harrisburg, PA 17105-8722

Name

Title

Company

Address

City

State & Zip

Affix
Stamp
Here

**Bureau of Workers' Compensation
Pennsylvania Department of
Labor and Industry**

1171 South Cameron, Room 103

Harrisburg, PA 17104-2501

5.9a

Attn: Registration Division

Please send me:

☐ Employer Withholding Registration Packet

☐ Sales Tax License Application

Name _____

Title _____

Company _____

Address _____

City _____ State _____ Zip _____

Post card provided by The Oasis Press, 300 North Valley Drive, Grants Pass, OR 97526   4/94

Attn: Bureau of Workers' Compensation

Please send me:

☐ Information and general forms regarding workers' compensation

Name _____

Title _____

Company _____

Address _____

City _____ State _____ Zip _____

Post card provided by The Oasis Press, 300 North Valley Drive, Grants Pass, OR 97526   4/94

Attn: Bureau of Small Business & Appalachian Development

Please send me:

☐ Poster, *Abstract of Equal Pay Law*

☐ Poster, *Employment Provisions, Pennsylvania Human Relations Act*

☐ Poster, *Abstract of the Child Labor Law*

☐ Poster, *Summary of the Pennsylvania Minimum Wage Law*

☐ Booklet, *Pennsylvania Small Business Operations and Resources Guide*

☐ Booklet, *Doing Business with the Commonwealth of Pennsylvania*

Name _____

Title _____

Company _____

Address _____

City _____ State _____ Zip _____

Post card provided by The Oasis Press, 300 North Valley Drive, Grants Pass, OR 97526   4/94

Attn: Corporation Bureau

Please send me:

☐ Information on fictitious name registration

☐ Order form for corporate forms on diskette

☐ *Pennsylvania's Corporation Laws — A Guide to Compliance*

Name _____

Title _____

Company _____

Address _____

City _____ State _____ Zip _____

Post card provided by The Oasis Press, 300 North Valley Drive, Grants Pass, OR 97526   4/94

✂ Cut out these post cards along the dashed lines. Just write in the information on reverse side, add your return address, then apply the proper postage and drop in the mail.

Affix
Stamp
Here

Name
Title
Company
Address
City
State & Zip

**U.S. Department of Labor
ESA/Office of Public Affairs**
Room C 4325
200 Constitution Avenue, NW
Washington, DC 20210

Affix
Stamp
Here

Name
Title
Company
Address
City
State & Zip

**Attn: Communications Dept. – CWS4
Pacific Bell Directory**
101 Spear Street, Room 429
San Francisco, CA 94105

Affix
Stamp
Here

Name
Title
Company
Address
City
State & Zip

**U.S. Department of Labor
OSHA Publications Office**
200 Constitution Avenue, NW
Washington, DC 20210

Affix
Stamp
Here

Name
Title
Company
Address
City
State & Zip

Unicor Distribution Services
3150 Horton Road
Fort Worth, TX 76119

Attn: Communications Dept. – CWS4

Please send me:

☐ A complimentary copy of *Small Business Success*

Name _____

Title _____

Company _____

Address _____

City _____ State _____ Zip _____

Post card provided by The Oasis Press, 300 North Valley Drive, Grants Pass, OR 97526   7/94

Attn: Unicor Distribution Services

Please send me:

☐ The Business Development list of publications (SBA 115A) offered by the U.S. Small Business Administration

Name _____

Title _____

Company _____

Address _____

City _____ State _____ Zip _____

Post card provided by The Oasis Press, 300 North Valley Drive, Grants Pass, OR 97526   7/94

Attn: U.S. Department of Labor – ESA/OPA

Please send me:

☐ Your most current version of *Your Rights Under the Fair Labor Standards Act* (WH Publication 1088)

Name _____

Title _____

Company _____

Address _____

City _____ State _____ Zip _____

Post card provided by The Oasis Press, 300 North Valley Drive, Grants Pass, OR 97526   7/94

Attn: U.S. Department of Labor – OSHA

Please send me:

☐ A list of free OSHA publications available from the OSHA Publications Office

☐ A list of OSHA publications available from the Government Printing Office for a small fee

Name _____

Title _____

Company _____

Address _____

City _____ State _____ Zip _____

Post card provided by The Oasis Press, 300 North Valley Drive, Grants Pass, OR 97526   7/94